PIT PROPS
AND
PONIES

By

Wilma S Bolton

Aunt Sadie   24/5/2008

Another look down memory Lane

*Love
Hannah*

Printed by Reid Printers Limited Blantyre
         Published by Wilma S. Bolton
This edition copyright © 2007 by Wilma S. Bolton

www.wilmabolton.com
ISBN 978-0-9552998-1-0

HAMILTON MINERS' MEMORIAL

History will recall and record the mining industry and its people. No matter the conclusion, when all who come after us read the story, the miner's name will be A BADGE OF HONOUR.   *(Anon.)*

This book is dedicated to the proud memory of the Lanarkshire miners and their families.

INTRODUCTION

A large percentage of the population of Lanarkshire and also countless thousands of people of Scottish descent living throughout the world have coal-mining ancestors. For most of us their lives remain something of a mystery; if we could only but turn back the hands of time for just a short while to speak to them, what a tale they would have to tell us. Unfortunately, this is not an option, but we can still find out a great deal about them, for the clues to the story of their lives are lying just waiting to be discovered in the reference libraries of our towns and cities, and also in the attics, cupboards and drawers of our homes.

My object in writing Pit Props and Ponies was to try to document the lives of our coal miners as accurately and truthfully as far as is possible. This has involved years of research and many discussions with miners and their families; but time is now fast running out to record the first hand accounts of the last remnants of the coal mining communities. It is up to us to ensure that their memories and experiences are documented and when the evidence is pieced together bit by bit, it is only then do we see the story of the suffering of our miners and their triumph against the overwhelming odds emerging from the past.

Pit Props and Ponies presents through factual stories and articles the evidence of the grinding poverty, overcrowded insanitary housing, dirt, disease, dangerous working conditions and the exploitation of our local coal miners. It also tells of the loyalty and raw courage of the miners working in conditions the likes of which we cannot even begin to imagine. It is about of the life of the Lanarkshire coal miner and his trials and tribulations as he struggles to survive and provide for his family.

It is a true account of who he was, where he came from, what he stood for and most of all what he stood up against; for this above all shaped his thinking and the thinking of his descendents long after he was no more and the coal mines had vanished into the mists of time.

ACKNOWLEDGEMENTS

The publication of this book would not have been possible were it not for the magnificent contribution from the descendents of the local coal mining communities who have so willingly given their precious family photographs and recorded their equally precious family memories for inclusion in this book and to each and every one of them I give my heartfelt thanks.

Special thanks to Don Boyle and Wullie Kerr for their priceless stories of life in the miners' rows and to Don for his poetry and Wullie for his photographs and wonderful sketches, also to Andy Bain, Phil Bradley, Mrs A. Dell, Alisha Farnan, John Farnan, Lesley Farnan, George Hay, the Hamilton Advertiser, Guthrie Hutton, Mrs Helen Jalono (USA) Betty Longmuir, Mary Neilan, Jean Robertson, Neil Scott, Sir Simon Watson Bt. and so many others, too numerous to mention, for assistance, photographs and contributions so kindly given for inclusion in this book.

Special thanks also to Audrey Wallace and Norman Tait for making available the Ballantyne collection of photographs taken in 1904 and which were developed by Norman from old glass negatives and also to George Archibald and Campbell Drysdale at the Scottish Mining Museum, Newtongrange for all their assistance, advice and photographs.

A special thanks to Pearl Murphy, David Young and Angela Logan of Hamilton Town House Reference Library for their invaluable advice and assistance and for making documents and photographs so readily available. Also to Miss Morag Corrie daughter of the late playwright, poet and ex miner Joe Corrie for her kind permission to include in the book two of her fathers wonderful pit poems.

Several anonymously published photographs, poems and articles appear in this book and I would be pleased to include acknowledgements in these cases for future editions.

ABOUT THE AUTHOR

Wilma Bolton's father Jimmy Russell and his four brothers were coal miners as were her grand father and great-grandfather. Her paternal great grandmother Joanna Kerr was in all probability descended from bonded colliers (slaves) living in Midlothian. Her father was a great teller of tales and some of the stories she has written about, she originally heard from him as a child.

Her interest in the lives of our local coal miners was kindled after she discovered while researching her family history, that her great grand uncle James Spiers had been one of the 73 men and boys killed in an explosion at Udston Colliery, Hamilton on the 28th May 1887.

Subsequent enquiries revealed that this explosion, (the second largest coal mining disaster in Scotland) had been largely forgotten and because of this, she decided to investigate the number of men killed in Hamilton Parish. After ten years of research, Wilma now has the names and details of approximately 1200 men, boys and young girls who were killed while working in the coal mines of Hamilton. She approached South Lanarkshire Council and was delighted when they agreed to place a memorial plaque to those who were killed on the base of the miners' statue which stands outside Hamilton's Brandon Gate.

Having felt that an accurate account of the appalling conditions endured by our local coal miners and their families had never been fully documented, she set about writing her first book Black Faces and Tackety Boots when she retired from her job as a staff nurse at Hairmyres Hospital, East Kilbride. The book which contained many true stories about the lives of the local coal mining communities, also included approximately 2000 names of our local old time miners; it was an instant success with copies being sent to countries all over the world.

Pit Props and Ponies is a social history of the Lanarkshire coal miners. To personalise it for readers and to enable them to find out more about their mining families, Wilma has included the names of approximately 2000 local coal miners who worked in the Hamilton, Blantyre, Larkhall and Quarter areas, some on them from as early as 1785. Also listed are names and the county of birth for quite a number of Irishmen who came over during and after the potato famine to work in the coal mines of Hamilton. Wilma, who knows only too well how difficult it is to find out where Irish ancestors were born, included this information for family historians.

As a result of her research, she now has large files relating to all the individual Hamilton Parish collieries; several of which have over 200 pages, Quarter Collieries and village is her largest file and it contains 75.000 words. The files will eventually be available for the public to read at Hamilton Town House Reference Library and the library of The Scottish Mining Museum, Newtongrange.

CONTENTS

THE MINER'S LOT

I dive into the deepest pit,
  You'd tremble where I stay;
And through the rocks and glittering
  ore
  My arms must make its way.

I cannot breathe the summer air
  Nor see the roses blow,
No scent of flowers can meet me
  there,
No freshness where I go

Though every element declare
  That death's at every turn,
I fear no dark abyss if but
  My little lamp should burn;

Nor do I fear the threatening
  cliffs,
 Precipitous o'er my head,
Nor yet the wild and gushing
  stream
  That tears its rocky bed.

Nor yet the blue and ghastly flame,
  From which comes poisoned breath
Blown out to bring us suddenly
  Into the jaws of death.

I boldly bore into the hardest hill,
  And split the hardest rock
God grant the grave, I light the match
  And wait the dreadful shock.

I boldly dig from mountain depth
  The veins that lighten dearth,
And bring from out of rocky gulfs
  The marrow of the earth.

How beautiful at first but soon,
  We see an idol rising,
They worship it forgetting us,
  And God himself despising.

I open many a golden lode,
  And many a silver vein,
And when the rich take up the prize,
  What think you, is my gain?

Stiff rheumatism in my limbs,
  And oft a beggars slave
My bread with but a little salt,
  And oft an early grave.

True many a miner passing by
  Weeps when he sees my end
And having blessed my ashes, says
  "Rest well, rest well, my friend."

So glimmer on my little lamp,
  For certain, soon or late,
With many a brave and noble man,
  The grave will be my fate.

H.M. circa 1883.
(Hector McNeill, Larkhall)

WEE PIT POWNIE*

Wee pit pownie, harness and a'
A hutch at the bottom, ready for tae draw,
Ile* flask, tea flask, piece boax and a'
And we'll no' be hame tae the mornin'.

Pit pony (wee Jenny) and her driver photographed in an in unnamed Lanarkshire pit.
Photograph c. 1900, courtesy of Hamilton Town House Reference Library

Many of the memories of children from mining communities are associated with the return to the surface of the pit ponies during the "Fair" holidays. The ponies became the focal point of the mining communities with fathers and brothers proudly showing off their ponies to their families.

*The above verse used to be sung throughout Lanarkshire to miners' children.
* Ile flask: oil flask

Scottish Society to Promote kindness to pit ponies medal, 1911

PIT PONIES

Prior to the passing of the 1842 Coal Mines Act, women and children were the means of transporting coal from the face to the pit bottom or up to the surface. The coal was carried in wicker baskets strapped to their backs or pulled by women and children harnessed to hutches. With the passing of the Act, women were finally prevented by law from working underground and although the bill originally had proposed that children under thirteen were not to be employed, the interference of the powerful coal barons ensured that children as young as ten could still be employed. However, because women and also children below the age of ten were no longer employed another method of transporting the coal from the coal face to the pit bottom had to be found and so began the pit ponies underground career.

Pony being lowered down shaft

The job of the pit ponies was to take supplies and pull full and empty hutches to and from the coal face.

The ponies were taken underground at the age of four, after they had been trained to pull a weight behind them and had gotten used to wearing headgear and harness. They were either taken down in the cage or suspended underneath it and lowered down. Except for times of strike or at the miners' annual holiday, the pit pony lived underground in stables which were at least 6 foot wide with a workman (Ostler) to look after their needs. They normally worked underground till they were in their twenties and they shared the same dangers as the miners with countless ponies being killed in underground accidents. At Bog Colliery in January 1903, 15 ponies were found dead from suffocation after deadly fumes from a fire which had been which had been smouldering away for years in the soft coal seam permeated through to the stables during the night.

Buying ponies was an expensive business for the coalmaster and feeding them could cost as much as ten shillings and sixpence a week 52 _ p but they worked hard for their keep. In 1911 the Coal Mines

Act made it compulsory to supply protective headgear and eye guards for pit ponies. (It should be noted here that the coalminer was offered no such protection for his head despite the appalling death rate due to head injuries. It was to be the mid 1930's before safety helmets were given to miners and by then a large percentage of the mines were closed or on their last legs.)

There was a bond between the pit pony and his driver and stories about the antics of the ponies were legendary. Miners children were reared on stories from the mine and the tales of the pit ponies as related to them by their fathers had them roaring with laughter. Unfortunately few of these stories were written down but the following story taken from an article written by a John Henderson and published by the Hamilton Advertiser on 1st December 1923 gives us an insight into humorous side of working with pit ponies.

"A new pony about to be "broken-in" to the work underground is almost sure to provide a first class laugh. The heroic individual who undertakes this job is often as comical as the celebrated Doodles. The writer has either assisted at this ceremony or was an interested spectator. I always preferred the latter role.

Jock was our horse-breaker and a capital hand he was at the game. In the first place, when a new pony was brought from the stable suitable graithed, it was interesting and amusing to hear the comments of Jock.

"Dae ye ca' that a horse?" roared Jock, when a new "recruit" was brought for his inspection. "Ye widna get rags for it frae the candyman." And the grumbling soon began. "Na" na! ye'll no' dae, faur too much daylicht below ye," or very often the variation came—"the horse's belly is too near the sleepers to be any use."

However, Jock met his match one fine morning. He had criticised and as usual nearly scandalised us with his criticism of a new pony we had "christened" Bobby. Bobby was a nervous animal and probably Jock's criticism had accentuated his nervousness. Anyway, Bobby was hitched on to a hutch and Jock was standing in front of it. Bobby backed till he got to the hutch and with a tiger-like spring he landed fairly and squarely between Jock's shoulders. This was too much for our hero and on recovering he bolted out the road for safety—or so he thought. Bobby too bolted after Jock. Then the fun began, Jock careered along like a McCrae, Bobby following at the gallop. However, they had a good run and when Jock stopped out of breath, Bobby stopped too, probably wondering why Jock stopped. Pure nervousness was all that was wrong with the pony; but Jock, when he got that thump between the shoulders, thought otherwise.

All horses underground are, however, not of the Bobby type. Danny was just the very opposite of Bobby and for six hours after it was hitched up to a hutch it was as still as King William's pony as Glasgow Cross. Jock began an oration about horses in general and Danny in particular. Danny was a stoic though and when the insinuation came from Jock that Wilmot would not have him in a gift, our new equine friend never moved an eyelid. Jock stopped swearing and started dancing; still Danny moved not. Then he took off his belt and went forward to Danny and shook it in his face. Result—no notice taken. Danny then got the belt, but he made no motion beyond merely flicking his back with his tail. Jock got in front, put two feet together on the sleepers and pulled Danny till we thought the head was going to be pulled off. Jock then started laughing, in a little while after he was singing; when we left him he was in tears. Danny still kept his end up.

Four hours after we came back again and still the two were standing where we left them. Jock was raving and shouting in a very hoarse voice—"you'll no beat me, pit that in your pipe and smoke it." Danny just looked at what all the noise was about. Jock sat down to rest. Just then a wee laddie, with a piece of bread appeared about six feet from Danny. "Come on Danny," he said and immediately Danny moved and the boy, keeping in front of Danny, kept him going. We side-glanced at Jock and a more mortified individual we have never seen before or since.

Danny had beaten Jock and he knew it, but what Jock did not like, was the idea of a small laddie doing in five minutes what he could not accomplish in six hours!

We have seen Jock however; accomplish some difficult work in this line. Once he knew the nature of a pony it was not long until he got it into good trim. To his credit also, he never used any brutality, nor would he allow any to be used."

THE
BEST WEE PIT PONY IN QUARTER

On the 14th July 1911 during the miner's annual holiday, the management of Quarter Collieries held a competition to find the best kept ponies in their No's 1,4,6,7 and 8 Pits.

During this holiday week, the ponies were brought up and allowed to run free in fields set aside for them. The arrival of 115 ponies at the surface drew crowds from not only Quarter but the villages round about. Prominent at the fields were the pit pony drivers anxious to show off their "own pony" to their families. It was evident to all that the animals appeared not only well fed but well cared for and in charge of the arrangements was the head ostler and the judge was local vet James Pollock.

Each pony was proudly paraded in front of the vet by its own pony driver to be carefully examined. The judging took some time because of the amount of ponies but finally the names of the prize-winners were handed over to the winners by Mr John Davidson the colliery manager.

Pit No 1.	1st John Thomson, 56 London Street, Larkhall *
	2nd Charles Marshall, Croft Road, Larkhall
	3rd William Stewart, 62 Darngaber Row, Quarter *
Pit No. 4.	1st George McLachlan, New Buildings, Quarter
	2nd Alexander Nicol, Mid Quarter *
	3rd James Henderson, Chapelton. *
Pit No. 6.	1st William Pollock, Meikle Earnock
	2nd John Pollock, Limekilnburn *
	3rd James Maxwell, Fue Cottage, Glassford.
Pit No. 7.	1st William Crozier, 16 Commercial Road Strathaven
	2nd Daniel Currie, Limekilnburn
	3rd John Brown, 45 Darngaber Row, Quarter
	4th Peter McGregor, Millheugh *

Pit No. 8 (Splint Seam.)
    1st James Higgins, 1 New Buildings Quarter. *
    2nd John Nicol, 62 Portland Park, Hamilton *
    3rd John McLeavy, 4 North Street, Strathaven
    4th Robert Logan, Low Waters, Hamilton.

Pit No. 8 (Splint seam.)
    1st James Lowell, 42 North Street, Strathaven *
    2nd William Clark, Darngaber Row, Quarter,
    3rd John McLare, 4 Furnace Row Quarter.

Overall winner for best kept pony was Quarter youth James Higgins

*Denotes pony drivers who within a few years, were to enlist in the forces to fight in World War One. All nine survived the carnage. James Higgins won the Military Medal for bravery.

LINES ON A PIT PONY DRIVER
"THE LINTY"

It's doon the dook and o'er the hitch
They draw the coal wi' such a pitch,
Ye'd think yon driver was a witch,
   The lad they ca' the Linty.

Although he has but got ae wing,
He fair can make the hutches ding,
The want o cleek, there's nae sich thing
   Wi' honest Jim the Linty.

An then he's cheery a' the day,
An tae his horse ye'll here him say—
"Come on, my flow'r get on the way,"
    Yes, that's the way wi' Linty.

Colliers wi' heart their wark begin,
Their coals are never lying in,
And they guid wages aye can win
   When they have got the Linty.

The auld men tae their hurl enjoy,
Their presence dinna him annoy,
To oblige them rather brings him joy,
   Guid-hearted is the Linty.

If scarce the wagons chance to be,
Fill up my lads; we'll let them see,
We can take part in ony spree,
   Yes this way spoke the Linty.

When aff the road the hutches went,
He seldom for a roadsman sent,
But o'er the hutch the tail chain went,
   The horse lifted with Linty.

"Come on," he's say, "the hutch is fu'"
And when I lift ye tae maun pu',
The horse was wise, but wiser grew
   The longer he kent Linty.

For when the hutch was on the road,
The horse wid ga'e his heid a nod,
And start again wi' his fu' load,
   When driven by the Linty

If Linty took an idle day,
The colliers they wid sadly say—
"We're better if the house to stay,
    When ocht comes o'er the Linty."

For nane like him that horse can drive,
Nae matter how the fellows strive,
The horse gaes daft an' tears, and rives,
   When idle is the Linty.

Master and men think much o' him,
For he has had his hill to climb,
Forby he's minus of a limb,
   But clever is our Linty

Lang may he live to earn his bread,
And may he in this world succeed,
For in his heart there ne'er wis greed,
   God bless and prosper Linty.

Peter Brown, Circa 1911.

INSTRUCTIONS TO HORSEKEEPERS AT BLANTYRE COLLIERY 1891

1. The Dayshift Horsekeepers shall carefully examine each pony when returned to the stable at the end of the shift and shall write a proper report of such examination.

2. In the pits where a Night Bottomer is employed, he shall also act as Night Horsekeeper and shall carefully examine each pony during the night, and shall write a report of such examination.

3. The ponies shall be fed at proper intervals, and the quantity of feeding shall be regulated so as to prevent any waste being left in the mangers.

4. The Nightshift Horsekeeper shall feed the ponies each morning at four o'clock, and no feeding shall be placed in the mangers afterwards before "corning" time.

5. The Dayshift Horsekeeper shall give out to each Driver sufficient feeding for use at "corning" time only. No Feeding shall be given out to Drivers of ponies which return to the stable at "corning" time.

6. The Dayshift Horsekeeper shall carefully mix a table spoonful of salt with the feeding for each pony every day.

7. The corn chest shall always be kept locked, and no person shall be allowed to feed the ponies except the Horsekeepers.

8. Whenever there is an early yoke* the Dayshift Horsekeeper shall descend the Pit the same evening to water the ponies.   (*finish)

9. The Dayshift Horsekeeper shall keep the stable clean and in good order, and shall whitewash the walls once every six months.

10. He shall see that the ponies' feet are carefully examined at the end of the shift by the Drivers in charge and shall report loose shoes to the Smith.

11. He shall see that all the harness is in good order before the ponies leave the stable in the morning and at the close of the work shall see that each pony is properly cleaned by the Driver in charge.

12. The Nightshift Horsekeeper shall keep the harness clean and in good order.

13. No pony shall have a halter more that four feet in length from the head stall to the ring.

14. When a pony is drawn the harness shall always be sent to the surface at the same time.

15. Ponies returned to the stable suffering from sickness or injury shall be immediately reported to the Foreman Smith, who will send for the veterinary surgeon if necessary.

16. Each Horsekeeper shall see that all the ponies are properly secured and that the gates at the entrance of the stables are safely fastened before he leaves the pit.

17. Dayshift ponies shall not be employed on the nightshift without the permission of the manager. The names of ponies employed during the night shall be entered in the daily report.

18. Any person found abusing a pony shall be reported to the manager.

19. On Sunday the Horsekeepers' lamps shall be given out at 8 a.m. and shall be returned to the lamp-room at 4 p.m.

20. Dayshift Horsekeepers who also act as Lamplighters shall attend the relighting of safety lamps as required by Regulation No. 4 after 6 o'clock.

THE PONIES LAMENT

Nae mair tae roam ow'r Iceland's hills,	*no more
Where oft we felt the wintry chills.	
But doon the daurksome valley, where	
There's naethin'* like fresh country air.	*nothing
The snaw that fell frae yonder heich,*	*height
Upon oor backs nae mair shall licht,*	*light
But frae the ruif* some bits o' stanes,	*roof
Will fa' an' hurt oor skin an' banes*.	*bones
Wi' muckle* glee we skipped each hill,	*much
An' jumped the rivulets at will,	
But noo, on sleepers, rails an' trees*	*pit props
We'll slip an' skin oor tender knees.	
While on hills in days gone by,	
Oor roof was aye the open sky,	
The air was pure, the licht was clear,	
Though darksome days for us are here.	
We'll be the theme o' money a crack,*	*conversation
An' suffer many an angry smack,	
Though tired an' weary wi' the loads,	
We'll hae tae empty a' the roads.	
"Fareweel" we say, "tae hills an' dales,	
Tae snaw* an' rain an' wintry gales,	*snow
An welcome work amang the heat,	
Wi' achin banes* an' weary feet.	*bones

Unknown c. 1939.

In August 1939 four Icelandic ponies were taken down Gateside Colliery, Cambuslang to assist the men hauling heavy hutches in an area where the character of the coal seam made it impossible for the coal to be taken out mechanically. The four ponies were the first down the pit since 1926. The above poem appeared in the Blantyre Gazette several weeks later

Miner John Monie, Canderrigg Colliery, Stonehouse c.1953, photograph courtesy of John Young

IMAGE OF GOD

Crawlin' aboot like a snail in the mud,
Covered wi' clammy blae,
ME, made after the image o' God –
Jings! But it's laughable, tae.

Howkin' awa' 'neath a mountain o' stane,
Gaspin' for want o' air,
The sweat makin' streams doon my bare back-
banes,
And my knees a' hauckit* and sair.   *hacks*

Strainin' and cursin' the hale shift through,
Half-starved, half-blin', half-mad,
And the gaffer he says, "Less dirt in that coal
Or ye go up the pit, my lad."

So I gie my life tae the Nimmo squad
For *eicht and fower* a day,   *eight and four- 42 p*
Me! Made after the image o' God—
Jings! But it's laughable, tae.

                Joe Corrie. 1894-1968

A MINER'S STORY

If you have never worked underground, then it is difficult to visualise just what life was like for a miner. Fortunately for our generation, some of the miners wrote about their working life and their work was published in local newspapers. These stories are the coal miners' legacy, which gives to us an insight into the working conditions of our forefathers.

The following article appeared in the Hamilton Advertiser in 1931. We do not know the author's name for the article was anonymous; a practice common at this time. We are greatly indebted to this unknown miner for leaving us such a vivid description of his working day.

*   *   *

Attempting to describe a day in the life of a miner to Lanarkshire people may appear to be as ridiculous as "carrying coals to Newcastle." Nevertheless, there must be a vast number of county readers who although they have lived in close proximity to the mines since childhood, do not know what a day's work in the mine means, or how the collier earns his daily bread.

Statistics regarding miners, pits, production, sales, wages, oncosts, accidents, profits, losses and "Old Uncle Tom Cobley and all," may be had in barrow-loads anywhere for the asking. What the non-mining members of the community want to know is: "What kind of work does the collier do when he goes down the pit to send up coal?"

There are many different kinds of coal; different qualities, varying thicknesses of seams. The same colliery pitheadman might draw off a hutch from a twenty-inch seam, together with one from an eight-feet seam—both from the same cage-load. Men sometimes choke with dust in the Ell coal workings, while far underneath them their colleagues may be wet-to-the-waist in the Black Band seam. Two men may be producing 15 tons per day in a machine-cut place for 8s (40p) each, while a few yards away less-skilled workmen may be earning 12s (60p) a day in a pick-place with a "4-ton darg" (amount of mineral to be dug out) It all depends on the natural conditions. But why go on? The whole British coalfield is a medley of contrasts—hence so much understanding by the general public on the whole question of work and conditions in the mines. How can one describe a day's work in the mines? Let me try.

.

As I write I see the thin, grey wisps of steam rising from my pit moleskins drying on the back of a chair by the fire. Wet clammy, dirty, disagreeable moleskins they are. Today at 3.30 they left the colliery, thoroughly soaked with the slush and slime of No. 9 roadhead sumphole. In a blizzard of sleet and snow they travelled the mile-and-a-half journey home, over a slushy and rain-sodden road. This I know to be true, because I was with them—inside them! Tonight after much care, they will be declared fit for duty for tomorrow's shift. Unfortunately, I will again accompany them; and what will tomorrow's shift be like? I wonder if I could picture it for you.

My shift starts at 7 a.m., but I will be roused from my slumber at 5.30, and while I am donning my "pit togs" my wife will be busily engaged preparing my breakfast (a slice of toast and a cup of tea) and making up my piece (four slices of bread and cheese) and filling up my tea flask.

Punctually at 5.45 I will venture out into the inky blackness, whatever the weather and make my way to the colliery,--a dreary, dismal and deserted place—arriving there about 6.10 a.m. Here I will receive my lamp, explosive can and tokens, then ascend to the pithead, hide my coat and cigarettes and sit down for a final "puff" before descending the mine. Having called my "ben" or turn when I arrived on the pithead, I am now ready to descend. I enter the cage. I am tempted to describe this cage. However, suffice it is to say that the cage is a conglomeration of iron bars and bolts, its main function being to hold coal tubs. Swiftly, with many an awesome rattle and rumble, we speed on our downward journey.

At the pit-bottom I pause till I get my pit "een" (eyes)—in other words, I accustom my sight to the underground darkness. Here also, I get my pick blades or any graith (tools) "up" for repair, and set off on the long tramp underground to the coal face. The haulage (main) road is fully a mile in length. It has low parts and high parts—and wet parts and dry parts. This done, I will climb the brae, travel the inside haulage road and finally, panting and out-of-breath, find myself at the fireman's station. As is our custom, I will smoke (rest) here and ascertain from him is my "place" all right, i.e., roof saft, air good, the place free from gas, etc. Everything being "O.K.," I will descend the "dook" (decline road) and branching off at No. 9, arrive at my working place at 6.55 a.m. About twenty yards from the face I will take off my jacket, waistcoat, and heavy shirt with a real sense of relief, because by this time I will be sweating profusely. And as I sit by the roadside, one hundred and fifty fathoms beneath the sod, with the feeble rays of my safety lamp casting flickering shadows around me, perhaps I will stare in thoughtful contemplation at the great mass of sandstone opposite me and lose myself in wonderful imagining, thinking of the great period of time that has elapsed since the carboniferous age, with its luxuriant vegetation, made our great coal-fields possible.

Although informed by the fireman that everything was in order in my place, my first duty at the face will be making a careful examination of the roof and sides and a test for gas. I will also look to the "laigh" (low) side of the place to see if, by some miraculous chance the water which usually lies there has disappeared. Unfortunately, I will likely be sadly disappointed.

Having satisfied myself that there is no immediate danger and erected some "props" where needed, my "drawer" (partner) having by this time arrived, I am ready to start work.
My first task will be to "hole" the coal –cut away the shale from underneath the coal that is to be brought down. The height of the seam is two feet 3 inches and in order to "hole" the coal I will require to adopt a very cramped and uncomfortable position—in fact, as the holing proceeds, practically lie on my side.

The first hour will see us both engaged holing the wall (side of place) cutting far underneath the coal in order to throw the weight of the strata above on it and thus save blasting with explosives.

Much of this holed material will be "waste" and must be thrown behind to the place from where the coal has already been taken. Skilled work with the pick and vigorous blows with the mash will soon be the order of the day. (A most important point should be noted here—up to this time I will not have earned a penny, *as miners are only paid for coal production!)*

The "lift" of coal should produce about two tons when we get it down. This can only be accomplished by much labour and toil and loss of sweat—and sometimes temper. After that the coal has to be shovelled from the wall to the "roadhead" and then filled into the tubs. The tub, which is a miniature railway wagon, has to be drawn from the lye, about 200 yards from the coal-face. When filled and pushed out again it is worth about 1s 6d to us. We require to fill twelve of these to earn about 9s each—less off-takes.

The saddest words of tongue or pen in mining terminology are not "it might have been," but the words "drawing" or "brushing," and to say no more than that, is to create an erroneous impression. Nearly everyone is familiar with the picture of the pit pony pulling a tub up an incline. We recall the animal straining and panting as it pulls the heavy load. Drawing means substituting a miner at the back of the tub in place of the over-worked animal at the front. Hence the reason why drawers fail to become enthusiastic towards the proposals to withdraw pony labour from the mines!

The word "brushing" is the greatest misnomer in the world's list of misapplied technical terms—hence the reason why, in a court case some years ago, the sheriff suggested that the injured workman on partial compensation should *seek a light job at the brushing!*

Let me try to make plain what brushing means. Employ two navies to cut a road nine feet wide through a rock surface, taking the cut four feet deep and ask them to cut a fathom forward each day, spreading the excavated material to the right and left of the roadway to a height not to exceed two feet. Now turn the world upside down, and they are employed at the "brushing"!

While we are at work the roof will require constant attention and props must be set where needed to safeguard our 6-ton "darg," we may find it necessary to take some risks. Many of the mining accidents attributed to "carelessness" are really caused by the miner having one eye on the "bad stone" above and one on the pay envelope he will receive an the end of the week. They pay envelope wins for a number of times until one day….

Propping up the roof, photograph courtesy of Scottish Mining Museum.

Thus will our work continue until about 10.30, when a halt will be called for "bread" and with what joyful relaxation will come out of that gloomy prison, 2 feet 3 inches high, to take our meal of the day! And you can forgive us if we forget about the dangers of the mine, picks and shovels, tubs and coal, and everything connected with mines, while we discuss the prospects of our football favourites, the Parliamentary situation, tell of the thrills of the latest talkie picture, or ponder on the intricacies of an Edgar Wallace thriller.

Alas all things good and bad come to an end and we will return to the second and more arduous half of our shift. So far, except for sweat our clothes were dry. Now we will start on the wet side of the place where the slimy water lies at varying depths of from 2 to 8 inches. With many a curse and grumble we will set to work at our most disagreeable task. Every movement we make will send the water squelching from our boots and trousers, rendering us miserable and uncomfortable. A feeling of dejection will overwhelm us, physically and spiritually. The water will soften our hands and the small particles of coal sticking to our pick-shafts will make holing an agony. Despite our care, lumps of coal falling will splash us with water, giving our faces a wild unkempt appearance. These, already blackened with coal-dust, will soon present a most woe-begone expression— which, in reality, will be a faithful picture of how we will actually feel.

And here at the coal-face, straining our eyes to see in the shadowy, flickering gloom of the feeble light cast by our 10 candle-power safety lamp, we will battle and struggle against Nature, in agony and misery, for the next four hours, endeavouring to wrest by our muscular energies, sufficient sustenance for ourselves and our families.

There is much more I could tell, but lack of space does not permit. And thus having produced our daily 6 ton "darg" at the end of the day, we will perhaps wonder, as we journey tired and sore, clammy and wet, on that tortuous road to the pit-bottom, why our fellow-citizens allow so many "unnatural" forces to range themselves against us, and prevent us from enjoying the full fruits of our arduous, wearisome and laborious toils of the day.

And so, arriving at the pithead at about 3.30 p.m., I will set off home, glad at heart that another day's toil is over—but I forget myself—what miner can tell if he will ever see daylight again, once he goes down the mine in the morning.

THE COAL WORM

You see yon poor bedraggled sight
Whose weak eyes blink, at strong daylight,
His sweat pores clogged with coal dust fine---
Behold the toiler from the mine.

His dragging gait betrays his calling,
Exhausted, near to point of falling.
He staggers home, with scliffing feet,
And thanks his stars his shift's complete.

All day he toiled, where black damp lay,
Thick as fog, yet he must stay
In cramped position, hewing coal,
To keep his meagre wages whole.

All through the night his wheezing chest
Keeps him awake, while others rest,
Let this poor worm your thoughts engage,
And don't grudge him a living wage.

L.J.W.   Blantyre 1924.

ROSS COLLIERY FERNIEGAIR
Courtesy of Scottish Mining Museum

Pit props holding up the roof at the bottom of the shaft at Ross Colliery, Ferniegair, Hamilton, c. 1904
Photograph courtesy of Hamilton Natural History Society and South Lanarkshire Council

A fault in the coal seam at Ross Colliery, Ferniegair Hamilton, c. 1904
Photograph courtesy of Hamilton Natural History Society and South Lanarkshire Council.

ROSS COLLIERY 1938

This ton block of coal from Ross Colliery was put on show at the 1938 Empire exhibition at Glasgow. Outside left of photograph Thomas Campbell and outside right Guy Brownlie. The names of the other 4 men are unknown. Photograph courtesy of Thomas Campbell's daughter Mary Neilan.

Although academically gifted Thomas Campbell left school on the morning of his 14th birthday in 1913 and started on the backshift at Ross Colliery Ferniegair where he worked as a pitheadman until the pit closed in 1945.

With the mining industry almost finished he went to work at Hallside Steelworks and then later on at John Brown's shipyard where he worked until he was 65.

Note the shine on his working boots. He polished them every night ready for work in the morning.

Thomas Campbell's certificate of competency to give and receive signals.

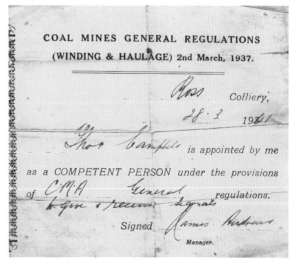

COAL MINES GENERAL REGULATIONS

(WINDING & HAULAGE) 2nd March, 1937.

Ross Colliery,

28·3 19__

Thos Campbell is appointed by me

as a COMPETENT PERSON under the provisions

of C·M·A General regulations.

to give & receive signals

Signed James Andrews

Manager.

JOHN NEWALL, OVERSMAN, ROSS COLLIERY

John Newall was born in 1862 at Low Meadowside, Monklands and started working in No 11 Pit Burntfoothill, Patna, Ayrshire when he was only 11 years old. He was to remain at this pit for 15 years until he moved to Brownlieside Pit, Clarkston where he spent the next 25 years working as a roadsman and then a fireman.

When Brownlieside Pit closed down John worked in Fife for 2 years and then at Auchengeigh Colliery where he worked for 3 years.

In 1913 he found employment in Ross colliery as a fireman and later he sat and passed his undermanagers exams and obtained promotion to oversman (underground manager).When this picture was taken in 1929 John was 67 years of age and still working as oversman at Ross.

Photograph c. 1929, courtesy of Richard Newall

MEN KNOWN TO HAVE WORKED AT ROSS COLLIERY

John Croft, (1902) *John Cross*, Portland Place, Hamilton, (1890) *Michael Dougan,* Campbell Street, Hamilton (1927) *David Easton,* Orchard View, Ferniegair, (1946) *Alexander Frew*, 7 Watson Street, Blantyre (1927) *Robert Galloway* (1929) *Alexander Laird*, undermanager (1929) *William Lang,* 39 Union Street, Hamilton, (1931) *Robert Lyle*, 53 Kenmar Road, Whitehill, Hamilton, (1945) *George McDougall* (1929) *Duncan McDougall*, (1944)*William McFarlane,* manager (1923) *James McGuiness,* 7 Castle Street, Hamilton, (1913) *Patrick McLaughlan*, Stevenson Street, Calton Glasgow (1927) *William Mackie,* manager, (1923) *William Miller,* 2 Marshall Street, Larkhall (1938) *Thomas Pennycuik* (1923) *John Rice*, pony driver, 12 Stanley Street, Burnbank, (1943) *James Ritchie,* 85 Glasgow Road, Strathaven, (1944) *Michael Rodgers,* 122 Calder Street, Blantyre, (1927) *Dennis Scullion,* 52 Strathaven Road, Eddlewood, (1944) *James Waddell*, cashier, (1923) *Dougald Waddell*, 17 Johnstone Street, Hamilton, (1924) *Joseph Wilson,* fireman, (1943)

Local miners waiting to go underground. Note the unprotected cage.

THE RIOTS AT ROSS ROWS
FERNIEGAIR
1894

In 1894 the coal masters reduced the miner's already low wage by 25% with the result that they withdrew their labour and came out on strike for the first time as the direct result of a ballot. The strike which began on 26th June was to continue for nineteen weeks.

From the onset, the decision by the authorities to involve the police in what was a peaceful strike had caused bitter feelings among the mining communities. The unnecessary introduction into the district of 120 English police officers from Lancashire was quite rightly interpreted as a blatant intimidation of the mining communities.

The very sight of the English police officers offended the Scottish miners and their misgivings were well founded. From the day of their introduction into the coal fields, the brutality used by these officers against peaceful strikers and their families was unbelievably vicious as the mining communities at Ferniegair were to find out to their cost on the 17th September 1894.

Ross Colliery had been a bit of a problem for the striking miners due to a number of the men continuing to work under police protection. Because of the strength of feeling running on both sides of the conflict, the owners of the colliery had placed some large chains across the entrance to Ross Rows in an attempt to prevent any pickets entering the Rows.

On 17th September a delegation of 300 pickets left Hamilton at 03.00 to walk to Ross Rows in an attempt to persuade the working miners to come out on strike. As they marched into Ferniegair they were spotted by *Constable Buist* who at once left for Ross Rows. The first thing he noticed when he arrived was that the padlocks and chains were broken so he ran to Ferniegair to telephone for assistance. On his way back he met a horse drawn brake with *Inspector Stewart* and several other police officers heading for the Rows and when they got there they found the pickets in the main street between the rows. Jumping out of the brake Stewart warned them that they were to move back to the public road at Ferniegair but the pickets ignored him and split up with half going to the back of the rows to wait for the men leaving to start their work and the other half went to the footbridge used by the workmen to get to the pithead. The crowd was getting bigger and noisier by the minute as men, women and children poured out of their homes to see what was going on and then joined in the booing and shouting at the police officers.

Standing on the outside of the railings of their house watching the proceedings were striking miners *Hugh Murphy* and his sons, Henry (who was fully dressed) and James who had only just come out of his bed was standing in his drawers and shirt. Without any warning the police baton charged the crowd raining blows down on men, women and children alike. *Hugh Murphy* who had moved back to his own door was then confronted by a baton wielding police officer who ordered him to *"go in."* When he protested that he was" *already in*" the police officer retorted that he would put him in further and laid into him with the baton. *James Murphy* carried his father into the house followed by several other miners trying to escape from the violence of the police. The police however entered the house and arrested *James Murphy*.

The police left the scene to escort James to Hamilton but the crowd surrounded the brake. For a second time the police charged into the crowd lashing out with their batons, feet and fists. Among the injured were union officials *Sam Colvin* and *David Gilmour*. Miner *Thomas Brownlie* was batoned and kicked by the police while he was standing at a neighbour's door and another two men were arrested; *Henry George* and *Alex.. McFadyen* and they were eventually escorted to Hamilton.

Some of the men had headed towards the bridge, but they were met by the County Police who asked them to leave and while they were in the process of doing this, the Lancashire Police charged the crowd with shouts of B----y Scotties and Irish B------s and batoned the crowd from the back giving many of them a severe beating.

Henry George's brother *Thomas George*, who lived nearby at Nisbet's Buildings, Ferniegair, was making his way down the Ross Road with a child in his arms when he was confronted by two police officers who knocked him against the railings, gripped him by the throat and swore at him.

One of the men arrested during the assault on the crowd was being removed to the police station in a brake with a large police escort. As they drove past the school at Ferniegair children in the crowd started shouting "Bannockburn" at the English police constables who were so incensed, they stopped the brake and charged into the crowd, beating with their batons anyone they could catch, including women and children.

Things began to quieten down when the crowds dispersed. Later in the day during a union meeting at Larkhall, word reached the men that a police brake containing ten police officers had been attacked just above Merryton. Twenty minutes later the brake containing nine officers drove into the centre of Larkhall. All nine men had received a bit of the same kind of treatment handed out by the police to the people at Ross and Ferniegair that morning and as they were driven to the police station covered in dust and blood from their wounds, they were booed and hooted by the crowds lining the streets.

The police officers reported that they had been attacked by 200-300 youths who had apparently *"reached a white heat condition of rage"* and they felt *"nearly killed"* and they were convinced that one of their numbers, a *Constable McFarlane*, one of the oldest constables in the district must be dead after he fainted and fell off the brake as it headed for Larkhall.

The brake was then sent out to find *Constable McFarlane,* who when he was rescued, appeared more dead than alive. The injured officers were taken to the Inspector's house at the police office which had been hastily turned into a hospital with Drs *Alexander* and *Lyons* attending to the injured men.

Almost simultaneously with the attack on the ten police officers, another attack by 1500 miners returning from Larkhall was being carried out on police at Ross Colliery. Half the men stopped at the Ferniegair entrance to the colliery and the other half proceeded to the entrance at Haughhead. The policemen were stationed at both entrances in considerable numbers and among them were some mounted officers who were sent down to Haughhead to assist the men there. At the same time the crowd at the Ferniegair entrance made an attack with sticks and stones. Charged by three mounted officers and twenty baton wielding officers the men ran in the direction of Allanton and Larkhall. Getting into the fields on either side of the road they stopped and showered the police with stones. The police never managed to get within striking distance of the miners who eventually escaped over the fields leaving the officers licking their wounds.

The men who were arrested went on trial at Hamilton Sheriff Summary Court three weeks later charged with "having, on the 17th September formed part of a riotous mob, obstructing police, and assaulting them by throwing stones, picks, pick shafts and *"pailing stobs"*(fencing). They pleaded not guilty. The Murphy's were tried first and despite evidence from eyewitnesses that they took no part in the riots they were found guilty. *Sheriff Davidson* considered that *James Murphy* took part in the mobbing and rioting to a minor degree and fined him 30/- or 21 days. *Henry Murphy* was found guilty of discharging stones from a catapult and for this which the Sheriff said was only less than a firearm, he was sent to prison for 30 days without the option of a fine.

The following day Ferniegair miners *Henry George* and *Alexander McFadyen* faced trial and again despite evidence which pointed to them being innocent, they too were found guilty and fined 40/- or 30 days imprisonment.

Many witnesses were called during the trial to testify that *Henry George* had in no way taken part in the riots, including *George Anderson* manager at Ferniegair Colliery who spoke of him having an excellent character. *Henry George* was an honest upright citizen, a member of the Salvation Army, highly respected in the locality and a man who was without stain on his character. It was said in court that only a short time before the strike he had been highly complimented by *Baillie Hamilton* after helping to capture some prisoners. The pleas fell on deaf ears for he may have been a model citizen but he was also a miner and therefore in the eyes of many, a second class citizen and this opinion had been deliberately fostered by the coal masters who with propaganda, had effectively demonised the miners in order to blinker the public to the terrible conditions they were forced to live and work in. After nineteen weeks on strike the men were eventually forced by starvation to accept the 25% reduction and returned to work.

WITNESSES AT THE TRIAL

For the prosecution…Constables *Buist, Murdoch, McLenan* and Inspector *Stewart*, Hamilton, Lancashire Constabulary. Constables *Riley, Crichton, Culshaw, Clitheroe, Dobson, Holden* and Sergeants *Willoughby, Roberts* and *Smith*.

For the defence…. *Charles Daly*, 3 Grammar School Square, *William Hart,* New Wynd, *James Kelly,* New Wynd, *John Shaw,* 78 Chapel Street, *Luke Garrity* 36 Castle Street, *James Mullholland*, Campbell Street, *James Moore* 45 Townhead Street, *William Queen,* 105 Castle Street, *William Smith*, Holmes St, Hamilton, *William Prentice*, Barrack Street all Hamilton. *Hugh Lambie, Thomas Hannigan* and *John Howie*, Allanton Rows. *George Anderson,* manager Ferniegair Colliery, *John Dick,* Forsyth's Buildings, *Peter Dick,* 10 Old Row, *Hugh* and *Peter Docherty, John Findlay, Thomas George*, Nisbet's Building, *James Hamilton*, 19 Front Row, *Ralph Irvine, Mrs Lindsay, Andrew Mackie, Mrs Pettigrew* Forsyth's Building and *Alexander Scott* all of Ferniegair, *James McVey*, manager Ross Colliery and *Jeremiah Rice* and *Hugh Murphy* both Ross Rows.

LINES ON THE STRIKE

'Tis now about nine weeks or there
Since miners, burdened o'er with care,
Came out on strike to seek redress,
Their hearts buoyed up with hopefulness.

But cupboards now are scant and bare,
And mothers' hearts are unco sair;
The weans in vain now cry for bread,
As they are happit into bed.

The men are getting sick at heart,
And wondering when they'll get a start,
For slavish chains are ill to wear,
But, tyranny, too, is hard to bear.

Now capital on Labour frowns,
And all its rightful claims disowns;
Each seems to think he's in the right—
The strongest party wins the fight.

Oh! surely wealth and power might give
Mankind a wage on which to live
Upon this earth a happier life,
Without this dire, continual strife.

The masters stand in their own light
The longer they maintain the fight
And though in union they conspire
'Tis adding fuel to the fire.

The rights of labour to restore
The cycle of time resolves once more;
And now there's hastening on the wing
An age when labour will be king.

The drones that sit on luxury's lap,
The parasites that suck the sap,
The fungus that on others thrive,
Will be ejected from the hive.

Then wealth and labour will unite,
And give to all what's requisite;
Then love their spirits too, will blend,
And peace will triumph in the end.

Anon. August 1894.

KNOWN FATALITIES AT ROSS COLLIERY

DATE	NAME	AGE	CAUSE OF DEATH
02.10.1884	WALTER BROWN	21	Face injuries
--.06.1885	JAMES TWEEDIE	39	Jammed between hutch and prop
22.10.1888	ROBERT HAMILTON	18	Fall of coal at face, 2 tons
16.10.1889	JOHN WRIGHT	63	Fall of coal at face
01.08.1891	JOHN ANDERSON	28	Explosion
"	GEORGE ANDERSON	23	Explosion
14.01.1893	JAMES KIRKHOPE	17	Dragged down shaft
02.03.1893	CHARLES REID	24	No details
12.11.1896	SAMUEL McCOOK	25	Roof fall (neck broken)
07.01.1897	THOMAS DAVEY	53	Roof fall
15.02.1898	WM. HENDERSON	13	Roof fall (fractured skull)
28.12.1900	WILLIAM MURPHY	50	Explosion (severe burns)
04.12.1903	JOHN MARTIN	28	Fall of coal at face (chest injuries)
03.02.1904	JAMES COX	55	Roof fall, 3-4 tons (multiple injuries)
24.05.1904	JOHN BOND	37	Runaway hutches (fractured pelvis/ leg)
09.03.1907	ALEX. PATERSON	56	Minor head injury (septicaemia)
13.04.1907	ALEX. TAYLOR	51	Roof fall (asphyxia)
16.04.1907	JOHN NISBIT	38	Blasting accident (decapitated)
19.11.1909	THOMAS R. ROBB	24	Fell 120 feet down shaft.
20.08.1912	WILLIAM WHITE	41	Roof fall (head injuries)
25.05.1917	DAVID MORRISON	37	No details (head and neck injuries)
01.06.1918	ROBERT DYET	35	No details (burns to face arms and leg)
07.10.1924	WILLIAM NISBET	25	Roof fall (fractured pelvis)
13.12.1925	PETER BROWN	53	No details (fractured pelvis)
23.10.1928	SUTHERLAND McKAY	37	Explosion (burns to arms, face, and neck)
15.03.1934	MALCOLM McCORMACK	26	Explosion (burns to upper body)
04.07.1944	CHARLES FRASER	42	Roof fall (multiple fractures)

JOHN NISBET KILLED 16.04.1907

John Nisbet lost his life in a horrific accident while working at Ross Colliery as a mining contractor. He was carrying out blasting operations with three other men on a haulage road of the Main coal seam and after setting three shots of gelignite to bring the coal down he lit the fuse and they moved back a safe distance until the shots went off. After hearing what they interpreted as a double and a single shot the men waited for a safe interval and then *John Nisbit* went in to examine the working place. The moment he reached the face a charge of gelignite went off decapitating him. His fellow workmen were badly shocked but uninjured.

Only that morning John had attended the funeral of the oversman *Alexander Taylor* who had been killed in a roof fall three days before. The death of *Alexander Taylor* was the second tragedy to hit that family. In 1899 his 16 year old son Sandy an ostler's assistant had fallen 60 feet to his death down the pit shaft.

John Nisbet who had lived at 3 Middleton Street, Ferniegair was married with five children and had been a member of the 2nd Volunteer Battalion Scottish Rifles for twenty years. His funeral service was at Hamilton Parish Church and the pipe band of the 2nd V.B. played a lament at the graveside at Hamilton's Bent Cemetery.

COLLYER'S WEEDOW

'Twas jist when my youngest was born,
  When Rab was the wean at my fit;
On a cauld winter's Setterday morn,
  That oor ane was kill't in the pit.

I was sittin', I min', by the fire
  Wi' Leezie, the wean, at my breist;
When in cam' wee Wull Macintyre,
  Wi' a face, ay, as solemn's a priest's.

"I doot, Mrs Sim," he begood,
  "There's an accident ower at the Mains;
For aroun' the pithead there's a crood
  O men buddies, weemen and weans."

"My God! its oor Geordie," I cried,
  As I banged to my feet on the flair;
Then wrappin' the wean in the plyde,
  I was oot o' the hoose like a hare.

At the heid o' the Hurries big brae
  A solemn procession I met—
Eh sirs, 'twas a sorrowfu' day,
  A day that I'll never forget.

I was left a wi' a family o' five—
  An unco bit haun'lin atweel,
When ane has to plan and contrive
  To cleed them, and keep them in meal.

Yet I managed to keep oot o' debt,
  By eydently workin' awa,
At the harvest, or ocht I could get,
  That wid earn me a shullin' or twa.

Tho' worried and wrocht aff my feet,
  And like to be bate for a spell,
I saw that my weans gat their meat
  Tho' I aften gaed hungry mysel'

At Nicht, when their rantin' wad cease,
  And a' was as quate as a moose,
I hae pictured them seekin' a piece,
  When there wisna a bite in the hoose.

Thank guidness! 'Twas only a dream;
  Tho feedin', and cleedin' were scant,
We never yet reached the extreme
  O' coming to actual want.

If maitters had come to the warst,
  I'd the "Board" to fa' back on. Ye see,
Guid kens! Frae the first to the last,
  It had aye been a terror to me.

But I hel' to the truth o' my breed
  That He wha the raven sustains,
Wad never neglect in their need
  A collyer's weedow and weans.

George Cunningham.
("Pate McPhun")

Pit props holding up the roof.

AT THE FACE

Scottish miners working at the coal face. Photograph courtesy of The Scottish Mining Museum, Newtongrange.

Sitting on his "hunkers" at the coal face the hewer digs the coal out with his pick. On his right his "neighbour" is putting up props to make sure the roof does not come down. Examples of the miners' graith can be seen in the picture. The man at the face has his pick and behind him can be seen his shovel for lifting coal. The miner putting up the props has his axe in his hand and his saw for cutting the props to size can be seen leaning against a prop supporting the roof. The props are all that stands between the men and eternity.

It was not until the Coal Mines Act of 1887 that it was made compulsory for the colliery owners to provide a sufficient supply of timber at the men's' place of work or in a convenient position. Prior to this Act miners had to saw their own timber to manageable sizes on the surface and then see that that the props "or trees as the miners called them" were taken down the mine. Many of the miners were too exhausted after finishing their shift to cut the timber and this was the cause of many fatal accidents.

THE BLACK SHINING PRIZE

Hewers drilling a coal seam at Ross Colliery, Ferniegair, Hamilton, c. 1904.
Photographs courtesy of Hamilton Natural History Society and South Lanarkshire Council

BRUSHERS AT ROSS COLLIERY, FERNIEGAIR

PIT PROPS HOLDING UP THE ROOF

Brushers at Ross Colliery Ferniegair, Hamilton, c. 1904 Photograph courtesy of Hamilton Natural History Society and South Lanarkshire Council

AT THE MINE

James Ruthven, winding engine man, Ferniegair Colliery
1935

The iron limbs of the engine strong,
　　Went clank-clanking all the day,
And snorts of steam, from its nostrils blown,
　　Rose up in a cloudy spray,
As steady kept in the horseman's eye
　　On his fiery steed and strong,
With curbing thong in his grip he chides,
　　Or thundering speeds along;
While from the hoofs of the charger flung,
　　Are columns of dust and sand,
At whirlwind speed though she dashes on,
　　The touch of his guiding hand
Can make her calm, like a child when calmed,
　　By pleadings of tenderness;
She stands quite still, at her master's will,
　　And stroke of his kind caress.

Be at his post stood the engineman,
　　Alert with a steady eye,
With whistle loud, and a snatch of song,
　　He stooped, and he made her fly
A simple touch from his master hand
　　Awoke with a thrill of might
The power that slumbered in her limbs,
　　Steel sinewed, strong and tight
She stirred; she slipped, then thundered on,
　　And spurned with her mighty heel,
Till iron casting, and groove, and slide
　Were ready to rock and reel.

The monster stroke shot out with a will,
    The coal went a-spinning round,
Loud sang the whorls to the wind aloft,
    And whistled a whirring sound
The signals clashed, and above the din,
    The clack of the cage rang out,
As up to the light, from the dingy depths,
    It came with a dash and shout
So lightly yoked to her traces tough,
All day with an action sweet,
The engine plunged with her mighty arms,
    And triumphant at her feet;
Flung were the treasures that make us great,
    Give us spheres to flourish in,
Nurse commonwealth in the lap of art
    So that all men feel akin.

Ho! ye who toil in a sunless mine,
    And pile up our comforts high,
I marvel much that the rich decline
    To list to your labour cry!
No scanty pittance be your reward,
    But thine the full flush of meed,
To make your labour, and lot, less hard,
    And lighter the pinch of need.
All honour be to the dusty face,
    The muscle and sinew sound
That slave for us—it is no disgrace
    To burrow beneath the ground.
Yours are the power to heap up wealth,
    Make us hammers, plough, and spade,
And wheel and axle to keep in health,
    The live currents of our trade.
We sing God-speed the heroic band,
    False veneer of caste disdain;
Let us venerate the horny hand,
    As well as the working brain.

        James Kelly
        Carluke
        Circa 1883

James (Jamie) Ruthven was born in Carluke and moved to Larkhall with his family when he was a small boy. At 18 he began working as an engineman at No. 4 Woodside Colliery and during his working life he worked in Bog, Bent, Dykehead, Cornsilloch, Ferniegair, Craighead and Springbank (Shotts) collieries.

In his fifty years as a winding engineman he was never once was involved in a cage accident involving miners although his daily load often exceeded 500 men.

A keen cyclist from the age of 14 he once possessed a penny farthing and when he was 68 he still cycled to and from his home at Maitland Bank, Burnhead, Larkhall to his work.

When he retired he had been working at Ferniegair Colliery for eight years

SAME PLACE - DIFFERENT TIME

Above, Front Row Ferniegair circa early 1900's; the chimney of Ferniegair Colliery can be seen at the end of the Row.

Below, Feb 2007, the public house has just been demolished and expensive houses have been built on the site of Front Row.

FERNIEGAIR COLLIERY AND VILLAGE

A very early picture of Ferniegair Colliery. Courtesy of Hamilton Town House Reference Library

The owner and developer of Ferniegair Colliery was Hamilton wholesale grocer and wine merchant James Nisbet. In 1857 he leased the mineral field at Ferniegair and by June 1859 the colliery which cost between £9000 and £10,000 to develop was advertising coal for sale in the Hamilton Advertiser. To celebrate the winning of coal, Nisbet treated his miners and their wives and sweethearts (104 in total) to a day trip to Rothsay.

Nisbet also built twelve two roomed houses to house his workforce most of whom came from outside Lanarkshire. James Nisbet however had borrowed most of the money for his business and an attempt to develop Greenfield Colliery Burnbank bankrupted him. Archibald Russell eventually bought control of Ferniegair Colliery and as the pit was developed and more men were employed extra houses were built to accommodate them and their families. Eventually Ferniegair Rows had thirteen single room houses, thirty-one with two rooms and seven with three rooms a total of fifty-one houses. There was one washhouse and dry closet (toilet) for every five families and water had to be obtained from stand pipes outside. There was no regular refuse collection and the dry toilets were emptied very infrequently.

There was very little in the way of local recreation facilities for the miners and their families until the opening of the new Miners' Welfare Institute on Saturday 10th May 1924. Delighted by the new facility the whole village turned out to watch Mr. T.C. Hardie managing director of Archibald Russell Ltd declare the building open.

Mr James Lochhead, of Messrs Cullen, Lochhead and Brown Architects, Hamilton had originally designed the building with a hall, billiard room, reading room, bowling green and tennis court with an estimated cost of £7000 which the committee hoped to obtain from the Miners' Welfare Scheme. However this failed to materialise and they were awarded a grant of £2000. To keep costs to a minimum and to obtain as good a building as the money could buy, the miners of the district were asked to volunteer their labour and they turned out in force to carry out the digging and levelling work and they also dug out and laid the foundations and the grounds.

To help with the building costs the Duke of Hamilton's trustees donated £59, a bit of an insult and a classic example of crumbs from the rich man's table considering the vast amount of money the Hamilton family had received in royalties from the local collieries. An anonymous gentleman donated £100 and with a few other small donations the hall was almost debt free when it opened.

At the opening ceremony the five longest serving colliery workers were to be presented with a token of gratitude for their years of hard work from the managing directors of Archibald Russell Ltd. Four of the men William McKendrick, aged 81, with 54 years service, Robert Reid, aged 72, with 61 years service, Philip McLuskey aged 77, with 67 years service, John Rowatt age 74, with 52 years service were present at the opening ceremony but the fifth man a James Ross aged 77, with 61 years service had just retired, was living at Glenbuck and too unwell to attend. Each man however was presented with a walking stick and no doubt they would need them for between them they had completed a total of 295 years in Russell's collieries.

Ferniegair was the fifteenth Miners' Welfare completed in Lanarkshire thanks to the Mines Industry Act. In Hamilton Parish five schemes were either being built or just about ready to commence. One of the largest was at Burnbank, for which the sum of £10,000 had been allocated. Low Waters scheme was to start in July at a cost of £7500. Eddlewood had been given £750 for the extension of their present recreation rooms and Earnock had been granted £860 for bowling green purposes.

The Miners' Welfare Institutes were funded by a levy of a penny a ton on every ton of coal produced commenced in 1922 to provide institutes and halls in outlying districts of mining communities where no such facilities existed. The miners themselves paid 2d each off their wages for the upkeep of their halls.

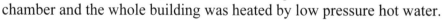

Ferniegair Miners' Welfare Institute was erected on the ground immediately adjoining the War Memorial. It had a billiard room and also a reading room which could be divided by folding doors into two sections for ladies and gentlemen's retiring rooms. There were male and female lavatories and a hall which seated 300. There was a cooking kitchen and heating chamber and the whole building was heated by low pressure hot water.

In February 1929 an extension was built to provide facilities for carpet bowls and in July 1933 a well equipped children's playground was provided by the same scheme at a cost of £780 and it was opened in front of a large crowd of children and parents by the miners' M.P. Duncan Graham.

Ferniegair Miners' Welfare Institute is now a community hall owned by South Lanarkshire Council and it is still very much a part of the life of Ferniegair village which has seen a building revival recently and is now a very desirable place to live, although to the original Ferniegair families it always was.

FERNIEGAIR VILLAGE AND DISTRICT MINERS' WELFARE
CHILDRENS' GALA DAY
22/7/1929

The big event of the year for the children of Ferniegair was The Gala Day which day began when the children met at Ferniegair School where the headmaster Mr Whitelaw, his staff, members of the Welfare Committee and Girl Guides got them marshalled into lines to begin the procession led by the Larkhall Prize Band. From the school they marched through the village on to Allanton and then back to the Public Park where they received buns, milk and a penny and after they had eaten their fill, the serious business of the day "The Games" got under way.

The following participants received their prizes from Mrs Whitelaw wife of the headmaster.

Boy's races---3 to 5 years 1st *T. Crighton,* 2nd *James Gibson,* 3rd *Peter Bolton.*
6 to 9 years--- 1st *Martin Wedlock,* 2nd *William Nimmo,* 3rd *James Crighton,*
9 to 11 years--- 1st *Cov. Brown,* 2nd *Thomas Wedlock,* 3rd *John Dobbie.*
12 to 14--- years 1st *R. Lawson,* 2nd *William Craw,* 3rd *Walter Agnew.*
Girls Races--- 3 to 5 years--- 1st *Jean Galloway,* 2nd *Nettie Wedlock* 3rd *M. Dawson.*
6 to 9 years---1st *Agnes Wedlock,* 2nd *M. Connachan,* 3rd *Nettie Couser.*
9 to 11 years--- 1st Nellie *McDougall,* 2nd *A. Davidson,* 3rd *A. Lindsay.*
12 to 14 years--- 1st *Bessie Lawson,* 2nd *Lizzie Crighton,* 3rd *Agnes Walkinshaw.*
High Jump (boys) --- 1st *Thos. Thomson.* 2nd *Robert Lawson,* 3rd *Wm. Gebbie.*
Sack race, (boys) --- 1st *Wm. Gebbie,* 2nd *James Moffat,* 3rd *Walter Agnew.*
Sack Race (girls) --- 1st *Mary McDougall,* 2nd *Cissie Nisbet,* 3rd *Lizzie Crighton.*
Skipping rope race--- 1st *Lizzie Wedlock,* 2nd *Mary Lawson,* 3rd *M. Cunningham.*
220 yards (youths--- 14-18 years 1st *Jas. Patterson,* 2nd *J. Tait.*
220 yards (adults) --- *1st J. Patterson,* 2nd *George Hutcheson,* 3rd *Pat Mulhearn.*
Men's--- 2nd *John Ballantyne,* 3rd *Sam Morrow*
Married women's race (50 years upwards) --- *1st Mrs Grey,* 2nd *Mrs Gibson,* 3rd *Mrs Murphy.*
Married women's race (under 30 years) ---1st Mrs *McDougall, 2nd Mrs Dunn, 3rd Mrs T. Brown.*
Unmarried women's race--- 1st Kate Dawson, 2nd Retta Martin, 3rd *Gladys Lawson.*
Five-a-side football--- (school boys) 1st *Alex Queen's* five, 2nd *Wm. Gebbie's* five.
Five-a-side football (adults) --- 1st *Caldwell Wright's* five, 2nd *John McCulloch's* five.
Judgment kick—1st--- *Alex. Dickson,* 2nd *Thomas Leggate,*
Tug-o-war--- 1st *Ross Colliery,* 2nd *Ferniegair Colliery.*
Handicappers---*Mr McDonald* and Mr *McFarlane,* Judges---Messrs *Galloway, Lafferty* and *Brownlie.*
Stewards--- Messrs *Millar, Laird, Leggate, Tait* and *Morton.*

THE DECLINE OF FERNIEGAIR AS A MINING VILLAGE

Seventy years after the first mine opened at Ferniegair, the worldwide industrial depression of the 1920's - 30's resulted in a slump in coal sales and over several years this gradually brought to near extinction many of the pit villages which only so recently had been thriving communities. Ferniegair was among the villages badly affected During the year 1913-1914 there was an average of 369 children being taught by 10 teachers including the headmaster at Ferniegair primary school. By March 1921 the number had dropped to 332 pupils and 9 teachers.

The closure of Bog and Home Farm Collieries on the 16th December 1927 with the resultant loss of 600 jobs left the mining communities of Ferniegair, Larkhall and Hamilton reeling. Previous to 1927 there had been a drip, drip, dripping away of the lifeblood of the village as its young people packed up in despair and left for distant shores hoping for a better life. Now that drip had turned into a haemorrhage and nearly every week saw the departure of another family or youth seeking work elsewhere. With the closure of Allanton Colliery in 1929 the school roll dropped to 210 pupils and 6 staff and it was becoming obvious that the village of Ferniegair was spiralling into an industrial and economic decline.

The small shopkeepers in the village were also seriously affected as their takings plummeted and they struggled to keep afloat with several going out of business.

By 1936 the condition of the houses of Ferniegair Rows had deteriorated to such an extent due to lack of maintenance that they were described in a Sunday newspaper article as "*an affront to decency.*" Families of seven and eight were living in one and two roomed homes with dry lavatories which were shared by 30-40 persons. The houses were rat infested and the only ones with running water were tenanted by three colliery officials. The women from the rows had to fetch their water from the washhouses out the back door and to reach them; they had to walk through a quagmire of mud.

The closure of Ross Colliery on 13th July 1945 and the collapse of Ferniegair Colliery's No. 1 shaft on the 27th February 1947 dealt the death blow for Ferniegair as a mining community. A short time after the collapse nineteen pit ponies were brought to the surface via No. 2 shaft but the rapid accumulation of black damp underground meant that the miners lost their graith (tools).

Right- James (Fernie) Nimmo who left Ferniegair in January 1928 to work in the coalmines at Colver, Pennsylvania. The two men on his right are his uncle and cousin both also called James Nimmo. Fernie never saw Scotland again. He died in 1938 age 34. Photograph courtesy of his son Jim Nimmo, U.S.A.

The pit however was doomed; the National Coal Board was not willing to pour good money into a mine which was almost 100 years old and nearing the end of its productive life. Of the 450 miners and surface workers, 250 were offered work at Cardowan Colliery with the rest being offered work at Ponfeigh, Kennnox Mine, Douglas, Woodend (Armadale) Polkemmet and Loganlea (West Lothian.) The National coal board compensated the miners for the loss of their tools.

Men over the age of 60 years who were unable to find employment or were retiring received 12 weeks wages. Ferniegair Colliery had given employment to countless men over a period of almost 100 years. Its closure meant that Ferniegair as a mining village no longer existed. Many of the miners were forced to seek work elsewhere and packed up and left.

Hootlet Row (Avonbank)

Pit joiner. MR AND MRS ROBERT BARR

Robert Barr was a native of Hamilton and spent his early days at Hootlet Raw (Avonbank) His wife came from Douglas and they married in Wishaw in 1876. Robert spent 46 years working at Ferniegair Colliery and when he retired in 1926 they were living at 29 Low Patrick Street, Hamilton. The above photograph was taken on the occasion of their golden wedding.

KNOWN FATALITIES AT FERNIEGAIR COLLIERY

DATE	NAME	AGE	CAUSE OF DEATH
23.07.1864	JOHN GILCHRIST	64	No details (broken legs and ribs)
06.03.1867	JOHN SMITH	60	Explosion (severe burns)
19.07.1870	JOHN WILSON	17	Struck by hutch (chest injuries)
13.05.1871	JAMES McMILLAN	55	Roof fall. 3 tons
07.09.1871	ROBERT PHEELY	13	Explosion (severe burns)
08.08.1872	JAMES McGINNIS	14	Roof fall _ ton.
28.08.1876	ALEXANDER ROSS	24	Roof fall (fractured pelvis)
14.09.1878	JAMES HAMILTON	62	Roof fall
03.04.1880	PATRICK CURRAN	15	Explosion (severe burns)
27.05.1881	JOHN McKENDRICK	47	Roof fall
14.11.1882	ALEXANDER AITKEN	38	Fell 72 feet down shaft
28.09.1882	JOHN WRIGHT	15	Roof fall (severe head injuries)
08.01.1887	ROBERT WANDS	17	Abdomen crushed by wagons
27.04.1896	THOMAS WHITELAW	22	Roof fall (multiple fractures)
09.04.1899	ALEXANDER TAYLOR	16	Fell 66 feet down shaft
14.03.1903	JOHN MILLER	31	Fell 120 feet down shaft
07.02.1904	JOHN KELSO	49	Coal cutting machine (multiple injuries)
22.03.1909	JAMES HUTCHINS	36	Roof fall
27.06.1909	FRANK TAIT	30	Explosion (severe burns)
"	GEORGE HUNTER	22	" " "
"	JOHN ADAMS	26	" " "
27.01.1910	WILLIAM JOHNSTONE	14	Roof fall (fractured spine - 3 months)
01.06.1911	WILLIAM KINNEY	32	Roof fall (severe back injuries)
17.08.1911	ROBERT McCUTCHEON	27	Roof fall (fractured spine)
18.09.1916	WILLIAM J. McROBERTS	34	Roof fall (fractured spine)
26.03.1917	ALEXANDER HAMILTON	40	Fall of stone (fractured spine)
01.04.1917	WILLIAM NEIL	25	Roof fall (asphyxia/multiple injuries)
10.04.1920	DAVID FARRELL	43	No details (fractured spine)
10.01.1922	JOHN KELLY	36	No details (fractured skull)
06.09.1929	THOMAS HYND BLAIR	45	Roof fall (fractured skull)
20.02.1933	JAMES TANNOCK	14	Crushed by wagon (ruptured bowel)
13.98.1934	DAVID HAMILTON	39	No details (asphyxia/multiple injuries)
17.03.1935	JOHN RUNDELL	32	Roof fall (fractured skull and thigh)
02.12.1942	DAVID CRAWFORD CRAIG	21	No details (fractured base of skull)

Ferniegair Colliery c. 1880. Note the children in the foreground of the photograph. News must have gone round the "Raws" that the photographer had arrived. Photograph courtesy of Richard Newall.

THE MINERS OF FERNIEGAIR ROWS 1871

John Barr (Ireland)
James Baxter (Ireland)
Andrew Beveridge. (Linlithgow, Whitburn)
John Campbell (Ireland)
John Campbell (15) (Lanarkshire, Airdrie)
Duncan Campbell (Lanarkshire, Glasgow)
Alex. Campbell (12) (Lanarkshire, Cambusnethan)
Robert Canning. (Ireland, Co. Derry)
John Carney. (Ireland. Fermanagh)
William Carney (12) (Ireland. Fermanagh)
James Casie. (Ireland)
John Casie (13) (Ireland.)
James Casie (11) (Ireland.)
James Cassidy (Ireland)
Thomas Cassidy (15) (Lanarkshire, Old Monkland)
David Clark (Joiner) (Lanarkshire, Dalserf)
Phillip Cosgrove (Irl. Co. Monaghan)
David Cummock (Irl. Co. Down)
Samuel Cummock (14) (Irl. Co. Down)
John Cunningham (Ireland.)
Daniel Cunningham (15) (Ayrshire Kilbirnie)
James Cunningham (13) (Lanarkshire, Bothwell)
John Davidson (Lanarkshire, Glasgow)
Edward Docherty (Ayrshire, Newton)
Patrick Fennen (Ireland)
Peter Fennen (Ayrshire, Muirkirk)
Patrick Fennen (15) (Ayrshire, Muirkirk)
Daniel Fennen (11) (Ayrshire, Dalmellington)
Alex. Ferguson. (47) (Ayrshire, Newton)
John Ferguson (21) (Ayrshire, Newton)
James Ferguson (14) (Ayrshire, Dalmellington)
Alex. Ferguson (19) (Ayrshire, Dalmellington)
William Ferguson (16) (Ayrshire, Kilmaurs)
William Fleming (Fireman) (Lanarkshire Blantyre)
John George (Ireland)
Thomas George (Lanarkshire, Bothwell)
William Graham ((14) (Driver) (Lanarkshire, Hamilton)
James Hamilton (11) (Coal Trapper) (Lanarkshire)
James Hamilton (Irl. Co. Donegal)
James Hand (Irl. Co. Cavan)
John Hilack ((Dalry, Ayrshire)
John Kilpatrick. (Ireland.)
Patrick Kearney (Irl. Co. Fermanagh)
James Kearney (13) (Irl. Co. Fermanagh)
Patrick Kearney (12) (Irl. Co. Fermanagh)
Daniel Kerr (Lanarkshire, Faskin)
Malcolm Kerr (14) (Lanarkshire, Shettleston)
Hugh Kirkland (Ayrshire, Tarbolton)
Andrew Lindsay (Lanarkshire, Glasgow)
George Lindsay (15) (Lanarkshire, Cambusnethan)

William Lindsay (14) (Cambusnethan)
John Lindsay (12) (Lanarkshire)
John McBane (12) (Lanarkshire)
Edward McCabe (Irl. Co. Cavan)
Patrick McCabe (Irl. Co. Cavan)
John McCann (Labourer) (Ireland.)
Thomas McCann (Ayrshire, Muirkirk)
William McBride (Wigtonshire)
James McGhie (Ayrshire)
James McGowan (Irl. Londonderry)
James McIntyre (13) (Coatbridge)
John McKendrick (Stirlingshire)
Jas. McKendrick (11) (Bothwell)
John McCann (Labourer) (Ireland)
Francis McStay (Irl. Co. Antrim)
Francis McStay (16) (Old Monkland)
Bernard Maguire (Irl. Co. Fermanagh)
John Maley (Ireland.)
James Miller (Glasgow)
James Morrison (Dumfries)
James Morrison (15) (Lesmahagow)
William Morrison (Lesmahagow)
Samuel Muir (Ayrshire, Irvine)
James O'Brien (Ireland)
Francis Park (Ireland.)
Alexander Porter (Irl. Co. Derry)
Robert Porter (14) (Coatbridge)
James Quinn (Irl. Co. Down)
William Quinn (Ireland.)
James Reid (74) (Ayrshire, Irvine)
John C. Reid (Lanarkshire Carnbro)
Charles Russell (Drawer) (Old Monklands)
Wm.& John Simmons. (Beith & Baillieston)
William Scoular (Old Monkland)
James Stewart (Ayrshire, Newton)
James K. Stewart (16) (Holytown)
Andrew Wallace (Lanarkshire, Shotts)
John White (Ayrshire, Stevenson)
James White (Ayrshire, Stevenson)
William White (16) (Ayrshire, Stevenson)
John Wardlaw (Lanarkshire, Carluke)
Andrew Wilson (Scotland)
William Wilson (15) (Ayrshire)
William Wilson (Ayrshire, Old Cumnock)
John Wilson (Lanarkshire, Bothwell)
James Wilson (Pit manager) (Dumfries)
Robert Wilson (15) Lanarkshire, Bothwell
Andrew Wilson (12) (Old Monkland)
Wm. Wilson (15) Ayrshire (Kilbirnie)
John Wright (Irl. Co. Monaghan)
Thomas Wright (Lanarkshire, Wishaw)

Spelling of names may differ from today's spelling

ALLANTON COLLIERY
JAMES M. RAMAGE
MINING CONTRACTOR

James Ramage was born at Low Quarter but moved to Larkhall were he worked for some time as under-manager at Bog Colliery before leaving to work at Kinneil Collieries Bo'ness. When he returned to Larkhall he began working as a mining contractor.

On 2nd December 1923 at Allanton Colliery Ferniegair, James and his sister Helen's husband James Hardie had just started work when there was an explosion of gas. Both men received severe burns and died two days later at Glasgow Royal Infirmary.

The deaths were not the first mining tragedy to affect the Ramage family, in 1904 when James was 16 years of age he had to register the death of his own father William Ramage (41) who fell 529 feet to his death down the shaft at Quarter No. 8 Colliery.

A newspaper account of the explosion records "*that both men were known to a wide circle of acquaintances and were kind-hearted and generous to those of their fellows in trouble and distress." Both were married with young families.*"

In Loving Memory
OF
JAMES MENZIES RAMAGE
(Beloved Husband of Isabella M'Callum),
WHO DIED AT ROYAL INFIRMARY, GLASGOW,
On Tuesday, 4th December, 1923
(The result of an accident received at Allanton Colliery, Hamilton),
Aged 35 Years.
41 RAPLOCH STREET,
LARKHALL.

"Blessed are the dead which die in the Lord from henceforth: Yea, saith the Spirit, that they may rest from their labours; and their works do follow them."—*Rev. xiv., 13.*

An early mine rescue team. Middle, top row James M. Ramage
Photograph courtesy of the Ramage family.

43

MEN KNOWN TO HAVE WORKED AT ALLANTON COLLIERY

Thomas Adams, Union Street, Larkhall *(1891) Alexander Airns,* Allanton Rows, (1890) *M. Anderson* (1924) *George Barr,* fireman, Walker's Building Muir Street, Larkhall, (1916) *W. Black* (1924) *R. Bulloch* (1924) *P. Bone* (1920) *John Brown,* Allanton Rows (1889)) *W. Clark* (1926) *A. Cook* (1920) *G.H. Couser* (1924) *Thomas Crookston,* oversman (1876) *T. Davidson* (1920) *Alexander Dick* (1870) *Richard Dick,* fireman *(1922) William Dobbie,* Allanton Rows (1896) *James Early,* Young Street, Hamilton (1891) *T. Fairley* (1920) *D. Fleming* (1924) *David Forsyth* (1846) *John Gaffney,* Low Patrick Street, Hamilton (1873) *John Gallagher* (1924) *J. Gilmour* (1924) *John Gilchrist* (1870) *H. Graham,* manager (1888) *D. Grant* (1924) *Matthew Grannahan,* brusher, (1920's) *Matthew Hill,* bogieman 38 Raploch Street, Larkhall (1917) *James Kirkwood* (1867) *W. G. Lanyon,* manager (1924) *John Lucas* (1891) *Peter Henderson,* undermanager, 2 Allanton Terrace, Ferniegair (1924) *R.. Jarvie* (1924) J*ohn Leishman* (1874) *T. London* (1924) *James Lynch,* Sheiling Hill Hamilton,(1870) *John Main* (1926) *Robert Miller* (1917) *Joseph Mitchell* (1890) *James Morrison,* oversman (1875) *John and Samuel Morrison,* Allanton Rows (1883) *John McAlpine,* oversman (1920*) Edward McCallum,* Low Patrick Street, Hamilton, (1873) *Malcolm McFarlane,* manager (1874) *Joseph McKendrick,* manager, High Merryton Cottage, Larkhall, (1918) *Alexander McLay*, clerk (1870) *C. McLaughlin* (1924) *Robert McQueen,* undermanager 145 Drygate Street Larkhall (1923) *J. Pollock* (1920) *Robert Rankin,* 12 Duke Street, Hamilton (1874) James Seggie, Deputy Rows, Allanton. *Cornelius Smith,* oncostman, 23 Brown Street, Hamilton (1917) *James Sporran,* 49 Townhead Street, Hamilton (1871) *Andrew Thomson,* undermanager (1924) *Archibald Thomson,* pit-sinker, Allanton Rows, (1897)
The above have been mentioned in the Hamilton Advertiser for various reasons. (Details available from author.)

ALLANTON ROWS FERNIEGAIR. C. 1900. From this photograph we can see quite clearly what the coal masters thought of their workers, How the women could possibly keep their homes clean with the quagmire at their door is beyond me, yet look at the lovely clean washing. The Rows consisted of 30 single end (one room) houses and 40 two roomed houses. 10 single ends were built back to back and the cost of rents varied between 2 and 3 shillings per week depending on the meanness of the house being let.

KNOWN FATALITIES AT ALLANTON COLLIERY FERNIEGAIR

DATE	NAME	AGE	CAUSE OF DEATH
31.03.1870	PETER McMEECHAN	42	Head crushed between buffers at surface.
17.07.1870	ROBERT BARR	18	Fire-damp explosion
22.07.1870	ALEX DICK.	19	Burns from fire-damp explosion. 5 days.
11.01.1872	JOHN SUMMERS	30	Roof fall killed instantly.
29.04.1873	ANDREW MEIKLE	50	Fell from scaffold when cage was down
10.07.1874	PAT. McFADYEN	19	Roof fall 15cwts killed instantly.
13.04.1877	JOHN McMANUS	53	Suffocated by fumes from underground fire
25.10.1878	THOMAS PARKER	44	Roof fall (no details)
27.03.1891	JAMES ROGERSON	15	Crushed by waggons (fractured ribs)
10.10.1893	PAT DONAHAY	60	Roof fall (no details.)
05.05.1893	ANDREW KYLE	32	Roof fall (no details)
11.11.1898	THOMAS BLAKELY	38	Killed by explosives (no details)
22.04.1898	ARCHIBALD SCOTT	16	Roof fall (ruptured bowel, peritonitis)
18.08.1898	JOHN HILL	46	Rundown by wagons. (abdominal injuries)
10.11.1898	SAMUEL BLAIKLEY	--	Killed by explosives.
01.08.1900	JAMES SMITH	19	Fell in front of wagons (fractured pelvis)
11.09.1900	MICHAEL HEALY	28	Crushed by wagons
29.03.1902	WILLIAM ROSS	45	Roof fall. (ruptured bladder)
15.10.1903	DAVID HUGHES	37	Roof fall (150 tons)
22.03.1905	JAS. R. HAMILTON.	20	Fell 240 feet down shaft.
29.08.1905	JOHN McLAREN	45	Roof fall (asphyxia)
"	RICHARD McLAREN	19	" " "
12.03.1907	JAMES COWAN	56	Roof fall (severe injuries to head and lower body)
30.09.1907	WM. MARTIN	14.	Roof fall (asphyxia)
08.10.1907	WM. McGOWAN	44	Run down by hutches.
03.04.1907	THOMAS BROWN	34	Run down by wagons (lacerated legs, shock)
18.05.1910	JAMES QUINN	--	Roof fall (no details)
04.09.1910	WM. MARSHALL	24	Roof fall (fractured skull)
15.04.1916	WM. LAMBIE.	34	Coal cutting machine (multiple injuries)
01.07.1916	WM. FLEMING	49	Roof fall (no details)
13.01.1917	ALEX. BONE	40	Roof fall 2 tons (neck broken)
14.01.1917	WM. RODNEY	40	Roof fall (fractured skull)
02.10.1917	THOMAS SCOTT	33	No details (fractured skull)
15.02.1918	DAVID STEWART	48	Killed by train (fractured skull)
19.12.1918	ALEX. LAMBIE	39	Roof fall. (fractured skull and meningitis.)
13.02.1919	WM. HAMILTON	65	No details (neck broken)
15.03.1921	CHARLES O'NEIL	53	No details
01.02.1923	NEIL WILSON	23	No details. (neck broken)
21.09.1923	CHARLES BARNES	24	Roof fall (head injury)
02.12.1923	JAMES RAMAGE	35	Explosion. (burns and shock)
"	JAMES HARDIE	33	" " " "
10.02.1924	ALEX. ANDERSON	14	Hutch accident (multiple injuries)
02.03.1924	ALEX. D. WELLS	34	No details (fractured spine and cardiac shock.
15.10.1924	PATRICK KELLY	30	Roof fall (neck broken)

THE MINERS OF ALLANTON ROWS 1871

James Adams. Joiner (Ireland)
James Addie (Airdrie)
John Allan (Ireland)
Thomas Allan (15) (Ireland)
John Allan (12) (England)
James Beggs (Campbletown)
Antony Burnet (Lanarkshire)
James Burns (Ireland)
Michael Burns (Ireland, Co. Antrim)
William Burt (Glasgow)
John Campbell (Greenock)
John Cherry (59) (Dalserf)
James Cherry (22) (England)
James Cowan (Stirlingshire, St. Ninians)
Robert Cullen. Fireman (Coatbridge)
Robert Currons (England)
James Currons (England)
Francis Clark (Ireland, Armagh)
Richard Clark, Fireman (Old Monkland)
Alex. Clark (15) (Cambusnethan)
Adam Clark (13) (Bothwell)
Thomas Cummings (New Monkland)
Dennis Curran (Ireland)
John Davie (15) Bothwell)
Peter Docherty (Lanark)
Robert Donnelly Ireland (Co. Derry)
John Donnelly (16) (Ireland, Co. Antrim)
Alick. Donnelly (14) (Hamilton)
Henry Donnelly (12) (Hamilton)
Laurence Donnelly* (8) (Hamilton)
Alexander Eirnes (Bothwell)
Richard Engwin,* (Cornwall, Lugdven)
Irice Engwin, (Cornwall, Lugdven)
Andrew Evans (Bothwell)
James Farl, Underground labourer (Ireland)
Arthur Farl (15) Underground labourer (England)
James Ferris (Ireland)
Alex. Forsyth, (Bannockburn)
David Forsyth, (Bothwell)
James Forsyth (14) (Bothwell)
Alexander Forsyth (12) (Bothwell)
George Gibb (Boness)
Robert Green. Blacksmith (Girvan)
Thomas Hamilton. Carter (Hamilton)
Edward Jeffries (England)
Edward Jeffries (12) (Fifeshire)

William Kilpatrick (Glasgow)
William Kilpatrick (19) Tollcross)
David Kilpatrick (14) (Tollcross)
Matthew Kirkwood (Denny)
James Lawrence (Old Monkland)
William Lindsay (Larkhall)
John Lindsay (Carluke)
John McGhie (Rutherglen)
Henry McGhie (Shettleston
David McKraith (Motherwell)
Hugh McLinden (Ireland Co. Sligo)
James McLinden (Blantyre)
John McLinden (Blantyre)
James Lynch (Ireland, Donegal)
Patrick McDougal (Ireland)
James McKendrick (Wishaw)
Edward Murphy (15) (Lanarkshire)
Thomas Maxwell (11) Carmyle)
James Neilson (New Monkland)
David Paterson (13) (Hamilton)
William Percie (Cornwall)
Patrick Rafferty (Ireland, Co. Down)
John Reid (14) (Hamilton)
Halbert Renwick. (Pitheadman) (Shotts)
James Russell (Bothwell)
John Russell (Hamilton)
William Russell (Ireland, County Antrim)
Robert Smith (Coatbridge)
Robert Smith (14) (Wishaw)
John Stevenson (Paisley)
Robert Stevenson (Ireland)
Hamilton Smith (Pit Roundsman) (Dalry)
David Swan (Inveresk)
Alexander Thomson (Old Monkland)
John Thomson (Whitburn)
George Thomson (Pitheadman) (Larkhall)
William White (Lasswade)
William White (11) Lasswade)
William Wilkie (Lanarkshire)
William Wilkie (11) Stirlingshire)
Neil Ward (Ireland, Donegal)
John Ward (Old Monkland)

*Laurence Donnelly is listed as working as a coal miner even although at the age of 8 years it was illegal. It was not uncommon for parents to add a few years on to the age of a boy (especially if he was tall for his age) so he could obtain employment.

*Richard Engwin (Angwin) and his wife travelled with their eight children from Cornwall to Allanton sometime between 1867 and 1870. In the census they are documented as Engwin but the name is Angwin. Marion Gebbie one of their descendants still lives locally at Ferniegair.

THE MINER BOY
IN
HIS FATHER'S COAT

What joys for boys, least some of them,
  When school at last they quit,
To follow where some others led,
  To work down in the pit.

That morning, when I dressed for work,
  I was as proud as punch;
One pocket held a flask of tea,
  Another held my lunch.

My faither's jacket I did wear,
  But it was not made to fit;
For anything was good enough
  For work down in the pit.

How I wish I had my photograph,
  That on it I might gaze,
Or show to others what were facts
  In my happy boyhood days;

Without a thought, without a care,
  As happy as a lark;
The coat it almost touched my heels,
  But the pit is very dark.

But to the earth I must return,
  And face the shining light;
It showed two feet beneath a coat—
  Oh, Lordy! what a sight!

My face, nae doot, was black enough,
  The sign that I could work;
But the truth I carried up my sleeve,
  I rubbed it with the dirt.

When Charles Chaplin jumped to fame,
  And made the people grin,
He was no handsome Beau Brummel,
  And I looked much like him.

His trousers they were out of style,
  And I guess I just looked it;
My jacket almost swept the road
  Coming from the pit.

The dumbest beast that walks the earth—
  This honour has the ass—
I wondered why it reared and shied
  And me it widna pass.

The puir auld man who held the reins
  He said I should be shot,
The very donkey acted queer,
  When it saw me in the coat.

It's no' the coat that makes the man,
  Is among the saying's true,
And every year is marked with change,
  But yet I'm telling you---

I would a silken vest despise,
  And the style some mashers got
Just to be a boy once more,
  Inside my father's coat.

It pays well to be handsome,
  And in costly clothes be dressed,
Ladies sweet and charming,
  By you may be caressed.

I could have served the farmer,
  But the word is seldom spoke,
The crows went cawing to their rook,
  When they saw me in the coat.

Oh I wish you saw my photograph,
  As sure as you have breath,
You would not need that any more,
  You'd laugh yourself to death.

Robert Maxwell,
Detroit, Michigan.
 USA
Circa 1931.

THE HOME FARM COLLIERY CALAMITY
JAN 1877

The wild unwelcome, bummin' o' that hoarse imperious
    horn. (1)
Through the chilly air is coming, on the morning breezes
    borne,
Tae the ears o' weary miners, and the bowers o' blessed sleep,
Fade awa' and Fancy sees again the dreary, dismal deep;--
The dismal, dreary mine, ye ken' is aye his foremaist care,
An' when *Morpheus draps* his sceptre, Fancy flits him ever   *Greek god of sleep drops*
    there,
As drowsily he lies a wee*, an' rubs ilk* weary limb,   *little *each
Half-feared tae face the daily fecht* in yon dark cavern grim.   *fight

Ay, grim an' gruesome, *weel I wot,* before my mem'ry's een   *well I see*
There rises mony a murky spot langsyne that I hae seen;
Oot through the mud, 'mang clouds o' smoke, the water
    tricklin' cauld*,   *cold
O'er back an' limb 'mid sweat an' steam, we toiled, and
    crulged, and crawled;
But, haith! oor miner maunna shirk—he *kens the awmrie's   *knows the cupboards bare*
    toom,* ---
He rises, dons his dirty sark*, and *lichts his doosy* dim;   *shirt * lights his lamp*
An' sune* a lot o' lively bairns are rantin'* roun' his knee,   * soon*noisy or boisterous
An' each his scrimpit* mornin' piece an' scanty cup *maun pree*   *scanty *must take*

Gaun doon the road, he muses, for he's wae* this winter   *sorrowful
    morn;
"We surely hae* as hard a lot as ony* mortal born!   *have *any
Tae fecht for bare existence aye, sae far below the grun'*,   *to fight* *ground
It's only an idle* day e'en noo we see the sun."   *not working
An' then he muses "Times 'Ill men'—we may be happy yet;"
I winna yaummer*—wee! I ken we arena easy beat.   *complain
Shall*poortith smoor* oor British pluck? Is pleasure a' oor   *poverty smother*
    aim?
We're Britain's heroes, fechtin'* for her treasure and her   *fighting
    fame!"

The heart's an unco humble ane that pride can never heeze;
Oor miner marches tae his post nor danger dreads nor sees;
But ah, the wicked "water sprite" they sang aboot langsyne
For thee had plotted fiendishly, thou Home Farm—fated
    mine!
Lang, lang oot o'er our miners she had hung a treacherous
    lake,
Noo, wi' a mighty surge that made the stoutest bosom quake,
It fell! O, God, abun us! like a horrid dream, we saw
The bonnie haughs o' Cunagar jist meltin' like the snaw!*   *snow

(1) The steam horn used to call the miners to work

Jist meltin' like the snaw, I say, an' fairly floatin' through—
Ah, whaur amid that mighty flood's oor hero-miner noo?
But fancy hears him murmuring; my puir wee, dear wee
    wife!
My bonnie bairns! an' sees the wild, ah unequal strife!
Lang, lang his loving wife at e'en* may look wi' tearfu' e'e.   *evening
But, ah, her hero-miner mair she'll never, never see!
An' aye her bosom bleeds anew, as 'mid the evening game,
The bairnies spier* sae wistfully—"Wull faither ne'er win*   *ask *find his way
    hame?

Thomas Stewart.
Larkhall. Circa 1878.

THE HOME FARM COLLIERY INUNDATION 1877

Situated on the lands of Merryton Farm, the Home Farm Colliery was the central link in the chain of collieries which began at the River Avon and terminated at the boundary of Hamilton Parish and Larkhall. There were two shafts, both sunk to the Splint coal and the workings extended towards the River Clyde.

The coal field was leased from the Duke of Hamilton by Hamilton & McCulloch & Co. who began sinking the shafts in 1864. An Ell coal seam 8 feet thick was found at a depth of 47 fathoms (282 ft) from the mouth of No.1 shaft, the Main at 38 fathoms, (228 feet) and the Splint at 73 fathoms (438 ft). The Ell coal seam rose up considerably and in 1877 at a point 600 yards from the pit bottom the seam was only 18 fathoms or 108 feet from the surface.

Lying above the Ell coal lay an 18 foot thick bed of stone and above it was a "channel bed" in which ran an immense stream of water draining from the high ground behind the pit.

In the middle of January 1877 a fall took place in the Ell coal and water was seen to percolate through at the point where the roof had come down. This was examined by McCreath the Duke of Hamilton's mining engineer who came to the conclusion that there was no cause for concern and advised propping up the roof. However on the night of the 16th January because of the amount of water finding its way down into the lower seams the horses and graith (miners' tools) were lifted from the Splint coal and on the morning of the 23rd January, fifteen horses in the Soft Splint coal and Main coal seams were removed because of the rise in the water level.

John McNeil was among the men withdrawn from the Splint coal seam on the 16th and for some days after that he worked on the face at the Ell coal and then worked with his brother *Hector McNeil* in the colliery's stone mine. *Hector McNeill* a union official had felt extremely uneasy about the situation and he approached the oversman *John Mair* voicing his concerns about the amount of water finding its way into the workings. Mair's reply that *"It'll be a lang time before it droons you; there's a lot to fill up yet; there is the Splint coal and the Main"* done nothing to reassure McNeil. Continuing to question the oversman he asked if any steps had been taken and John Mair informed him that *"Mr McCreath had been down; we had advice and we are going to try and build it in"*. McNeill persisted and asked him if *Ralph Moore* the Inspector for Mines had been called in he was told *"no and there was no need for him."*

On the night of Monday 23rd January several men including *John McNeill* were working night shift propping up the roof in the Ell coal seam where the fall had taken place and when they finished their work just before 6am they left, leaving *McNeil* who was working a double shift. At 6am *David Hinds, John McAllister* and *John Toll or Gregory* arrived underground and made their way to their working places at the face which was well away from the damaged roof.

Another 60 men and boys were also lowered down to the pit bottom and as they made their way in groups to the working face they heard a thunderous noise followed by the unmistakable sound of rushing water. Recognising immediately that there had been an inundation of water into the mine the men turned and ran for their lives.

The roof had collapsed at the point where the water had been entering for two weeks and millions of gallons of water which had been collecting at the channel bedrock fault was now pouring through the roof of the Ell seam; and as it moved through the workings, everything that could be moved, trap doors, hutches, pit props and rubble was carried through the mine by the overwhelming force of the flood.

The panic stricken miners were overtaken by the torrent and many were injured as they were swept off their feet and tumbled head over heels down the roadways. The men who were still standing were up to their chests in water and fighting a battle against the tremendous force of the water as they struggled to reach the pit bottom. With the depth of the water increasing by the minute the miners finally reached the bottom of the shaft and frantically signalled to the surface to be drawn up.

Just prior to the inundation, fireman *William Simpson* had examined the workings to ensure they were safe and he then sent three men through to *"the long wall"*. Just after they left, a noise and a change in air current made him think that they had forgotten to close the trap door and he sent *James Easton* to investigate. However sensing that something wasn't just quite right, he ran in along the level to check the doors himself. At this point the air current was strong and he ran on towards the heading, but further in he realised that the current had stopped. Racing back, he warned the waiting miners not to go any further until he re-examined the mine to see if was still safe to come in.

Lighting his safety lamp he set off with *George Forsyth* to see what was going on and they had reached the stables 240 feet from the bottom of the mine when they heard water *"rushing doon the brae"* bringing with it the props supporting the roof. He told *Forsyth* that he would try and warn the men in the mine and went down the shaft leading to the Ell coal and called out to the men in the workings to come up for the water had broken into the pit.

As he struggled to warn the miners working deep in the mine he was met by a wall of water pouring down the 1 in 18 gradient of the roadway and he was knocked off his feet badly injuring himself and breaking the bones of his left arm. Unable to get up he shouted for help and *George Forsyth* came and dragged him back to the pit bottom where he shouted to the men to get up the pit as the water had broken through. At this point he was joined by *Archibald Muir* and he sent him with *James Easton* to several working places to warn the men to get out. With the exception of *John McNeill, David Hinds, John McAllister* and *John Toll* or *Gregory,* all the men and boys underground managed to get back up to the surface despite the water being four feet deep at the pit bottom. Had it not been for the bravery of *William Simpson, George Forsyth, James Easton* and Archibald *Muir* the death total would have been a lot higher.

Up on the surface the shocked survivors stood at the pithead in groups all shivering and soaking wet discussing who were likely to have been saved and who had been lost. Bad news travels fast and soon the miners' terrified womenfolk were arriving at the pithead searching the faces for their loved ones.

At Cunningair Haugh, the site of the subsidence, the ground had collapsed to a depth of 100 feet and millions of gallons of water and an estimated 500.000 cubic yards of sand, gravel etc, had vanished down the mine leaving a hole one mile in circumference.

At 10 am, the water in the flooded workings had reduced and manager *William Kirkwood* and several men went down the shaft in an attempt to find the missing men but were unable to make any headway.

The sound of the water roaring into the mine could be heard for quite some distance off and *Hector McNeill* approached *Mair* the oversman and asked him if nothing could be done to rescue his brother and the other men. *Mair* told him that *"it's all up with your brother now"*

It wasn't until mid-day with the arrival of senior partner Mr Hamilton, Ralph Moore government inspector of mines and mining engineers *George McCreath* and *Simpson* that active steps were taken on their instructions to attempt to stop the flow of water by throwing bales of hay, trees and brushwood into the gaping chasm in the hope that this would block off the hole. Six hours had already elapsed from the time of the inundation and it was several hours before the work started although William Kirkwood had already made preparations by getting the foresters permission to cut down trees and brushwood and had obtained horses and carts to transport them. After countless tons of material were thrown over the side of the chasm the hole was finally sealed preventing any more water getting into the mine.

However when access was finally gained to the Pit it was found that the workings were so tightly packed from pavement to roof with silt and debris that it was as if they had never been and it appeared that the mine would have to be abandoned. Mine management and officials came to the conclusion that the men and 15 ponies were lost. Among the miners relatives there was a great deal of dissatisfaction and they were convinced that not enough had been done to try to save them or recover the bodies.

Four women had been left without their husbands and breadwinners and twelve children were now fatherless. *John McNeil, John McAllister* and *John Toll or Gregory* each left two children; *David Hynd* left six, the youngest *David,* was only 6 months. The families wanted answers as to what had happened in the pit and who was to blame but they had little chance of finding out as the law of Scotland at this time was that the Procurator Fiscal held a private enquiry into a disaster such as this and he then made a report to the Lord Advocate who made the decision if any prosecution would take place or if the whole matter should end. At no time did the public or mining communities involved have access to this enquiry and this was a great source of discontent among the miners because they felt that with the appalling number of men lost every year in accidents there should be a public inquiry held into each and every death, in the hope that recommendations would be made which would improve safety in the mines.

Alexander McDonald M.P.

After the inundation *John McNeil's* brother *Hector* pushed for a Public Inquiry into the accident. He held public meetings and demanded that the law be changed to ensure justice for the miners. At one such meeting in Wishaw town hall he spoke with great feeling of how he could count within the *"last six months between the cross at Hamilton and the cross at Larkhall, eight persons who had been sacrificed in the mine and there had been a public inquiry in none of them."* He condemned the system which allowed 40,000-50,000 men to be exposed daily to danger in the mines of Scotland without there being in place a law which would give them the right to a Public Inquiry if anything went wrong. *McNeil* organised meetings in all the local towns and *Alexander McDonald M.P.* presented question after question relating to the circumstances surrounding the deaths of the four men to the Secretary of State for the Home Department in Parliament. It was through the combined efforts of these two men that eventually a Public Inquiry was held before *Mr Joseph Dickinson* one of Her Majesties inspectors of Mines at Wishaw Court House beginning on the 28th June 1877.

As witness after witness took the stand, each had a story to tell of the accident and the events leading up to it. *James Ramage* a stone miner in the colliery told of how he was not at work that morning because his neighbour (*the man who worked with him*) *Dalziel* didn't turn up for work. He told of how he was *"a little afraid working in the mine on account of the talk about it. I placed my confidence in those over me. They shared the danger, but I could not say if they shirked their duty or not. I seldom saw them. I think a great many were ignorant of the thickness between the coal and the surface where they were working."* *John Hilson* gave evidence of how he had worked for 17 months in the area where the water had broken through. He said that *"from the 15th-16th January when the water first started finding its way in until the 23[r] January, he met the flow of water every morning while going to his work. It remained much the same in quantity up until Saturday the 20th."* *William Watson* another witness said it was his opinion that *"if John Mair had given the men wood, the pit would be working yet. He would neither allow wood or bratticing."* *John Mair* the overman whose evidence was crucial to the Inquiry failed to appear although he was called; he had left the employment of Hamilton & McCulloch because his services were no longer required.

The inquiry continued for 2 days and Dickinson's report was published the following January. The owners of the colliery Hamilton and McCulloch and Co. were exonerated from any blame for the loss of the four men. Dickinson stated that *"apparently all concerned knew what was going on. It was an occurrence upon which no infallible conclusion could be arrived. Some risk has to be run in earning a livelihood in mines." All alike, masters and men, including even the surveyors went on with their work as usual. The men might have availed themselves of their own power of inspection or of calling in the inspector but they did neither. The risk proved to have been underrated. I am therefore, inclined to think that, although the result was very sad, each person accepted the circumstances and should bear his own share of the consequences."*

These are fine plausible words indeed from Her Majesty's Inspector of Mines; words which pointed the finger of guilt at everyone except the owners of the colliery. Unbelievably he also included the miners in this judgement but he knew very well, as did the miners, that if they had complained and insisted on an inspection of the mine, then sooner rather than later, they would be out of a job and out on the street for causing bother. Union official *Hector McNeil* was the one man known to have approached the oversman *John Mair* with his serious concerns regarding the flow of water coming into the pit; Mair had ridiculed him.

Six months after the accident two 15 horse power horizontal engines and two 10 inch centrifugal pumps were positioned 30 feet from the edge of the chasm and 90 feet from the banks of the River Clyde. As the pumps got to work to remove the estimated 100,000,000 gallons of water from the gigantic basin, people travelled from all over the country to watch the spectacle. The Duke of Hamilton who stood to gain a fortune from coal royalties if the mine re-opened was a daily visitor, watching intently as the pumps removed 6300 gallons of water weighing 22 tons every minute from the huge chasm.

In November 1878, 22 months after the tragedy, the remains of *David Hynd* and *John Toll* were found in the long level, 400 fathoms or 2400 feet from the pit bottom by miners who were working to re-open the mine. The following day John McNeil's remains were found *"a considerable distance nearer the working face"*. One week later *John McAllister's* remains were found in workings which had been silted up from pavement to roof and all the remains had been found thickly embedded in sand and all were identified by their clothing.

Then as now it was compulsory to register a death but neither *David Hynd* nor *John McAllister's* deaths were registered; the other two victims had been registered at the time of the inundation. Three days after the recovery of her husbands remains *Ann Hynd* travelled to Hamilton to register his death. *John McAllister's* death remains unregistered. The reasons for the women not registering the deaths has not been recorded but *Ann Hynd* is remembered by her descendants as a stubborn very strong willed woman and it would appear that both she and *McAllister's* wife refused to register the deaths until the men were found. Aged 28 when her husband was entombed, Ann was left to bring up six children on parish poor relief; she never remarried.

Years later two of her married daughters *Mern (Marion) Grey* and *Isobel Brown* emigrated to Australia and *Ann Hynd,* distraught at their leaving was too upset to see them off from Larkhall railway station. Sitting sobbing in her home at Summerlee Rows she could hear the train leaving and running out of the house ran desperately down past the field to reach Summerlee Cottages where it turned as it headed for Hamilton, and there, with tears streaming down her face, she got a last glimpse of her beloved girls. She died when she was 90 years of age, without ever seeing them again.

During World War Two, Ann's youngest son *David Hynd Jnr.* opened the door of his home at 56 West Clyde Street, Larkhall to find two Australian soldiers standing on the doorstep. They were the grandsons of *Isobel* and *Mern* looking for somewhere to stay for a few days. The family were overjoyed to see them and the young soldiers met all their Larkhall relatives.

Both boys fought in Burma but were captured by the Japanese and died within days of one another while working as slave labour on the infamous Burma Railway line.

KNOWN FATALITIES AT HOME FARM COLLIERY.

DATE	NAME	AGE	CAUSE OF DEATH
15.01.1869	AUSTINE McMINN	---	Roof fall
17.07.1870	ROBERT BARR	18	Explosion (severe burns)
22.07.1870	ALEX. DICK	19	" "
23.01.1877	JOHN McNEIL		Inrush of water (drowned)
"	DAVID HINDS	36	" " "
"	JOHN TOLL/GREGORY	51	" " "
"	JOHN McALLISTER	50	" " "
18.05.1877	JAMES COWAN	13	Caught in spokes of a wheel (multiple injuries)
12.09.1884	JOHN NEILSON	12	Legs amputated after being run over by waggon
16.05.1893	JAMES ROBERTSON	18	Fell from screen to wagon. (spinal/head injuries)
27.06.1894	EDWARD BRANNAN	36	Fell 240 feet down shaft
"	MATHEW CORBET	38	" " "
"	WM. STEVENSON	22	" " "
27.04.1907	WM. NICOL	66	Run down by wagon.
30.09.1910	THOMAS AITKEN	38	Drawn into drum of coal cutting machine
11.04.1912	THOS. H. COWAN	34	Premature detonation of explosives. Part of face blown off
16.02.1923	EDWARD COLE	36	Explosives accident (head and face injuries)
--. 02.1923	RBT. BALLANTYNE	16	No details (fractured skull)
13.04.1924	ALEX. McKEOWN	20	Drawn into coal cutting machine

THE WEDLOCK FAMILY OF HOME FARM ROWS

Back row. Elizabeth, Matthew, Thomas, Mary Anne. Front row Richard, Mother Margaret Wedlock nee Walton, Margaret and William c 1897. At one time of the 11 houses at Home Farm Rows, nine of them were occupied by Wedlock's, or close relatives.

MERRYTON ROWS

The above picture of Merryton Rows was taken approximately 100 years ago and shows the single story row of miners' houses situated at Lanark Road end which were occupied by miners from both Merryton and Home Farm collieries. There were 22 houses, 7 with 1 room, 14 with 2 rooms and one house with 3 rooms. There were no gardens, washhouses or coal cellars. Coal very often had to be stored under the set in bed. There were no sinks; water was obtained from outside wells. The 2 open privy toilets were 60 feet behind the houses. Food was cooked in a pot over the domestic fire. A glimpse of the hard life miners' wives had to endure can be seen by the wooden washing bines and cast iron pots stored below the windows. At the top of picture smoke can be seen curling up from a fire being used to boil clothes in one of these pots. Note the mud and water in front of the houses. Photograph courtesy of Larkhall Heritage Group.

MINERS LIVING AT MERRYTON ROWS IN 1871

John Allan. (12) (Lesmahagow)

John, James, Wm. Jnr. and Wm. Browning. (Larkhall)

David Caldwell. (Pitheadman.) (Airdrie)

William Caldwell (62) (Dumfries)

Alexander S. Caldwell (11) (Cambusnethan)

David Copeland. Coalminer/Army Reservist. (Muirkirk).

David Dalgleish. (Glasgow)

Thomas Dick. (Glasgow)

Robert Ellis (Biggar)

Robert Galbraith (Motherwell)

Edward Heffron. (Ireland, Co. Tyrone.)

Alexander Mathie. (Renfrewshire)

John (12) Mathie (Lanarkshire)

John Mathie (Rutherglen)

Alexander Maxwell. (Rutherglen)

Dennis Neilson. (Govan)

John Ramsay. (Glasgow)

John Russell (Newarthill)

David Seggie. Underground Manager (Whitburn)

James Seggie. Pit Bottomer. (Airdrie)

James Seggie. (Whitburn)

David Sim. Stone miner (Glassford)

William Sim (13) Ponydriver (Bothwell)

Thomas Stark. (Motherwell)

Thomas Torrance (Lanarkshire)

William Wood. (Ireland, Belfast)

Charles Young (Glasgow)

It is obvious from the census returns that it was not a common heritage that made the miners rows such close-knit communities; it was the dangers shared by all the men who worked at the pit and the poverty and depravation which bound them close together. It is very unusual for census returns to include Irish details but enumerator John Thomson added the county of birth for many of the Irish miners in Allanton, Dykehead, Ferniegair, Haughhead, Merryton and Home Farm collieries and for this reason I have included the details for family historians

THE FORLORN HOPE
(A PITMAN'S STORY, BY EVAN McMURDO)

"Twas the thirty-first day of December,
  In the year eighteen-seventy-nine—
A day that I'll always remember—
  The day we fought death in the mine.

We'd been lowered down in the morning,
  Seventy-five men all told,
Most of them rough, swearing miners,
  Strong-limbed, light-hearted, and bold.

We soon dispersed to the faces;
  But the work had scarcely begun,
When we heard the rush of water;
  And father told me to run

We signalled, and were raised again
  Into the cold, wintry air;
The wind pierced me through like an arrow,
  For my arms and neck were bare.

The snow had been steadily falling;
  And we could see by the grey, morning light
That the sheds and unsightly dirt-heap
  Were clothed in a mantle of white.

Weeping wives soon crowded round,
  (Ill news always travels fast);
But as cage after cage was safely raised,
  We began to think all danger was past.

Bottomer Jack at last came up,
  And then the boys began to cheer;
He cried out "Don't cheer yet, my lads,
  There are some lost I fear.

"Five men still are missing,
  Who were working in the dook,
And I want two to come with me;
  I'm going back to look.

"And let them be unmarried men,
  For we might never more see daylight;
And there are widows enough already,
  And there may be more to-night.

I think I see him standing there
  With the boyish eyes of blue;
But immortal fame was never won
  By a hero more bold and true.

Jack and I had been good friends,
  And I said I'd go with him;
And then another volunteered—
  His sweetheart's brother Jim.

We three were lowered into the mine,
  And heard the water gushing into the sump,
And sweeter than music to our ears
  Was the steady thud of the pump.

The flood, we found, wasn't slackening,
  And it soon rose up to our knees,
As we carefully picked each footstep
  . By hutches and floating trees.

We never exchanged a single word,
  For we needed all our breath;
And folks aren't inclined to say much
  When they're face to face with death.

Jack, of course, was leading us—
  He knew every inch of the seam—
How that dreadful journey haunts me still;
  Aye, haunts me even in my dreams.

We soon left the main level behind us,
  And turned into an old airway;
Jack turned and told us to hurry—
  The first work spoken that day.

The road was narrow as well as low,
  And we had to crawl in single file;
And thus we followed each other
  For more than half-a-mile.

Again we stood on the level,
  And my very heart stood still;
For the road we should have come by
  Was flooded from roof to shill.

Jack said if the air-way got flooded,
  We, too, would be entombed,
And to a terrible lingering death
  The eight of us would be doomed.

We hurried towards the faces—
  Be sure we ran with a will;
The five had long since given up hope,
  And we found them sitting still.

The men were sitting with folded arms—
  Even young Bill had ceased to weep;
Exhausted Nature had claimed her due,
  And he had fallen soundly asleep.

We roused him and hurried back again,
  For there wasn't a minute to spare;
And we ran back the road we came,
  With Jack now in the rear.

We heard a grating, crushing sound,
  Whose meaning too well we knew;
We hurried past the dreaded spot,
  And all but Jack got safely through.

He was caught and terrible injured
  By that fall of wood and stone;
We turned, and tried to take him out,
  But he bade us leave him alone.

He said, "I feel I'm dying now;
  "Twill do no good 'though you stay,
So leave me here to die alone,
  And save yourselves, while you may.

"And Tom, you've always been my friend;
  Just give my hand a shake,
And if you learn to love my Nell,
  Will you wed her, for my sake."

I stooped and grasped the manly hand
  That would soon be cold and still,
And pressed my lips to his clammy brow,
  And faltered out, "I will."

The air-way was near flooded now—
  Jim and I scarce got through;
The five had hurried on before—
  Had gone and left behind us two.

The pit was never opened again,
  You'd search for it now in vain,
For the field in which the shaft was sunk
  Is covered with golden grain.

And Nell! Well, Nell is my wife now;
  We've been wed for many a year;
We've called our eldest boy 'Jack,
  That name to us is very dear.

And often in the evenings,
  When the children are tired of play,
They'll ask me to tell the story
  Of that terrible Hogmanay.

And Nell's eyes grow soft in the firelight,
  As I speak of her sweetheart that's gone—
The boy that led the Forlorn Hope,
  And died in the mine alone.

THE KETTLE

The kettle was used during the sinking of pit shafts and also to gain access to the pit when it was not possible to use the cage e.g. after an explosion had wrecked the cage.

It was used at the Blantyre and Udston disasters to repair the damaged shafts and to transfer the rescue teams and equipment underground and also to bring up the survivors and the bodies of some the victims; a kettle could hold 3-4 men.

At the Blantyre disaster two rescuers brought numerous bodies to the surface by sitting astride the side of the kettle and supporting the body in an upright position.

THE QUARTER COALIERS FRIENDLY SOCIETY ARTICLE AND ACCOUNTS BOOK WITH PAY
BOOKS FOR QUARTER Nos. 1.2.3.4. PITS 1855-57

FIRST TWO PAGES OF QUARTER COALIERS FRIENDLY SOCIETY ARTICLES AND ACCOUNTS
BOOK 1799

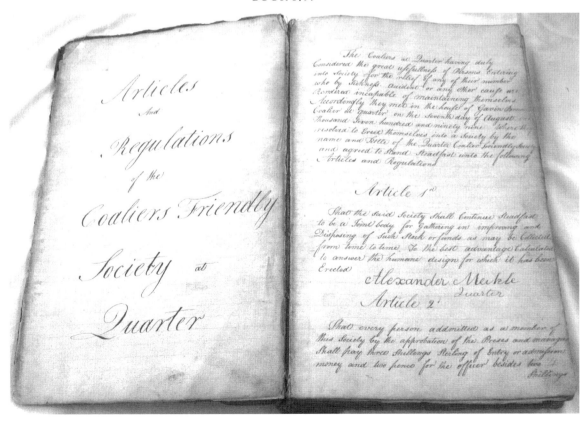

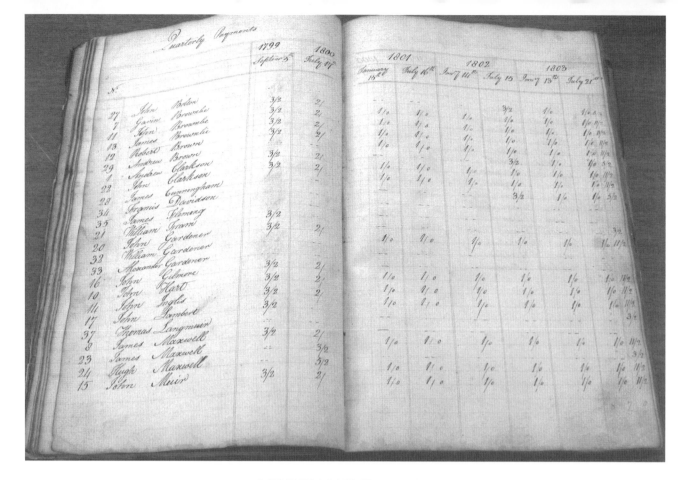

MEMBERS PAYMENT RECORD
QUARTER COALIERS FRIENDLY SOCIETY FOUNDED 1799
FREEDOM!!

The following paragraph contains the opening lines in the accounts book of the Quarter Coaliers Friendly Society which was established on 5th September 1799 following the release from slavery of all bonded colliers by an Act of Parliament on the 13th June 1799.

"The coaliers of Quarter having duly considered the great usefulness of persons entering into society for the relief of any of their number who by sickenings, accident or any other cause are rendered incapable of maintaining themselves. Accordingly they met in the house of Gavin Brownlie coalier at Quarter on the seventh day of August one thousand seven hundred and ninety nine where they resolved to erect themselves into a society by the name of Quarter Collier Friendly Society and agreed to stand steadfast unto the following articles and regulations."

ARTICLE 1
"That the said Society shall continue steadfast to be a joint body for gathering in improving and disposing of such stock or funds as may be collected from time to time to the best advantage calculated to answer the humane design for which it has been erected."

> *"Alexander Meikle*
> *Quarter"*

ARTICLE 2
"Cost 3/- on entry to the Society with 2d for the officer and 2/- per quarter paid twice yearly one half on 2nd Thursday of January and the other half on the 3rd Thursday of July annually which is to be general election day".

ARTICLE 3
"No person will be admitted a member of this society except he is of sound health, honest character and known diligence in their calling,, his age not to exceed forty five years and all below twelve years to be

admitted at half entry but to receive no aliment till they arrive at fifteen years of age. And none to be admitted whatever their age be whose circumstances appear so as they must immediately become a burden upon the society."

ARTICLE 4
"That this Society be properly and skilfully managed the Society shall proceed to elect one of the worthiest of their members as a Preses or overman who shall preside at all their meetings and have power to transact all their business, to call meetings on all necessary and emergency occasions, who is to have the first vote beside the casting or deciding vote in all cases of parity and in all times concerning the presses or deacon shall be chosen in forms as follows. The present Preses and managers shall lay out three men of the worthiest of their members to their knowledge in a leet six weeks before the annual election day as candidates for the ensuing presses and whoever of these can obtain the majority of votes shall be elected presses.

There were 23 articles and regulations, the above of which are examples. The benefits of joining the Society were alimony of 2/- (10 pence) weekly if ambulant but unable to work due to injury or ill health. If bedridden, then 3/6d (17 _ pence) would be paid. Applicants would also have to be a fully paid up member of the Society for three years before any aliment would be paid out. Any member who "*falls into a habitual practice of any Capital Sin such as drunkenness, swearing, Sabbath breaking, fornication, theft or adultery or any habitual practice of profanity which may bring a stain upon Society they shall be immediately extruded the Society never to be admitted except evident marks of their penitence for past offences and sufficient satisfaction to the Society for their better conduct for the future then they may be admitted as new members and pay the accustomed admission due."*

Members had to reside upwards of 2 miles from "the quarter" or they were to be deemed outwith the bounds of the visiting masters jurisdiction. If alimony was required due to ill health then he must produce a certificate signed by the minister or 2 elders of that community to which he adheres signifying whither he is bedfast or able to walk about so that aliment may be granted accordingly."

The following list of members records only the coaliers but there were other tradesmen admitted as members of the society e.g. John Inglis (Weaver) Broomknow who joined on the first day. John Fram, (farmer) Laigh Quarter, Hugh Maxwell and Andrew Brown (shoemakers) Quarter and James Maxwell, (weaver) Quarter became members in September 1799. The word coalier was used in the ledger until 1824 when it was replaced by collier.

The first eighteen men are founder members of the Society and all names given are listed as coaliers unless otherwise stated. The list is not in alphabetical order; it is in the order given in the book. There can be little doubt that the coaliers who founded the society and some of the men who joined in the early years would have been prior to the 1799 Act, bonded coaliers belonging to the Duke of Hamilton and just as much slaves as the Africans on the plantations of America. Had they left their employment they would have been hunted down and returned. Earlier generations of bonded miners who ran away could live and work as free men if they crossed the border into England or evaded capture for one year and one day. However even this avenue of escape was closed in 1708 when the law was changed to ensure that "*all escapees were able to be brought back even if as long as 8 years had passed*". To achieve freedom was well nigh impossible for any man found employing him would face a crippling fine and the runaway coalier would be liable for the expenses incurred returning him to his master and he was often imprisoned as a thief "*stealing himself from his master*". A letter written by the Duke of Hamilton to a sea captain asking him to return a boy from the mines states; "*it is contrary to the laws of this realm to keep any man's bond-servant without a certificate from his master or a testimonial from a judge*". In 1786, James Weatherspoon one of the Dukes bonded coalier's was reported to have absconded for a seven week period between June and August.

Children born to colliers were bonded or 'arled' to their fathers master at their christening. In effect they were bonded into slavery for the rest of their lives for a very small monetary 'gift' handed over at the ceremony by the master to the father. These children worked underground from a very early age. A woman became bound automatically to work in a pit when she married a collier. Women and small children worked underground at Quarter as they did in mines all over the country.

The emancipation Act of 1774, the preamble of which ran *"Whereas by the statute of law of Scotland as explained by the judges of the courts of law there, many colliers and coalbearers and salters are in a state of slavery and bondage, bound to the collieries and saltworks where they work for life, transferable with the collieries and saltworks,"* This Act imposed so many conditions to be observed by those to be freed that little advantage was taken of it and the masters were not giving up their rights without a struggle. A new Act drafted in 1799 retained some shreds of the old bonds but the miners, especially in the West of Scotland had recognised their plight and in Lanarkshire 600 colliers contributed 2 shillings each to send deputations to collieries in other districts and to employ a Mr Wilson, law agent of Cowglen Glasgow to conduct the opposition to the Bill. By their organisation and intervention the objectionable clauses were removed from the Bill and the colliers after 191 years of slavery had finally gained their freedom… but had they?

The coal masters, who had used every devious method possible to retain their stranglehold on their colliers didn't give up easily. Although in law the colliers were free men, the masters soon devised other methods of retaining absolute control over them. Tied houses meant if a miner lost his job he was evicted with his wife and children on to the street. He was ruled by fear and this effectively stopped him from protesting about conditions and wages. Fortnightly or monthly wages kept the miners in debt to the colliery store. By deliberately retaining their wages for this period, they forced their workers to be perpetually in debt to them, ensuring that they could not afford to leave their employment.

The influx of desperate starving refugees from Ireland exacerbated the situation. The labour market was flooded with men looking for work to support their families and this changed the balance of supply and demand. Where previously it had been difficult to obtain colliers, there were now thousands of desperate men clamouring for work. The coal masters used the situation to their advantage by repeatedly reducing the rate paid to the men until they were living well below the starvation level. The obligatory deductions from wages, the doctor's fees, school fees (whether you had children or not) fines, chimney sweep, pick sharpening, powder, oil, etc, reduced their earnings even further. In theory the collier was a free man but in reality he was still a slave.

QUARTER COLLIERS KNOWN TO BE BONDED SLAVES TO THE DUKE OF HAMILTON 1785-86

James Baillie, Robert Brown, James Brownlie, John Brownlie, John Curr, John Gardiner, Thomas Hamilton, John Lambert, James Lambert, James Maxwell, John Murray, Arthur Renwick, John Wilson, John Wilson Jnr. John Wotherspoon, James Wotherspoon.

THE FIRST MEMBERS OF QUARTER COALIERS FRIENDLY SOCIETY

SEPTEMBER 5TH 1799 Andrew Clarkson, John Wotherspoon, Arthur Renwick, Sen., James Wotherspoon, John Wilson, Gavin Brownlie, James Maxwell, Archibald Wotherspoon, John Hart, John Brownlie, James Brownlie, Robert Brown, John Muir, John Gilmore, (Coal Grieve) John Lambert, Sept. 12th 1799 James Wilson, Sept 20th John Gardiner (Cleeksman) Sept. 26th John Clarkson. 1800 William Wilson (Smith). 1802 John Bolton. 1803 Duke Tinsell, William Gardiner (Coal Grieve). Francis Davidson. 1805 William Renwick, Thomas Longmuir (Cleeksman) John Wilson (Smith) Hugh Maxwell Jun., James Maxwell Jun. 1806 William Wotherspoon, William Hamilton, Robert Hart, William Diet, Hugh Wilson (Carter) Alex. Brown (Labourer) James Meikle, (Cleeksman) John Forrest, James Wilson (Labourer). 1806 John Hamilton (Coalier in Larkhall). 1807 George Weir (Miner at Quarter) Henry Lowden (Coalier at Marlage) David Weir (Coalier at Marlage). 1808 John Hamilton, Angus Maxwell, James Crossbie, Robert Brownlie, James McHale, Andrew Hamilton, William Weir (Coalier at Marlage). 1809 John Gardiner, Peter Cunningham. 1810 John Meikle (Coalier in Righead). 1812 William Bruce, John McFale (Coalier at Righead). 1818 Archibald Wotherspoon. 1819 Thomas Forrest. 1821 John Gardiner (Coalier in Righead) James McFale (Coalier in Righead) John

Wotherspoon (Coalier in Larkhall) Peter Spalding (Coalier in Larkhall) John Gold, Andrew Gold. 1822 John Lammie (Collier* in Larkhall) 1824 James Gold, 1825 James Wilson, Samuel Crawford (Collier in Raploch) William Wilson Jnr., (Smith) Michael Forrest, John Maxwell, William Law, Matthew Lammie (Collier in Raploch) William Scott.1826 John Gold Jnr. John Wilson, Donald Livingston. 1828 John Hall, William Donaldson, Matthew Donaldson, James Russle. 1832 Mark Gold, Andrew Gold Jnr. James Fleming, Andrew Forrest, Robert Wilson, John Bolton, Matthew Walker (Coal grieve). 1834 Edward Miller (Collier in Avonbanks) James Miller (Collier in Avonbanks) Joseph Small (Collier in Avonbanks) Francis Gilberson (Collier in Avonbanks). 1834 James Meikle. 1835 Gavin Brownlie Jnr. Hugh Wilson (Pitheadman) William Wilson.1836 Robert Wilson, William Fleming. 1837 John Dixon. 1838 John Meikle Jnr. John Bolton Jnr. William Robertson.
* Coalier changed to collier.

The Quarter Coaliers Friendly Society Accounts appear to stop in 1885 and although names appear in the book at later dates they do not appear to be related to the Society.

THE QUARTER COALIERS FRIENDLY SOCIETY
DEBIT ACCOUNT FROM
JULY 1825 TO AUGUST 1826

By aliment to John Gilmour	- 2/-
By aliment to Hugh Maxwell, Sen.	£4 3/6
To Duke Tincle*	£2 19/-
To John Findly	- 12/6
To John Mackie	- 11/-
To James Brownlie, Sen.	- 13/6
To Arthur Rinnick	- 4/-
To John Wotherspoon	- 4/-
To John Bolton's aliment and funeral	£2 4/6
To Thomas Longmuir	- 18/-
To Robert Hart	- 14/-
To John Mackie	£1 7/6
To John Hendrie	£1 1/6
To one aliment book	- 1/-
To repairing the new flag	- 7/-
To closing of books	- 6/-
To clerk and office bearers	- 15/6
To music expenses	£2 - -
To two bottles of whisky at rouping colours	- 4/-
Given to James Mackie for his bill	£10 - -
To balance in the treasurers hand	£10 17/3
	£ 39 14/3

*Duke Tincle also listed as Tinsel.   Stock of the society   £101 17/3

1865 QUARTER COALIERS FRIENDLY SOCIETY
ANNUAL GENERAL MEETING

On 6th July 1865 the Annual General Meeting of the above society was held at the house of William Meikle. The following masters (officials) were elected for the ensuing year.

William Scott, (clerk) John Fleming (presses) William Thomson (treasurer) Michal Forrest,

John Meikle Jnr. and John Brownlie (keymasters) John Meikle, John Forrest, Francis Gilchrist, John Bolton, Alexander Meikle (ordinary masters) James Cathcart (officer) It was decided that there was to be no fair that year.

*   *   *

THE NAMES OF THE QUARTER COAL AND IRONSTONE MINERS 1855-1857

The above pay book complete with coal thumb prints records the names of men working at No. 2 Ironstone Pit Quarter for two week period beginning 24th May 1855.

The following men were listed in surviving pay books as working in Quarter Nos. 1.2.3.and 4 Pits between the years 1855-57. Several names are listed as working in more than one pit. This could have been that the men moved from one pit to another or it could have been relatives with the same name. Many of the names are Irish and as the spelling depends on the man writing them down a percentage of them are spelt phonetically; with the result that several of the names are spelt with Irish accents, e.g. Kinneth Kerney instead of Kenneth Kearney and William Scat instead of William Scott

The years 1856 - 57 saw a great influx of Irish workers into Quarter, so many, that the main street Darngaber Rows was referred to as "Dublin". These immigrants had fled a country devastated by a famine of biblical proportions following successive failures of the potato crop. With their families, they would have experienced starvation and indescribable suffering during the period 1846-50 and also in the immediate post famine years. In a letter to the Duchess of Hamilton, coalmaster Colin Dunlop remarked that many of these Irish miners came from Connaught; this was an area where one third of the population were wholly dependant on potatoes.

The potato famine was the result of a culmination of a social, biological, political and economic catastrophe which in Ireland, resulted in the deaths of an estimated 500,000 to 1,000,000 people and the emigration of approximately 1,500,000 people to Britain and America.

QUARTER NO.1 IRONSTONE PIT (BOGHEAD)

Andrew Anderson, John Anderson, John Arthur, Peter Barr, William Barr (Bottomer) Alexander Barrowman, John Berry, Robert Berry, John Bolton Snr., John Bolton Jnr., John Bolton (Roadsman) Robert Bolton, John Black, James Brie, John Brown, Robert Brown, William Browning, James Brownlie, Thomas Bruce, (Drawer) William Byars, Alexander Bryce, Thomas Burns, Felix Cain, John Cain, Philip Cain, Barney Callahan, James Cathcart, Thomas Cherry, William Cherry, Hosie Clark, James Clelland, Thomas Clelland, John Clorman, Hugh Clorman, John Cowans, George Cowan, John Colquhoun, Edward Cuthbertson, Robert Cuthbertson, David Craig, Sam Craig, Thomas Crawford, George Davidson, John Dawson, Thomas Docherty, Alexander Drinnen, Peter Duff, James Duffy, Alexander Duncan, Antiny Early, Austin Early, Peter Early, John Finlay, Richard Finlay, William Finlay, John Fisher, John Fleming, Michel Fleming, William Fleming, John Forsyth, (Roadsman) William Fraser, Daniel Frame, Robert Frame, Henry Frew (Brusher) Alexander Frew, Alexander Frew Jnr. James Frew, John Frew, Barney Gallahar, James Garvey, James Gilbert, Colen Gilbertson, James Gilmour, Andrew Gray, Andrew Gold, John Gordon, Samuel Hainey, William Hainey, Adam Hamilton, Thomas Hamilton, William Hamilton, James Harper, Robert Harper, Thomas Hebren, Walter Henrie, Alexander Horn, John Inglis, William Johnston, James Kay, (Drawer) James Kain, John Kain, Kinneth Kernny, John Kain, James Lammie, John Lafferty, Dugal Lawson, Dugal Lyon, Robert Lunden, Daniel McClundie, John McCollins, Frank McCullan, William McCullan, John McDermont, Henry McDown, John McFarlane, John McGinnis, John McGrogan, Sam McHavie, John McIlhan, Paddy McKachnay, Peter McMillan, Hugh McLammond, Hugh McLammond, Daniel McLundie, John McLean, Cynis Smith, John Mare, David Martin, James Maxwell, Robert Maxwell, William Meikle, Walter Menzies, William Moore, John Moire, George Moses, Robert Morten, John Muir, Henry Mullen, John Mullen, Barney Murphy, John Murphy, Barney Murray, Andrew Nesbit, William Nelson, William Neilson, Thomson Noble, John North, Robert North, Thomas North, James Orr, John Pall*, Sam Patan, William Patrick, Hugh Polland, William Pollock, James Potter, John Potter, James Prentice, Robert Pritchard, William Prentice, Andrew Rae, (Bottomer) John Rafferty, Joseph Ralston, David Ralston, George Reid, James Richmond, Robert Ritchie, Joseph Robertson, John Russell, William Russell, Charly Shaw, James Thomson, John Thomson, Noble Thomson, William *Scat, William Scoat*, John Short, Alexander Smith, Arthur Smith, Thomas Smith, William Stevenson, (Roadsman) John Stewart, William Stewart, Hugh Swinney, Cornelius Sullivan, John Thomas, James Thomson, Peter Waddle, Hamilton (Hamey) Ward, Sam Wallace, Thomas Wallace, Robert Watson, John Weir, James White, Alexander Wilson, James Wilson, David Wingate, (Fireman) John Winning, Alexander Wilson, John Wilson, Robert Wilson, William Wilson, David Wingate, John Wiper, Henry Wood, John Wood, William Wotherspoon.

*Michel (*Mitchell*) Fleming was a contractor sinking pits and contracting underground. *Pall is probably Paul and Scat and Scoat will be Scott

BOGHEAD NO.1 CLAYBAND 1857
Dugal Lawson, James Smith.

QUARTER NO.2 IRONSTONE PIT

John Alexander, Thomas Archibald, John Arthur, William Barr, John Barr, James Barclay, Samuel Barclay, Thomas Binns, John Black, James Bolton, David Braid, Gavin Brownlie, John Brownlie, Gavin Bruce, Fahey Cann, James Carlin, William Cherry, Hosie Clark, Earchibald Clelland, James Clelland, Hamilton Campbell, James Campbell, John Caine, Thomas Carson, Hugh Conor, Thomas Cowie, Thomas Cowan, George Cowan, John Craw, David Craw, Thomas Dochertay, Thomas Farrel, Peter Finlay, John Frame, Thomas Frame, Peter Finlay, Richard Finlay, William Finlay, Peter Finlayson, John Fleming, William Fleming, Michel Fleming, James Frew, Henry Frew, John Forsyth, John Gilbertson, Andrew Gold, John Gold, James Gold, George Gordon, William Hamilton, James Harris, James Howie, William Howie, William Johnstone, James Keay, Matthew Law, Robert Maxwell, Francis Muir, David Moore, John Muir, William Mitchell, John McBride, William McClament, John McGarry, Patrick McGarry, John McGinnes, John McIntyre, John McLaughlin, Robert McMillan, William Menzies, Alexander Neilson, George Neilson,

Kenneth Neilson, Sam Paterson, James Potter, Andrew Rae, Alexander Rae, Joseph Ralston, David Ralston, Francis Regan, Arthur Renwick, Alexander Ross, Richard Finlay, William Scoat,* John Smith, Arthur Smith, William Stevenson, James Stewart, William Stewart, Cornelius Sullivan, John Swinnie, Edward Swiney, David Thomas, James Thomson, William Thomson, William Watson, Robert White, James White, Alexander Wilson, Arthur Wilson, Andrew Wilson, Duncan Wilson, George Wilson, James Wilson, John Wilson, William Wilson, John Wotherspoon, Charles York.

QUARTER NO. 2 COAL PIT 1857

John Fleming, William Johnston, Robert North, John Thomson, John Wilson.

QUARTER NO. 3 COAL PIT

Robert Alexander, Robert Bolton, James Brien, James Brownlie, Gavin Brownlie, Robert Buchanan, John Cain, Jacob Cather, John Cather, John Cherry, William Cherry, David Crow, Alexander Donaldson, Patrick Donalay, John Duffie, Richard Finlay, Mitchel Fleming, William Fleming, Andrew Frame, Alexander Frew, James Frew, Edward Gardiner, Francis Gilberton, John Gold, Peter Grogan, Peter Gourlay, Adam Hamilton, George Harvie, Alexander Harvey (Pitheadman) William Johnstone, Matthew Law, Alexander Liddle, William Meikle, John Meikle, Matthew Mitchell, William Mitchell, John Murphy, John McGraw, (Bottomer) Hugh McLundie, William Neilson, John Paterson, Andrew Rae, David Ralston, William Stevenson, William Stewart, Peter Waddle, Robert Wilson, John Wiper, Arthur Wilson. Andrew Wilson, John Wilson, William Wilson, David Wingate.

QUARTER NO. 4. COAL PIT. (BOGHEAD)

Michel Fleming, William Fleming, David Cuthbertson, William Holland and William Neilson listed as sinking No. 4 Pit in 1856.

NAMES OF SOME OF THE MINERS WORKING IN QUARTER IN APRIL 1898

S. Barr, J. Clelland, J. Cragie, J. Creechan, John Davidson, George Davidson, R. Davidson, W. Davidson, W Day, A. Dunn, W. Davidson, W. Daly, J. Ewing, R. Finlay, A. Fleming, Alexander Hodge, W. Inglis, D. Farquer, A. Fleming, W. Gemmill, W. Kane, R. Kelly, P. King, J, Lang, J. Lane, George Lawson, G. Maxwell, Alexander Meikle, J. Meikle (Larkhall) J, Meikle (Quarter) John Meikle, W. Meikle, Charles McDowell, P. McGourty, D. McKendrick, James McQueen, W. McQue, Hugh Orr, W. Pollock, G. Pollock, J. Pringle, J. Prentice, James Queen, John Queen, J. Renwick, J. Scott, W. Thomson, J. Watson, J. Waugh, R. Waugh, Peter Waugh, James Wilson.

BANKSMEN

John Dickson, Gavin Douglas, Thomas Higgins. Peter King, Gavin Maxwell, Richard Moffat, Frank Neil, John Renwick, James Ramage, William Robertson, James Todd.

*   *   *

As technology improved and deeper pits were developed, many of the Quarter miners moved on to work at Ferniegair, Hamilton and Blantyre.

QUARTER NO. 7. COLLIERY
14th July 1870

During the summer of 1869 Colin Dunlop & Co. commenced the sinking of a coal pit on the lands of North Carscallan near to the Quarter Iron Works. Coal was reached at a depth of 74 fathoms or 444 feet, but unexpectedly the following April, a fault in the form of a seam of stone 11 fathoms (44 feet) thick was encountered resulting in the loss of the coal seam.

In order to catch the coal on the rise, a mine had been driven for a distance of 50 fathoms or 300 feet and a blind pit* was in the course of being sunk from the stone seam to the works underneath for the purpose of ventilation.

The work was being carried out by five men, *John Watson, Thomas Ramsay, Gavin Williamson, Richard Sneddon* and *Thomas Ward.* The men had been blasting and as there was no reputation of gas in this pit they had been working with naked lights.

A shot was fired and *John Watson* then went to the main shaft and signalled to the engineman to lower a hutch from the surface to the mine level. The signal had hardly been given when a devastating explosion occurred and flames and debris shot out from the mouth of the pit, blasting away some of the surrounding woodwork.

The full force of the blast was felt not at the pit head, but further down the shaft, destroying much of its wooden lining and forty fathoms or 240 feet of centre bratticing*. With this bratticing gone the ventilation to the mine was seriously compromised, cutting off the air supply to any survivors underground.

The engineman Thomas Miller was caught by the blast and although suffering from concussion he immediately stopped pumping water from the mine and reversed the procedure pouring hundreds of gallons of water down the shaft. The theory behind this procedure being that the water would push air down in front of it hopefully give any survivors a better chance of staying alive.

The assistant underground manager *Robert Speirs* Jnr. and *Francis Gilchrist* volunteered to go down the pit to see if they could find any men still alive. Because of the devastation caused by the explosion they were making slow headway. Despite the dangerous state of the underground atmosphere which was loaded with after-damp from the explosion, the men ventured further and further into the mine. When they eventually managed to reach the mouth of the stone mine their efforts were rewarded when they found *Ramsey, Williamson, Sneddon* and Ward all alive but severely burned about the head and face. There was however no trace of *John Watson* and the rescue party could only assume that he had died instantly in the blast. The four badly injured survivors were brought to the surface and taken to their homes where *Williamson* and *Ward* later died from their injuries.

All that night and the following day, teams of workmen worked flat out repairing the damage and finally they managed to temporarily restore the air current by inserting canvas where the 260 feet of bratticing had been destroyed.

It was feared that there could be another victim. The pitheadman *William More* had been sitting on the woodwork at the pit mouth at the time of the explosion and couldn't be found despite a thorough search. His cap was then noticed to be hanging on the gangway below the pulley wheels, 36 feet above where he had last been seen. It was assumed that he had been caught by the blast and had been projected down the shaft.

By the following day the ventilation was restored enough for a search to be made for the two missing men. At nine in the morning the body of *William More* was discovered lying on projecting timbers 66 feet from the bottom of the shaft by fireman *James Frew.*

Two hours later *Robert Speirs* and *Ralph Moore* H.M. Inspector of Mines were surveying the works when they found the remains of *John Watson* which were so dreadfully burned, bruised and disfigured as to render identification impossible. *More's* body was also in a similar condition.

All four victims were married men; *William More* (22) who resided at Maryfield, Low Waters, left four fatherless children. *John Watson* (22) although married, was at that time living in lodgings at Low Quarter; a common occurrence then with men moving about looking for work. *Gavin Williamson* (21), who resided at Meikle Earnock, had been married for only a few months and *James Ward* (35) resided at Earnockmuir.

The resulting investigation into the cause of the explosion came to the conclusion that shortly after the firing of a shot in the blind pit, a blower had opened up and the gas had been ignited by John Watson's naked light flame.

*Blind pit. ----*An underground shaft which does not reach the surface. A shaft from an upper to a lower level.*
Bratticing. ---- Partition for directing the ventilation current.

The remains of Mid Quarter miners' rows. Photograph c. 2007 courtesy of Wullie Kerr.

LAND OF HOPE AND GLORY!!
1879
THE QUARTER EVICTIONS

The original Quarter coal mines were small and owned by the Duke of Hamilton but in 1854 he leased the mineral field to Messrs Dunlop of Clyde Ironworks who immediately commenced boring operations. It wasn't long before an excellent bed of Black-Band ironstone was discovered about 15 fathoms below the Main coal. Seams of Slatey and Clay Band ironstone were found at Darngaber and Boghead.

Pits were sunk to both the ironstone and coal seams and in 1856 two furnaces were built for the manufacture of pig iron and were put in blast in March 1857. A third furnace was built in 1867, a fourth in 1875 and a fifth followed in 1875. The average production of pig iron from each of the Quarter furnaces was 8 _ thousand tons per year.

By the late 1870's, most of Quarter's ironstone was worked out and supplies were being brought from the company pits at Blantyre, Boghead and Drummine. The limestone required in the production came from Blantyre and Lesmahagow.

The combined yearly output of coal from four out of the five of the coal pits in operation in 1879 was 120,000 tons and the coal besides supplying the furnaces, also found its way on to the world market via the Hamilton / Strathaven Railway line.

Approximately 150 men were required to supply material for each furnace and upwards of 500 hands of all kinds were employed by Messrs Dunlop & Co. who had a relatively good name with regards to the way they treated their workmen. Indeed they were known as model employers and conditions for their coal miners were much better than any other employer in the district.

However by 1879, Dunlop was getting greedier and the treatment of the miners employed at Quarter had been progressively deteriorating. Wages had been cut again and again and the men were now at a starvation level of 3s 2_ d or 16 pence per day less offtakes. This was less than the daily rate paid in 1855. Miners' agent David Gilmour estimated that the reductions enforced on the men had resulted in Messrs Dunlop having increased their profits by £5000 in one year.

Attempts to form a union were met by brutal intimidation of the miners and their families by the company. The most vulnerable men *"usually the worst off, with large families"* were singled out for dismissal. Between the end of 1877 and the summer of 1879, fifty miners and their families had been evicted from their homes for no reason other than attempting to join a union.

Among the men sacked during this period was 20 year old *James Keir Hardie* who had been employed at Quarter No. 4 pit until he was singled out for his union affiliation. Descending in the cage to start his work one morning he had been half way down the shaft when the cage stopped and then ascended. Waiting at the surface was a stormy-faced manager who told him to get off the company's grounds and that his graith (tools) would be sent to him. *"We'll hae nae damned Hardies in this pit,"* and he kept his word; he also sacked Hardie's two brothers for good measure. They were of course evicted from their company house. Hardie had been labelled an agitator and he accepted the label and spent the rest of his life fighting the cause of the justice and fair wages for the working man.

During June 1879, the County Union agent held meetings at the colliery and the men agreed unanimously to revert to a five day policy and to form a branch of the union. The companies answer was to dismiss a number of the men involved the following day and ordered them to vacate their houses immediately. The manager Mr *Munro* also attempted to put the miners and their wives into a state of fear and alarm by letting it be known that he had another forty eviction notices prepared. His plan backfired because the remaining 400 miners, incensed by what they perceived to be a declaration of war against innocent women and children, immediately withdrew their labour until the dismissal and eviction notices were withdrawn.

The Lanarkshire Miners' County Union circulated a plan of action in a pamphlet which was distributed amongst the counties 30,000 miners. It informed them that they would be asked to be present in the village on the day of the evictions to witness the miners and their wives being turned out of their "*wretched dwellings.*"

The following Tuesday the manager attempted to trick the men into going back to work by knocking the window of a miners house and sending him round the rows to tell the miners that the eviction notices were withdrawn and that the men were to resume their work the next morning.

David Gilmour was informed of this action and he immediately went to Quarter and advised the miners to ignore the communication as no agreement had been reached.

The following day *Gilmour* was back at the colliery and he was met by six Hamilton policemen who had cycled to Quarter for the men starting back their work. However not one miner turned up. The policemen returned to Hamilton and *David Gilmour's* enquiries soon found out that there had been no agreement with Mr *Colin Dunlop* junior to withdraw the dismissal and eviction notices. On hearing this, the miners agreed to continue the strike.

The next day the legal process of eviction started when *George Kemp* messenger at arms served twelve miners with summonses to appear before Sheriff Davidson on the Tuesday. The miners and their families, aware that he was only doing his job, accepted the summonses with the utmost civility.

On June 12th a mass meeting was held at the Quarry, Hamilton and the miners listened intently as Robert Smellie spoke of how "*in this sixtieth year of the reign of Her Most Gracious Majesty and throughout the length and breadth of the country not only in Great Britain, but also in the far Colonies, preparations were being made to celebrate the Diamond Jubilee of Her Majesty's reign; they had something more serious to consider. Again and again during the past three or four months they had all read of the vast strides the workmen of this country had made during the past sixty years--- strides so great that a stranger not acquainted with the real state of affairs would think that workmen of this country lived in a perfect paradise; that there was no poverty, no tyranny; that they lived in a land flowing with milk and honey and they were free men in a free country But information would be put before the meeting that day that would show that they did not live in a land flowing with milk and honey, neither were they free men.*" Bob Smellie in his speech spoke of the events leading up to the strike and warned the men that evictions were the expected outcome at the Sheriff Court. He said "*that if seven days after were allowed for these men and their families to clear out, they would have on the 22nd day of June the glorious spectacle of Her Majesty followed by thousands of loyal subjects through Piccadilly, and millions there to witness the show, while the miners of Quarter, with their wives and little ones were being evicted from their houses and left on the roadside. That was if the miners of Lanarkshire allowed the evictions to go on and he thought that they would not.*" He asked for assistance for the striking Quarter miners and their families and told how "*that morning they had entertained between 400 and 500 Quarter children to dinner and he was glad to say that all the children turned out clean and tidy, took the milk and bread gleefully.*"

David Gilmour was the next man to address the men and he told of how "*twenty years ago when Mr Dunlop Jnr. was a boy of eleven, he was made to beg the pardon of a servant and what this woman was able to make him do he hoped the 30,000 miners of Lanarkshire would make him do also.*"
Chairman Robert Smellie then finished the meeting by saying that "*the officer who carried out the evictions would have some trouble. The probability was that there would be some fun. He was not going to say what was going to be done, but there would be fun. If the evictions were carried out 30,000 miners would take part in the Jubilee demonstration.*"

This statement must have made the blood run cold in the veins of every member of the Hamilton establishment. For months, every detail of the Jubilee demonstration had been planned with precision. Everybody who was anybody or who thought they were, were taking part in the greatest show in the town's history.

The months of planning were now about to come to fruition. Householders with houses fronting on to principal streets were asked to have their dwellings lit up at night and the inhabitants of the town were advised to co-operate by decorating their houses and places of business the night before the procession.

The huge parade was to include the Queen's Own Yeomanry and band, the Provost, Magistrates, Town Council and officials. The Volunteers were to be there with their band, the Boys Brigade, Hamilton Brass Band, several Joint Friendly Societies, a pipe band, the Dramatic Club, the Operative Masons, Operative Joiners and Hamilton Co-operative Society's vans were among the organisations parading through the town.

There was also to be a sports day and each school child was to have a commemorative medal; a half crown (25p) was to be given to 112 pensioners and a fireworks display was being held at the New Cross.

Prior to the parade, a banquet was to be held in the Town Hall for the Provost, Magistrates and Town Council followed by the Provost reading his Jubilee Day address to Her Majesty from the balcony of the Town House. After the speech and amid great pomp and ceremony, the procession of dignitaries would be driven in horse drawn carriages to the Palace Grounds where they would join with the other guests and organisations in Queen Victoria's Diamond Jubilee celebration parade through the town------ -------- and so would 30,000 uninvited miners ---------------THE EVICTIONS WERE CANCELLED AND THE SACKED MINERS REINSTATED.

Quarter Collieries manager's house. The last manager was Sanny (Ducie) Meikle. The miners gave him the nickname Ducie because he reminded them of the Italian dictator Mussolini (il duce) Photograph courtesy of Wullie Kerr.

COLIN'S HOT BLAST

Written shortly after the erection of blast furnaces at Quarter by Colin Dunlop & Co. of Clyde Iron Works.

We bodies roun' Quarter may lift up our heads,
For we've gotten licht now to blazon our deeds;
We sat in the shadow for mony a year past,
But now we're enlightened by Colin's hot blast!

Among mineral men we've a standin' and name,
And for coal and pig-iron a far-carried fame—
With Gartsherrie, Dundyvan, an' Clyde we are classed,
Aye since the erection of Colin's hot blast!

The inventions brought out in this wonderful age
Will form a bright era on history's page;
Of the many inventions not one has surpassed
The ingenious contrivance of Colin's hot blast!

The wise king of Canaan said, under the sun,
In science or art, nothing's new's to be foun';
If in century nineteenth his life had been passed,
He had seen something novel in Colin' hot blast!

In the workin' o' metals nae doubt he was skilled,
And Hiram, his founder, in mouldin' excelled
But on Jordan's clay plains, where his vessels were cast,
He had nae roarin' furnace like Colin's hot blast!

It acts as a midwife on auld Mother Earth,
And brings forth by labour her valuable birth;
For the treasure concealed in her bowels so vast,
Are a' brought to light now by Colin's hot blast!

The utensils of peace, and the weapons of war—
The plough, scythe and spade, the sword, rifle, and spear—
A' lie in embryo in that lava-cast
Which runs frae the red jaws o' Colin's hot blast!

In the days of the feud and the foray langsyne,
On our mountains red beacons of warnin' did shine;
Now our hillsides are studded—grim war being past—
With industrial beacons like Colin's hot blast!

In the lang nichts of winter, when winds whistle high,
And the dark scowlin' tempest bedims a' the sky,
Our horizon's illumined—north, east, south, and wast
With the light- giving flashes of Colin's hot blast!

And, oh! What grand pictures at midnight are showed
On the dark troubled face of the storm-driven cloud;
There is nae photographer on canvas can cast
Sic vivid reflections as Colin's hot blast!

Ghosts, witches, and bogles, wha haunted our roads,
Some dressed in black cleedin' and some in white shrouds,
Which made travellers eerie and look a' aghast,
Are banished for ever by Colin's hot blast!

When the farmers abune the wudhead taigle late,
O'er a gill about markets and shows to debate,
Till Forbes gi'es warnin' his set hour is passed,
The pole-star they steer by is Colin's hot blast!

When the miner on pay-nichts steps into town,
To forget ilka grievance and dull care to drown,
As he airts his head homeward his guide stan's southwast,
In the clear-burnin' safety-lamp –Colin's hot blast!

When Jock, the gay, ramblin' amorous wicht,
Has vowed to meet Jenn under clud o' the nicht!
Tho' the moon's in the wane, and the carry o'ercast,
He's a guid travellin' buat in Colin's hot blast!

When the harvest is late, an the stuff ill to win'—
The days short an scow'ry—stooks dreich to get in—
We gather our fragments, sair driven an' dasht,
With the moon's sparkling substitute—Colin's hot blast!

Tho' our cornfields and pastures are blacken'd by smoke,
And our sheep and horned cattle assume a dark coat,
Yet meal, milk and butter are held in request,
By the gudewives wha dwell near to Colin's hot blast!

The production of limestone, of coal and of mine*,
Cause a great circulation of guid British coin,
To the sons of industry its import is vast—
Tis a great public benefit, Colin's hot blast!

A.H*. Quarter. July 1862,

- "Mine" –the technical name given to the calcined ironstone, when put to the furnace.
- * A.H. Andrew Hamilton. Farmer and Historian.

LAIGH QUARTER, BUILT IN 1681

Above - captured forever, smoke from Quarter coal spiralling from the chimneys and the beautiful white washings hanging out to dry at Laigh Quarter. Photographs courtesy of Neil Scott. Circa 1920's Below Laigh Quarter showing the houses at the top of the above picture; note the hen.

FROM COAL FACE TO BATTLEFIELD
THE QUARTER SOLDIERS
OF WORLD WAR ONE

*Robert Cook, coalminer
born Laigh Quarter, 1897.
He served as a Private in
the Royal Field Artillery
during World War One.*

Photograph courtesy of Robert Cook (son)

Of the 7,866 men employed in the coal mines owned by The United Collieries who went to war, 2,264 were killed in action and 289 died of wounds. The following names are of the miners and officials from Quarter and surrounding villages and towns who worked at United Collieries, Quarter and who served in the armed forces during the First World War.

NAME	REGIMENT	RANK
ALSTON, Andrew	Royal Army Medical Corp	Private
ALLAN, Robert	Royal Field Auxiliary	Private
ANDERSON, William	-------	Private
ALLAN, William	Scottish Horse	Trooper
ANDERSON, Thomas	Black Watch	Private Killed in action
ADAMS, James	--------	Private
ALLISON, James	Argyle & Sutherland Highlanders	Private
ALLAN, John	Scottish Rifles	Private
AITON, Ephraim	Highland Light Infantry	Private
AIRNS, Andrew	Dublin Fusiliers	Private
ALEXANDER, Alex.	---------	Private
ALEXANDER, William	---------	Private
BULLOCH, John	Scottish Rifles	Private
BEATTON, Baird	Cameron Highlanders	Private. Killed in action
BROWNLIE, Andrew	Royal Scots Fusiliers	Lce.-Corporal
BALLANTYNE. Adam	Scottish Rifles	Private
BOYLE, John	Gordon Highlanders	Private
BALLANTYNE, Neil.	Scottish Rifles	Private
BULLOCH, William	The Royal Scots	Private
BLAKELY, Nathanial	Scottish Rifles	Private. Killed in action
BOYLE, Frank	Argyll & Sutherland Highlanders	Private
BROWNLIE, Daniel	Scottish Rifles	Private

Name	Regiment	Rank/Notes
BRAZENALL, Wm.	Royal Naval Division	Leading Seaman
BROWNLIE, James.	---------	Private. Killed in action
BALLANTYRE, Rbt.	Argyle & Sutherland Highlanders	Private
BROWNLIE, Wm.	Black Watch	Private. Killed in action
BLACK, Archibald.	--------	Private
BURNS, H.	--------	Private
BANKS, Walter.	Black Watch	Sgt.-Major. D.C.M
BRADY, John.	Argyle & Sutherland Highlanders	Private
BROOKS, James.	Dublin Fusiliers	Private
BARR, Thomas.	--------	Private
BRADY, James.	Scottish Rifles	Private
BROOKS, Peter.	Scottish Rifles	Private
BROWN, Neil.	--------	Private
BARCLAY, Wm.	Scottish Rifles	Private
BARCLAY, James.	Royal Field Artillery	Private
BULLOCH, Wm.	--------	Private
BLAKELY, Wm.	Scots Guards	Private
BOWNLIE, Gavin.	-------	Private
BARR, Thomas.	-------	Private
BROWNLIE, David.	-------	Private
BELL, John.	Highland Light Infantry	Private
BROWN, John.	Black Watch	Private
BURGESS, Josh.	Gordon Highlanders	Private. Killed in action
BLAIR, Daniel.	Scottish Rifles	Private
BAUCHOPE, John.	Royal Engineers	Private
BORELAND, Hugh.	The Royal Scots	Private
BARR, Alex.	Royal Navy	A.B.
BALLANTYNE, John.	Royal Field Artillery	Private.
BANKS, Smillie.	-------	Private
COCHRANE, Henry.	Argyle & Sutherland Highlanders	Private
CROOKSTON, David	--------	Private
COLLINGTON, James	--------	Private
CURRIE, Robert.	Gordon Highlanders	Private. Killed in action Deville wood 19.07.1916
CAMPBELL, Pat.	Royal Scots Fusiliers	Private
CASEY, Pat.	------	Private
CLARK, John.	Gordon Highlanders	Private
CAVANAGH, James.	Royal engineers	Private
CONNOR, Robert.	Lovat Scots	Private
CAMPBELL, Hugh.	The Royal Scots	Private
CAMERON, John.	Highland Light Infantry	Private
CREECHAN, Michael.	Scottish Rifles	Private
CORNESS, Thomas.	King's Own Scottish Borderers	Private
COOK, Robert.	Royal Field Artillery	Private
CRAIGIE, Matthew.	Army Service Corps	Private
CUNNINGHAM, Robt.	-----------	Private
CASSIDY, Pat.	-----------	Private
CLARK, Pat.	-----------	Private
CONNOR, Hugh.	Royal Scots Fusiliers	Private. Killed in action-Neuve Chapelle. 12.3.1915
CAVANAGH, John.	Army Service Corps.	Private
CULLEN, James	-----------	Private
CLINTON, John.	Scottish Rifles.	Private
COURTNEY, Walter.	Army Canteens	Private. Died 20.7.1917
CRAIG, William.	Scots Guards	Private
CREECHAN, Henry.	Cameron Highlanders	Private
CAIRNEY, Dan.	Scottish Rifles	2nd Lieutenant
COUCHLAN, Hugh	Highland Light Infantry	Private. Killed in action- France, 20.2.1916
CONNELLY, James.	Scottish Rifles	Private
CANNING, James.	Munster Fusiliers	Private

CONNELLY, Thomas.	Scottish Rifles	Private. Killed in Action
CRAIG, William.	------------	Private
CUNNINGHAM, David.	Royal Field Artillery	Private
CONNAR, Peter.	------------	Private
CONNELLY, John.	Dublin Fusiliers	Private
CONLIN, Thomas.	Highland Light Infantry	Private
DUNN, James.	Seaforth Highlanders	Private
DICK, John.	Kings Own Scottish Borderers	Private
DOUGLAS, Abraham.	--------------	Private
DAWSON, W.	Scottish Rifles	Private
DEMPSY, John.	---------------	Private
DICKSON, Thomas.	---------------	Private
DICKSON, Terence.	---------------	Private
DEVINE, James.	Scottish Rifles	Private
DEVLIN, James.	Seaforth Highlanders	Private. Killed in action— Frelingheim. 26.10.1914
DEVANEY, Bernard.	---------------	Private
DYKES, Andrew.	---------------	Private
DUFFY, Patrick.	Dublin Fusiliers	Private
DIXON, James.	Black Watch	Private
DUNN, Wm. C.	Black Watch	Private
DOUGAN, Matthew.	Scottish Rifles	Private
DUNN, John.	Argyll & Sutherland Highlanders	Private
FLEMING, John.	The Royal Scots	Private
FALLOW, Archibald.	Black Watch	Private
FLEMING, Thomas.	Gordon Highlanders	Private
FREW, David.	----------------	Private
FINDLAY, Andrew.	----------------	Private
FLEMING, George.	Argyll & Sutherland Highlanders	Private
FORSYTH, John.	Gordon Highlanders	Private.
FALLOW, Matthew.	------------------	Private
FRASER, H.	-------------------	Private
FERGUSON, James.	Scottish Rifles	Private
FLEMING, William.	Scottish Rifles	Private
FLEMING, William.	Royal Scots Fusiliers	Private
FARRELL, Walter.	Royal Navy	Stoker
FERGUSON, Thomas.	Scottish Rifles	Private
FLEMING, WILLIAM.	-------------------	Private
FRAME, William.	-------------------	Private
FULTON, David.	Transport	Sergeant
GILBERT, James.	Scottish Rifles	Private
GILMOUR, Andrew.	Kings Own Scottish Borderers	Private
GOURLAY, Wm.	Black Watch	Private
GOURLAY, James.	Royal Engineers	Private. Killed in Action, Cambrai 9.4.1918
GRANT, John.	------------------	Private
GIVENS, John.	Scottish Rifles	Private. Killed in action, 14. 3. 1916
GILBERT, David.	Argyll & Sutherland Highlanders	Corporal
GIFFEN, Thomas.	Scottish Rifles	Private
GIBSON, George.	------------------	Private
GILLON, John.	Scottish Rifles	Private
GOUDIE, William.	Argyll & Sutherland Highlanders	Private
GARDINER, Geo.	------------------	Private
GRAY, Frank.	------------------	Private
GLANCY, James.	Scottish Rifles	Private. Killed in action 14.7.1916
GEMMELL, Robert.	Royal Engineers	Private
GLANCY, James.	Machine Gun Corps	Private
GLANCY, Michael.	Scottish Rifles	Private
GOLD, Andrew.	------------------	Private
GRIFFE, James.	Gordon Highlanders	Private

HART, Hugh.	Seaforth Highlanders	Private
HILL, David.	Scottish Rifles	Private
HAMILTON, Wm.	Royal Scots Fusiliers	Private. Military Medal
HIGGINS, James.	Royal Irish Fusiliers	Private. Military Medal
HARTNESS, Wm.	------------------	Private. Military Medal
HARDY, JOHN.	------------------	Private
HAMILTON, Jos.	------------------	Private
HODGE, Jacob.	Highland Light Infantry	Private
HARRISON, Conn.	Highland Light Infantry	Private
HAMILTON, Archd.	Scottish Rifles	Private
HUMES, Fred.	Royal Naval Volunteers	A.B.
HALEY, Pat.	------------------	-------
HADDOW, Robert.	------------------	-------
HUGHES, John.	------------------	-------
HIGGENSON, Alex.	Scottish Rifles	Private
HIGGINS, Arthur.	Gordon Highlanders	Private
HAMILTON, Thomas.	Royal Engineers	Private
HIGGENS, Frank.	Scottish Rifles	Private
HAMILTON, Gavin.	Scottish Rifles.	Private
HOOLIHAN, Michael.	------------------	Private
HAMILTON, Jas.	Royal Field Artillery	Private
HORNAL, Robert.	Highland Light Infantry	Private
HAMILTON, Thomas.	------------------	Private
HENDERSON, James.	Cameron Highlanders	Private
IRVINE Samuel	------------------	--------. Military medal
JAMIESON, James.	Seaforth Highlanders	Private
JARVIE, Alex.	King's Own Scottish Borderers	Private
JAMIESON, Alex.	------------------	Private
JONES, Edward.	------------------	Private
JAAP, William.	Scottish Rifles	Private
KENNEDY, Wm.	The Royal Scots	Private
KANE, Geo. F.	Highland Light Infantry	Private
KIRKLAND, Andrew.	Royal Navy	A.B.
KELLY, Wm.	------------------	Private
KELLY, Hugh.	Royal Field Artillery	Private
KEENAN, Owen.	Highland Light Infantry	Private
KIRKLAND, Andrew.	Royal Garrison Artillery	Private
KIRKLAND, John.	Scottish Rifles	Private
LITTLE, Thomas.	Cameron Highlanders	Private
LAMBIE, John.	------------------	Private
LAWRIE, John.	Highland Light Infantry	Private
LOWE, Geo.	Scottish Rifles	Private
LINDSAY, Dugald.	Scottish Rifles	Private
LAW, Robert.	Dragoon Guards	Private
LAMOND, Wm.	------------------	Private
LAWSON, Wm.	------------------	Private
LOGAN, David.	------------------	Private
LAW, Adam.	------------------	Private
LOWELL, Wm.	Royal Dublin Fusiliers	Private
LOWELL, James.	Highland Light Infantry	Private
LUCY, John.	Scottish Rifles	Private
LAWSON, Robert.	------------------	Private
LAFFERTY, Robert.	Royal Scots Fusiliers	Private
LUCY, Frank.	Royal Scots Fusiliers	Private
LAW, Adam.	King's Own Scottish Borderers	Private
LEIPER, John.	Royal Navy	A.B.
McLAREN, George.	The Royal Scots	Private
McNAUGHT, Alex.	The Royal Scots	Private
McKENZIE, John.	The Royal Scots	Private

McPHERSON, James.	Seaforth Highlanders.	Private. Killed in action—Neuve Chapelle, 9.5.1915.
McKENZIE, William.	Scottish Rifles	Private
McDOWELL, Alexander,	Seaforth Highlanders	Private. Killed in action— Arras 02.1.1917.
McKELLAR, John.	Argyll & Sutherland Highlanders	Private. Killed in action Ypres 13.7.1917.
McCAIG, John.	Royal Engineers att. R.F.A.	Private
McGUIRE, Hugh.	Royal Marines	Private. Died of wounds—Valenciennes, 11.9.1918.
McQUEEN, John.	-------------------	Private
McGOURTY, John.	Irish Guards	Private. Killed in action— Arras 03.6.1918.
McGEECHAN, William.	Royal Engineers	Sapper
McEWAN, William	Seaforth Highlanders	Private
McLARE, George.	Argyll & Sutherland Highlanders	Private
McLACHLAN, Frank.	Connaught Rangers	Private
McKENZIE, Alex.	Black Watch	Private
McGEECHAN, Andrew.	Scottish Rifles	Private
McLEVY, Michael.	-----------------	Private
McANDREWS, John.	-----------------	Private
McVICKERS, William.	Cameron Highlanders	Private
McCANN, Edward.	Army Service Corps	Private
McGINNES, William.	Dublin Fusiliers	Private
McKAY, David.	Scottish Rifles	Private
McCOURT, Pat.	Royal Field Artillery	Private
McCABE, John.	Argyll & Sutherland Highlanders	Private
McGHIE, John.	Black Watch.	Private
McCOLL, Andrew.	------------------	Private
McLEAVY, Pat.	Royal Engineers	Sapper
McDAVID, Alex.	Scottish Rifles	Major-Bugler
McLEAVY, James.	Scottish Rifles	Private
McGONAGLE, James.	Gordon Highlanders	Private
McCANN, Charles.	Royal Field Artillery	Private
McGRAW, Peter.	Argyll & Sutherland Highlanders	Private. Military Medal and Bar
McGRAW, George.	---------------------	Private
McCAIG, Frank.	Scottish Rifles	Private
McGREGOR, Peter.	Scottish Rifles	Private
McGINNES, Michael.	Royal Scots Fusiliers	Private. Killed in Action
McLARE, Alex.	The Royal Scots	Private
McARTHUR, John.	---------------------	Private
McQUEEN, Robert.	Royal Air Force	Private
McCONNELL, Alex.	---------------------	Private
McBETH, Henry.	Scottish Rifles	Private
McBETH, Arch.	---------------------	Private
McFARLANE, John.	---------------------	Private
MORRAN, William.	Royal Field Artillery	Private
MOORE, Walter.	---------------------	Private
MOFFAT, John.	Scottish Rifles	Private
MILNE, Alex.	Gordon Highlanders.	Sergeant-Major
MORRAN, Thomas	Argyll & Sutherland Highlanders	Private
MAIR, Daniel.	Royal Engineers	Sapper . Military Medal
MURDOCH, John.	---------------------	Private
MOORE, Robert.	---------------------	Private
MAXWELL, Charles.	Dublin Fusiliers	Private
MITCHELL, Robert.	Scottish Rifles (Bantams) Private	
MOORE, Alex.	---------------------	Private
MOFFAT, Andrew.	Royal Field Artillery	Private
MASSEY, John.	Scottish Rifles.	Private
MURRAY, Frank.	Highland Light Infantry	Corporal. Died on Service— Persian Gulf 17.7.16.
MURRAY, Hugh.	Highland Light Infantry.	Private
MURPHY, John.	---------------------	Private

MUIR, John.	--------------------	Private
MUIR, John.	---------------------	Private
MURPHY, James.	--------------------	Private
NUTT, Richard.	Scottish Rifles	Private
NEIL, JAMES,	Scots Guards	Private
NICOL, Alex.	Scots Guards	Private
NAIRN, Robert.	Gordon Highlanders	Private. Killed in Action – Romeries, 23.10.1918
NICOL, Robert.	Highland Light Infantry	Private
NICOL, John.	---------------------	Private
NICOL, George.	---------------------	Private
O'DONNELL, Patrick.	Royal Engineers Driver	
OGG, James.	--------------------	Private
Wm. Paterson	Argyle and Sutherland Highlanders	Private
PARK, George.	--------------------	Private
PARK, Hugh.	Highland Light Infantry	Private
PATERSON, James.	Cameron Highlanders.	Private
PATERSON, William.	Royal Engineers	Sapper
PATERSON, David, C.	------------------	Private
PAXTON, William.	Lanarkshire Yeomanry	Private
PARKER. Robert.	---------------------	Private
PROSSAR, Andrew.	Scottish Rifles	Private
PARKER, Robert.	------------------	Private
POLLOCK, John.	------------------	Private
ROBERTSON, Rbt. W.	Royal Army Medical Corps	Private
REID, Robert.	------------------	Private
RENWICK, David.	Cameron Highlanders	Private
RENWICK, Halbert.	Royal Scots Fusiliers	Private. Military Medal
RENWICK, John.	------------------	Private
ROSS, William.	Black Watch.	Private
ROSS, Robert.	Royal Army Medical Corps	Private
ROCKS, Joseph.	Scottish Rifles	Private
ROCKS, Charles.	Scottish Rifles	Private
REILLY, James.	Army Service Corps	Private
ROBSON, George.	Highland Light Infantry	Private
ROBERTSON, Harry.	Highland Light Infantry	Sergeant
RADIGAN, John.	Scottish Rifles	Private
RUSSELL, Robert.	Black Watch	Private
ROBSON, James.	Gordon Highlanders	Private
ROBERTSON, John.	------------------	Private
RUSSELL, John.	Black Watch.	Private.
ROBSON, George,	Scottish Rifles (Bantam)	Private. Killed in action— France 19.10.1916
RAMSAY, Graham.	--------------------	Private
RUSSELL, William.	Royal Scots Fusiliers	Private
RICHMOND, Hugh.	--------------------	Private
ROSS, James.	Royal Engineers	Sapper
RHONEY, James.	--------------------	Private
RENWICK, John.	--------------------	Private
SCOTT, Hugh.	Cameron Highlanders	Private
STEWART, James.	Argyll & Sutherland Highlanders	Private
STEVENSON, David.	Gordon Highlanders	Private
SINCLAIR, Alex.	------------------	Private
STRACHAN, James.	Scottish Rifles	Private
STRACHAN, JOHN.	Scottish Rifles	Private
STEVENSON, William.	Royal Army Medical Corps	Private
SCOTT, Peter.	Gordon Highlanders.	Private
STEWART, Alex.	Scottish Rifles	Private
SHARKEY, THOMAS.	Royal Dublin Fusiliers	Private
SMITH, John.	Royal Irish Fusiliers.	Private

STEVEN, Wm.	------------------	Private
SHRUBB, William.	Seaforth Highlanders	Private
SCOTT, Richard.	------------------	Private
SCOTT, William.	------------------	Private
STEWART, William.	Black Watch.	Private
STEWART, John.	Cameron Highlanders	Private
STEVENSON, Wm.	Argyll & Sutherland H/landers	Private
SEMPLE, John.	Scottish Rifles	Private
SOMMERVILLE, John	Scottish Rifles	Private
STEWART, William.	Royal Garrison Artillery	Private
SYMONS, Adam,	Royal Navy	Leading Seaman
SYMONS, David.	Argyll & Sutherland H/landers	Sergeant. Killed in action—Loos 26.9.1915
TAYLOR, George.	Scottish Rifles	Sergeant-Major
THOMSON, Isaac.	------------------	----------
THOMSON, Alex.	Black Watch	Sergeant
TORRANCE, Abram.	The Royal Scots	Corporal
THOMSON, John.	Cameron Highlanders	Private
TWADDLE, John.	Seaforth Highlanders	Private
THOMSON, Thomas.	Scottish Rifles.	Private
TODD, John.	Argyll & Sutherland Highlanders	Private
URE, James.	The Royal Scots	Private
VINT, William.	Argyll & Sutherland Highlanders	Private
WARDROPE. Thos.	------------------	Private
WILSON, William.	Scottish Rifles	Private
WEIR, Joseph.	------------------	Private
WYLIE, James.	Scottish Rifles	Private
WEIR, Robert.	Scottish Rifles	Private
WEIR, James.	Scottish Rifles	Private. Drowned, 21.5.1916
WALES, Thomas.	------------------	Private
WALLACE, Archd. F.	Highland Light Infantry	Private
WEIR, James.	Scottish Rifles	Private
WILSON, Hugh.	Scots Greys	Private
WILSON, John.	Argyll & Sutherland Highlanders	Private
WILSON, John.	------------------	Private
WILSON, Robert.	Scottish Horse	Private
WILSON, John.	------------------	Private
WEIR, Robert.	Scottish Rifles	Private
WILSON, Thomas.	------------------	Private
WHITESIDE, James.	Dublin Fusiliers	Private
WHYTE, James.	Scottish Rifles.	Private
WEIR, William.	------------------	Private
WARDROPE, James.	------------------	Private
WHITE, Joseph.	Gordon Highlanders	Private
WALKER, Thomas.	Gordon Highlanders	Private. Killed in action Hill 60 7.6.1917
WILSON, John.	Scottish Rifles	Private
WILSON, William.	The Royal Scotts.	Private
WILLIAMS, George.	Scots Guards	Private
WILSON, Arthur.	The Royal Scots	Private
WILSON, Robert.	------------------	Private
WILLIAMS, Alex.	Highland Light Infantry	Private

JAMES HIGGINS, MM

Photograph courtesy of John Carrigan (grandson   *..... James Higgins's Military Medal.*

James Higgins was born on the 5th January 1887 at 20 Carscallan Rows, Quarter, his father Patrick was a coal hewer and his mother was Mary McPake. He had five older brothers, Thomas, Patrick, Francis, John and William; he also had a younger sister Kate who was born in 1890. James was four and Kate only a baby when their father died.

At the age of 13 years of age James started working at Quarter Collieries; to begin with he was a pony driver then he went on to work as a hewer. In 1911 he won first prize for having the best kept pit pony out of a total of 115 ponies at Quarter Collieries.

In 1913 he married Winifred Sharkey and the following year their first child Thomas was born. James had a lot of hobbies; he was a great dancer and loved to play bools, winning medals for both. He was a member of the Quarter Colliery Band, an avid junior football player and loved to grow vegetables in his plots. Highly respected in Quarter, James, or Coochie as he was known, was the man other miners came to for advice; he was also a good provider for his family never missing a shift at the pit.

Three weeks after the outbreak of the First World War, James enlisted in the Connaught Rangers and after his initial training was transferred to the Royal Irish Fusiliers serving with them for almost four years, during which time he was awarded the Military Medal for outstanding bravery while saving the lives of four men. On the 13th May 1918, he was admitted to a military hospital in France with mustard gas poisoning and returned to the front almost nine weeks later on the 19th July. Transferred to the Royal Inniskillen Fusiliers, he remained in France until 12th December 1918; he was demobilized three weeks later. His brother Frank a private in the Scottish Rifles also survived the war.

James returned home from France with irreversible lung damage caused by the mustard gas but he returned to work at Quarter Collieries. In 1921,, with his health getting worse he applied for a war pension but was turned down. By 1929 his health had deteriorated so much he had to give up his job as a coal hewer and with 8 children Thomas, Patrick, John, Mary, Winifred, Agnes, Catherine (Kit) and Margaret (Meg). James and his wife must have found life very hard. In 1930 an application to the Department of War Pensions for a disability pension was turned down but on appeal he was awarded the paltry sum of 8/- (40p) a week for himself and 2/- (10p) for his wife. He died from chronic lung disease aged 51 years in 1938 when his youngest child Meg was only 12 years old. As a war hero he could have had a military funeral but he left instructions that there had to be no military presence.

LINES WRITTEN IN THE TRENCHES

(By a Stra'ven Callan*)

In the trenches in the night time
Wide awake I lay and thought,
Listening to the crack of rifles
And the nightly feud of shot.

Sometimes fainter, sometimes louder,
Till at times the sound it seemed
Like a storm of bullets coming
Nearer where I lay and dreamed.

In the trenches seeing nothing
But the night sky overhead,
Where the moon kept watch till morning
Over the unburied dead.

And the stars in solemn wonder,
Looking down on earthly powers,
Seemed to shed a light of pity
On this poor sad world of ours.

Far away at home in Scotland,
Where we left our loves and joys,
Wives are thinking of their husbands,
Sweethearts dreaming of their boys.

Fathers, yes and also mothers
Speak with pride and eyes that shine,
Of their sons who've gone to battle
Fighting in the firing line.

But could they be hear and listen
To the noise of screaming shell,
As it rattles through the valley
Where grim death and murder dwell

Could they see the limbs of bodies
Sticking out from 'neath the soil,
Horrid work of human slaughter,
Fit to make a fiend recoil.

What a shock the sight would give them,
Here with death on every side,
Here where there is a need for pity
More than there is room for pride

See the scores of dead men lying
Fast decaying in the stench,
Out there where 'tis death to venture,
Just beyond the firing trench

This then is the field of glory
Twas to this your sons you sent,
Fathers, yes and mothers
'Twas to this hell's punishment.

To be slain and lie there rotting
To be buried like manure
That the schemes of kings and statesmen
Might tomorrow still endure.

And again create fresh bloodshed
When it suits a head of state
To attempt some new ambition
Born of power and greed and hate.

How they cheered us, how they shouted
When from home we marched away
Shook our hands and called us heroes
What a mockery to-day!

Seems the send off that they gave us
All a tragic waste of breath,
Here in this red field of slaughter
In this harvest field of death.

R.H.
Strathaven
Circa 1916.

* *Callan. A youth.*

QUARTER COAL MINERS

John (Jock) Allan was born in Larkhall and started work at Quarter Collieries when he was 13 years of age. In 1913 he joined the Territorial branch of the Scottish Rifles and when war was declared in 1914 he was among the first to be called up to serve his country. His pal John (Tiffty) Bulloch was called up the same day and both men were to serve throughout the war. They fought at all the major battles including the Somme and the battle of Festubert where their battalion was almost wiped out.

They were transferred to the South Welsh Borderers. This regiment also suffered appalling casualties and John found himself transferred again this time to the Kings Own Scottish Borderers.

Quarter miners Jock Allan and Danny McGlynn sitting on the fence at Quarter crossroads. c. 1958
Photograph courtesy of Wullie Kerr (grandson)

Jock was shot five times and on one occasion he lay wounded on the battlefield feigning death while the German soldiers bayoneted any British soldier they thought was still alive. After recovering from his injuries he was transferred again, this time to his own regiment The Scottish Rifles.

Jock married Lillian Davidson from Carscallan Rows (Monkey Raws") Quarter at the end of the war and lived at Laigh Quarter for many years before moving to William Drive, Eddlewood. They had four daughters Margaret, Mary, Lily and Annie and three sons Tam, Wullie and John. He worked in several of the Quarter pits and also worked at Thinacre and Avonbanks drift mines.

Jock was a bit of an amateur boxer and fought under the name of Yankee Allen, a name given to him because his mother was born in America. He worked for 46 years in Quarter coalmines and when he retired he received £200 and watch from the National Coal Board.

*   *   *

Taken from an unusual angle this photograph shows miners Robert (Rab) Miller and his brother-in-law Wullie Miller returning home from work. Rab a coal hewer was born in 1901 in Larkhall and worked for most of his life at Quarter No. 2 Pit. When he retired at 65 he was working at Knowtop Mine.

George Smith

George Smith a was one of 16 children born in a 2 roomed house at 8 Store Row Quarter to miner William Smith and his wife Elizabeth Perrow. George and his brother John spent most of their working lives in Quarter Collieries. George who had the nickname Powie lived at Furnace Row with his wife Jenny and two daughters Audrey and Sheila. Like many miners he loved growing vegetables in his plot (allotment). His pit pony Star, grazed in the field next to the plots and his girls loved to give it bread and water. George's life as a pit pony driver came to an abrupt end in the late 1950's when his back was seriously injured by a runaway hutch at Knowtop Mine. With his health ruined by years of working underground he died in 1972 aged 63 years.

WULLIE KERR'S MEMORIES OF AVONBRAES MINE QUARTER

Wullie Kerr spent much of his early teenage years at Quarter where several of his pals lived and he knew the area very well. Having left Woodside School in 1959 he had no intention of going into the pits so he started working for the Duke of Hamilton at the High Parks (now Chatelherault Country Park) until he could join the RAF.

Wullie spent many a happy hour at Avonbraes Mine sitting with the bottom winding machine operator Andrew Hamilton, the father of his best pal. Andrew Hamilton was a gentleman and Wullie thought the world of him and loved to be in his company. When he had spare time he would go to the mine and sit in front of the warm fire listening to Andrew's stories and watching him working the haulage winding engine bringing the hutches full of coal out of the mine.

Andrew could tell where the hutches were by the sound of the winding wheel drum and the engine room rang with the sound of the bell as the miners underground signalled their instructions to him. To use the signalling system the miner, would touch the wires with his knife. One ring signalled go, two was slow down, three stop. At the end of the shift the miners used to ride up to the surface on the hutches.

At the entrance to the mine was a cut down oil drum which the men used as a urinal and the miners who were well known for playing tricks on each other would occasionally wrap a couple of loose wires round the low voltage signalling wire and drop the other end into the water in the drum. When one of the men came to the surface to use the drum he would receive an electric shock from the stream of urine. The men responsible would be hiding waiting to hear the howls of pain from their poor victim.

*   *   *

Quarter store was built by coal master Colin Dunlop and due to the remoteness of the village; miners had no alternative but to buy their groceries at inflated prices. When the miners were paid at the pay office at Quarter Cross they would go home to their wives with their wages. The wives would then go to the store and pay their groceries which they had received on credit during the week. The pay office would run out of money to pay the miners and someone would be sent to the colliery owned pub and store to take money back to the pay office and so the money went full circle.

Quarter store and The Bully Inn, c. 1957. Photograph courtesy of Wullie Kerr

AVONBANKS/AVONBRAES MINE
QUARTER.1962

*L-R   Unknown, John Smith of Strathaven Road, Eddlewood, Hamilton, and unknown, deep inside
Avonbraes drift mine, Quarter, c.1964 Photographs courtesy of Andy Bain*

Avonbanks Mine Quarter was owned by The Duke of Hamilton and situated on the banks of the River Avon.   It was developed where the Ell coal seam reached the surface and was a drift mine or ingaun e'e. The first coal from the mine came up for sale in August 1824 and it was hauled by horses via a railway to a depot at the Old Avon Bridge where it was then sold. The coal from the Duke's early Quarter Pits was brought over the White Bridge, (a wooden structure made of pine) and also sold at this depot. The wooden bridge collapsed and was replaced by a stronger stone one in 1829.

The miners living at Laigh Quarter also used the bridge to get to their work. In 1841 an explosion of fire-damp resulted in the death of 13 miners; the youngest victim being only 10 years of age. The mine which had two entrances one at Hootlet Raw and the other at the Larkhall side of the White Bridge, was abandoned in 1856. It was reopened by the National Coal Board under the name of Avonbraes mine in 1950 and closed in 1964.When the mine was being re-opened some old miners' tools and a woman thick leather shoe were found, an indication that women had also worked in the mine.

Captain, one of the three ponies employed at Avonbraes Mine, Quarter. 1964.

The colliery topped the National Coal Board's safety league having gone through the year without a worker suffering a serious injury. Photograph courtesy of Hamilton Advertiser.

Front Row left Matha Mason, William Stewart, unknown, Back row Left to tight, Jock Cochrane, Peter Bain, Wullie Miller, James Bain, Johnny Currie.

James Bain (52) 2 Douglas Place Eddlewood, hewing coal by hand in Avonbraes Mine
Photographs courtesy of Andy Bain

Blacksmith Robert Muir shoeing Mary one of the six ponies at Avonbraes Mine

Avonbraes Mine 1962. Captain pulls a load of coal away from the coal face
Photographs courtesy of Andy Bain

The White Bridge
Two miners at the mouth of Avonbraes Mine

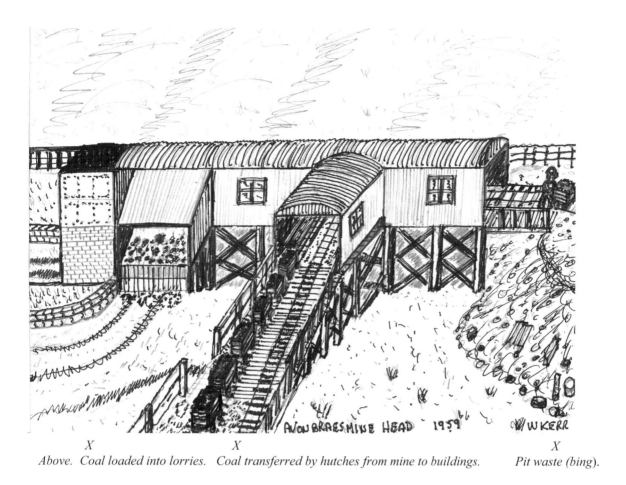

    X   *X*   *X*

Above.   Coal loaded into lorries.   Coal transferred by hutches from mine to buildings.   *Pit waste (bing).*

Avonbraes Mine buildings and haulage ramp looking from the Larkhall side of the River Avon towards Quarter.
These wonderful sketches of the mine were drawn by William Kerr from memory. He has not seen the mine
since the early 1960's. Bottom hut winding enginehouse, middle hut blacksmith's shop

If the haulage rope snapped this safety system derailed the runaway hutches preventing them from running back down the steep haulage railway. As can be seen in previous illustration there were three pairs of safety bars.

The entrance to Avonbraes Mine lay on the Larkhall side of the River Avon. The low voltage wires used for the signalling can be seen on top of the walls of the mine. The tin drum at the mine entrance was used as a urinal by the miners. The stairs at the left were known as Jacobs's ladder. Sketches courtesy of Wullie Kerr.

Above, remains of winding enginehouse middle of picture the remains of two of the brick pillars of the Avonbraes Mine haulage ramp situated on the Quarter side of the White Bridge, Chatelherault Country Park. Below on Larkhall side of the White Bridge the mouth of the Avonbraes originally called Avonbanks Mine can be seen quite clearly. Originally there was another entrance to this mine at Hootlets Raw. Photographs courtesy of Wullie Kerr formerly of Eddlewood Raws and now living in Paisley.

Above the pillars of the original White Bridge (c. 1829) of Avonbraes Mine now used to support the wooden structure used by thousands of walkers every year in Chatelherault Country Park. Below standing on the bridge looking up towards the site of the haulage ramp which transported countless tons of coal to the mine head at the top of the Avon gorge on the Quarter side of the river. Photographs courtesy of Wullie Kerr.

KNOWETOP
MINERS
QUARTER

Miners from Knowetop Mine, Quarter.
L-r Frank Kane, Solly Fleming, unknown, unknown, Jimmy Dunn, Tammy Stewart. Photographs by the late Joe Dell c. 1966 courtesy of Mrs A. Dell.

An unknown Knowetop Miner with one of the last pit ponies in Scotland.

Limekilnburn hamlet circa 1955. L - r three Bulloch children, Maureen Jones, Miller children, Jan Miller pushing pram and Mrs Kerr. Photograph and identification of children courtesy of Margaret McTaggart

Bonspiel at Limekilnburn curling pond, c. 1920. It is documented that some of the players were miners. Photograph courtesy of Andy Bain.

A SELECTION OF INFORMATIVE LETTERS FROM THE HAMILTON ADVERTISER ARCHIVES.

MINERS. ---The lock-out in this district has now continued for six weeks, with all the attendant misery and distress that usually accompanies such strikes. Wretchedness is everywhere prevalent and poverty is apparent in almost every face—hunger has now become, with the miner, an everyday attendant; and his clothing, generally of the best, has, in too many cases, turned into a mere covering of rags. These poor fellows have struggled manfully amid all the wretchedness of this protracted struggle with a spirit and determination worthy of men occupying a much higher position in life. The masters seem determined to starve out the men, thinking that then they will be glad to go to their laborious duty at any price; but to all appearance there is a likelihood that the masters will be first starved out, seeing that almost every "bing" in the district, is cleared away, and the market crying out for coals, which must be supplied, not to speak of the contracts which must be fulfilled. It is but right to think that these industrious men should have their 4s 6d. per day for fulfilling one of the most dangerous callings to which man can be placed, seeing that when the pick sharpening, school-fees, doctor's fees, oil, &c., are taken from that wonderful 4s 6d. there is left only about 18s per week to come into a family of perhaps four children, a wife, and the husband, to find them in food, clothing, house-rent and taxes. Meetings are being held every day, which are numerously attended by most expectant audiences; speeches are fluently and earnestly delivered by the energetic members of the union. At the meeting on Wednesday forenoon, reports were heard from all the pits in the district, which were unanimous in the cry, "no concession." Mr McDonald addressed the meeting at great length, showing distinctly the propriety of continuing steadfast in a cause which would do undoubted good both to the men and the country for many months to come…… Hamilton Advertiser. 11/4/1863. Page 2.

Sir, --The other day as I was walking along the Glasgow Road, I observed a cart approaching with what seemed to be a bed in it and, on its coming up, I saw a man lying thereon. Upon inquiry, it turned out that he was a poor fellow who had met with a terrible accident in a coal pit, on his way to the Royal Infirmary. The afternoon was lowering, and although everything had been done to make the man as comfortable as the circumstances permitted, still had the rain come on as it threatened, the consequences might have been most serious. Now sir, it struck me as being rather in discordance with the habits of the age that men with broken bones, and bodies crushed, should be thus exposed to the inclemency of the weather in an open cart, and in this condition, be necessitated to make a journey of 12 or 18 miles in such a jostling, shaking, rumbling conveyance. The process must be in the highest degree painful and precarious. Upon reflection, it seemed to me, that the thing admits of a very simple remedy. Were vans placed at different stations throughout the local coalfields, constructed on proper principles, and fitted up with proper apparatus, the journey could be made comparatively painless and comfortable. And such vans could be instituted by very simple means. Supposing Hamilton, Wishaw, Holytown, &c. were made the centres of their various districts, and the workmen in each district to contribute, say sixpence each, machines of the very best construction could be procured. Once built, they would necessitate no further expense, and when an accident did occur, which required transmission to Glasgow; the matter should be managed much more seemly and humanely than by the present primitive mode. The suggestion may appear simple, perhaps trivial; still I think it is on the side of humanity. I am yours, &c. C. Ref. Hamilton Advertiser. 12.8.1865. Page 2.

Sir, in regard to the explosions I maintain that masters or employers are not free from blame. My argument is this, why do masters employ men who are entirely ignorant regarding the nature of gas, or the use of a safety lamp? While such men are employed, there will be no end to explosions and loss of life. I say that every man who is employed to go down a fiery mine ought to have a practical knowledge regarding the nature of gas, and how to use a safety lamp. The only men the masters engage as qualified men are what they call their firemen who have to look out for the safety of the miner. And as the gas is apt to accumulate suddenly owing to the changes in the atmosphere and sometimes by caves and falls from the roof and the fireman has so many men to look after, it is a mere impossibility that the mine can be wrought in safety, unless the miners have a thorough knowledge of the subject. Unless our Government inspectors use some means to rectify this, the safety of the miner, I am afraid, will remain as it has been.—I am etc., A MINER. Ref. Hamilton Advertiser. 19th July 1879. Page 2.

Above Cadzow Roman Catholic Chapel and school Eddlewood. Built in 1883 it had to be demolished in 1933 after being seriously affected by subsidence from the underground workings of Cadzow Colliery.

Below Gilmour Memorial Church, Glasgow Road Burnbank, In 1883 when the church was being built, it started to sink and the walls crack because of underground workings. The planned spire had to be left off the steeple.

AND THE WALLS CAME TUMBLING DOWN

In 1873 the Bent Colliery Company started sinking operations in the lands at Bent, Hamilton and on 26th April 1878 a 7 foot 4 inch thick seam of the finest quality Ell coal was reached at 106 fathoms (636 feet). The lands were owned and leased to the coal company by the Duke of Hamilton, Dr Naismith of Auchincampbell, Hamilton Parish Church and all three would receive royalties for each ton of coal extracted from under their lands. The coal field extended to three hundred acres.

For the first 228 feet the sinking of the colliery had been relatively problem free, but when they reached a 75 foot thick bed of white sandstone known as *"cutters"* which had an infamous reputation for its water bearing cracks, they came up against huge problems. The sandstone was *" like a sponge"* and water shot through a 1 _ inches diameter blasting hole like a high pressure fountain at the rate of 500 gallons per minute which soon increased to 1400 gallons. It took months of pumps running night and day before the water was under control.

At its peak, the Bent Colliery employed 500 men and annually produced 200,000 tons of first class coal which sold well to the local and international markets; but old Mother Earth never takes kindly to the plundering carried out by the human race and it was inevitable that the removal of millions of tons of coal from deep within her would have consequences which would eventually manifest on the surface.

Within a few years, subsidence on the surface began to cause major problems in the area. In 1884 the Caledonian railway bridge at Park road started to show serious signs that it was in imminent danger of collapsing. The stone bridge had a big flay arch and this had to be substituted by iron girders to prevent it collapsing.

The Bent Coal Company, the Trustees of Auchincampbell Estate and others who owned the ground and were receiving royalties for the coal being extracted beneath it were now being sued by fuers who found their property was being damaged by the coal workings.

In 1891 at a meeting of the Town Council, Baillie Hamilton remarked that if a stranger passed through Hamilton he would think *"it had been wrecked by an earthquake"*. The Council were forced to spend large amounts of money repairing gas and water mains which were torn apart by subsidence. By March 1892 the condition of some of the buildings in Orchard Street and Union Street were so dangerous the tenants were ordered out and the owners given no option other than pull the buildings down. By July further damage occurred in Orchard Street and also at Park Road; even the Bent Colliery Company were not exempt. The gable end of the manager's house had to be shored up. Park Road E.U. Church required a large wooden buttress propped up against its walls which also had to be bound with iron bars which were inserted through the interior from side-wall to side-wall.

Three months later residents in the Park Road/Orchard Street areas were wakened out of their sleep by their houses shaking violently and a loud rumbling sound which was coming from deep within the earth. One man jumped out of bed convinced that there had been an explosion at Bent Colliery and as he ran out of his bedroom he met his terrified servant running up the stairs.

Cracks were appearing in many of the buildings in the vicinity of the workings of Bent Colliery and the Town Buildings were damaged.

In April 1893 two trains and a pilot engine collided at Orchard Street Bridge after an empty train was derailed when the track subsided. At the home of Mr Blyth manager of the Bent Colliery the front wall of his house in Park Road subsided breaking a gas pipe and the house was in grave danger of burning down when escaping gas ignited sending a jet of flame shooting out of the top of the rainwater conductor pipe.

Buildings were being damaged or destroyed by underground workings all over Hamilton. In 1883 at Burnbank, tenants of a three storey tenement at the corner of Glasgow and Whitehill Roads were living in terror as the building started to subside when the "stoops" were being removed in Greenfield Colliery. The building was shored up with wooden buttresses and the chimney stalk on the corner house was removed to lighten the load on the wall. One of the tenants was wakened in the middle of the night by the sound of the joists snapping. The new United Presbyterian Church (now the Gilmour Memorial) which was in the course of construction showed cracks in several places. The steeple which was being built had to be finished off without the addition of the planned spire.

Hamilton Academy

In June 1911 to the horror of the Town Council the costly new Hamilton Academy which was in the process of being built by prominent Hamilton building firm T. Anderson and Sons started to show evidence of serious cracks from subsidence before the building was even halfway up. To prevent any more subsidence and to secure the foundations, Hamilton School Board purchased the coal reserves in the vicinity of the school from the Bent Coal Company.

In 1926 a substantial and relatively new sandstone tenement building in Wylie Street, Hamilton was the subject of a court case at Hamilton Sheriff Court. Council for the building's owner revealed that the property had "*been completely wrecked by underground workings.*" The pit in question, the Bent Colliery, had been responsible for a great many properties quite literally falling down due to subsidence. The owner of the Wylie Street property found himself in court charged with failing to carry out improvements in the backcourt of the tenement. His lawyer told the court that the owner had been left the property (and a big mortgage on the building) by his father and he wished that he had left it to someone else for it had been a drain on him for several years. He stated that he could not even get his expenses from renting the houses because the tenants refused to pay due to the condition of the building. In his desperation he had even written to the Town Council offering them the building but they had declined. It appears that they did not want it not even for the land it stood on. The building was not demolished until the 1960's

Wylie Street Hamilton

The effects of subsidence caused by the underground workings of Fairhill Colliery can be seen in the angle of the roof of Laighstonehall House in the background of the photograph below. This mansion was formerly the home of coalmaster Sir John Watson's son and heir John Watson.

Other large houses in the area met the same fate as the underground workings from Bent, Eddlewood, Fairhill, Neilsland and Cadzow collieries wreaked havoc on the surface. At Hollandbush only two out of four large mansions survive; Ivygrove which stands on Mill Road across from St. Ann's School shows evidence of subsidence and Hollandbush House which was owned by John Watson Ltd and sold on to the South Church to be used as a manse. Today it is in private hands. Fairview and Oakenshaw were demolished approximately mid 1950's, both were owned by John Watson and beyond repair due to damage caused by mineral workings. The South Church at the top of Mill Road also shows evidence of subsidence.

Laighstonehall House which can be seen in the background of the above photograph is showing signs of serious subsidence. In front of the house is McAffers tomato houses. Children L-r Wilma and Eileen Russell c. 1947 Photograph taken from back door of prefab house at 133 Mill Road

The Hamilton Town Hall and its stunning clock tower which stood at the New Cross junction of Duke and Quarry Streets was an architectural treasure lost to subsidence.

The multipurpose building contained greater and lesser halls, the police court, police station, procurator fiscal's office and a fire station. By 1930 it was in grave danger of collapsing on to the busy street below and the Duke Street wall had to be shored up and barricaded off to protect pedestrians. The clock tower was eventually taken down and the clock was a sore miss to the people of Hamilton who were so used to checking the time, it was years before the habit of looking up stopped.

R- The town hall in 1930 with the tower teetering on the brink

The remains of the building continued to be used as the Burgh Police Station. It was replaced by a new police station in Campbell Street and finally demolished in the 1960's. Bairds now occupies the site.

The greatest loss to the town of Hamilton and to the countries heritage was without a doubt the magnificent Hamilton Palace which was described by H.V. Morton as *'the most regal home in Britain, 'the big brother of Buckingham Palace'.* Permission was given to the Bent Colliery Co. by the Duke of Hamilton to remove from directly below the palace the pillars of coal holding up the roof of the Ell seam and the Splint coal.

This act of greed resulted in the loss of one of the most important buildings in the country.

The millions of pounds from coal royalties which poured into the coffers of the Dukes of Hamilton had been squandered on grandiose living and gambling.

R- *William Alexander Louis Stephen Douglas-Hamilton the 12th Duke* who almost bankrupted the family with his gambling. When he died in 1895 his distant cousin Alfred Douglas-Hamilton became the 13th Duke of Hamilton and as well as the title and some estates he inherited £1,000,000 of debt which he cleared off in 13 years, no doubt with a great deal of assistance from the coal miners who scraped a living from digging out coal from under his lands. When the Duke moved with his family to Dungavel outside Strathaven the scene was set for the destruction of this unique building.

The 10th Duke of Hamilton built as a chapel and family tomb the magnificent Mausoleum in the Low Parks. The building cost £130,000, took 15 years to build and was completed in 1855. It was another victim of subsidence but fortunately even although it had sunk 5.5 metres it has been saved as has the Chatelherault at High Parks which was once used by the Dukes as a hunting lodge and dog kennels.

It is worth comparing the £130,000 paid for the Mausoleum and the total cost to the Duke of Hamilton to employ twelve men and three women at his Skellyton coal mine near Dalserf in 1805. The cost of a year's wages for fifteen people.... £10.10s.6d (£10.53 _ p).... It's an ill divided world.

THE COSY CORNER, MILL ROAD, HAMILTON 1963
Photograph courtesy of Hamilton Town House Reference Library.

The above picture shows the entrance to Laighstonehall House, once the grand home of coalmaster Sir *John Watson's* son and heir *John* and birthplace of his grandson *John Watson*. Born into a life of wealth and affluence the child was educated at Westgate and Eton Young *John Watson* was only a child when his father died and he became 3rd Baronet of Earnock. Tragically at 20 he was killed in action during W.W.1. I sometimes wonder if this privileged little boy ever got to enjoy his life and this location half as much as the local children, many from mining families, for whom the memories of this corner will forever be etched on their hearts.

Just behind the right hand entrance wall were two magnificent chestnut trees and on the opposite side of the road growing on the high ledge of the Cadzow Colliery branch mineral railway banking was another. In the autumn when the chestnuts ripened and the fallen leaves lay four inches deep on the road; local children would spend hours kicking the leaves looking for the shiny copper harvest.

When every leaf had been overturned and every chestnut found, eyes would turn upwards searching among the high branches for the biggest and best chestnuts. Once spotted, a selected piece of wood would be swung skywards in an attempt to dislodge them. Up went the stick and everyone scattered in case they got hit by more than chestnuts on the way down. Whoops of delight would signal success and with shouts of triumph there would be a dive for the prize.

Even today, 55 years on, the same old feeling of excitement that I experienced as a child resurfaces when I spot a chestnut lying on the ground. During the1970's I managed to transport myself back to those halcyon days of the 50's by taking my four small children out chestnut hunting. A high wind during the night would guarantee we were out of our beds at 6am and by 7am we were off walking to the Cosy Corner, returning home an hour later with bags and pockets full of chestnuts. My children still reminisce about this annual chestnut hunt which took place until the trees succumbed to gale force winds during a winter storm.

Thirty years later and now with grandchildren, the search was on again. Each autumn we would go to a long chestnut lined avenue leading to a tenant farm on the periphery of Hamilton. However in 2002 this stopped abruptly when, with my five year grandson Andrew Seeds, I was confronted by the landowner Sir John Inglefield-Watson Bt. of Earnock who informed us we were trespassing and asked us to leave. Pleas that we were doing no damage and that the child had travelled from Yorkshire to pick up chestnuts with his granny fell on deaf ears. We left, with me wondering if when a child, he had ever had the pleasure of going home with his pockets bulging with chestnuts and if he had, how he could ever deny a wee boy the thrill of searching for them.

"A NAKED LIGHT"
UDSTON COLLIERY HAMILTON
MONDAY 15/5/1882

It was just after half-past five on Monday 15th May 1882 and the day shift at Udston Colliery was almost finished. Most of the 200 miners employed at the pit had gone home and the men who remained underground were packing up for the day.

In the Main coal seam, young *Robert Marshall* was hanging about in the roadway waiting for miner *David Coutts*. Normally *Robert* would have walked home with his father but three hours earlier, word had been brought down the pit that his sister was seriously ill and his father had gone home.

David Coutts was a stranger to the colliery, a Motherwell man, he had started in the pit only the previous Friday and was staying in lodgings at 10 Windsor Street, Burnbank while he looked for accommodation. In the meantime his wife and children continued to live in Motherwell.

Donald Mathie 31 and his son *James* had finished their shift and were making their way along the roadway heading for the pit bottom with Burnbank men *Felix* and *James Teirney* for company.

Charles Morrison and his son *William* were the only two miners still working and they were busy putting an end down into an old drift when their work was interrupted by a visit from colliery manager *William Archibald* and oversman *John Bolton* who had been supervising the job. Finding that the *Morrison's* had all but broken through the wall, *Archibald* asked the two miners to leave because they were using naked lights.

William Archibald and *John Bolton* made a hole in the wall with a jumper and were nearly through when to their absolute horror, *Charles Morrison* returned for his pick which he had left behind. Just as *Archibald* shouted to him "put that light out" the wall was breached and a rush of foul air from the old workings came into contact with *Morrison's* naked light. The lethal mixture of gas and air from the old workings ignited, sending a wall of flame exploding through the colliery. *John Bolton,* his hair and clothes on fire from the blast, dived for a corner and the other three did likewise, each finding their own place of safety.

With their lights blown out and the pit in pitch blackness, the men, deafened by the blast and in various stages of shock were now in great danger of being gassed by after-damp. Injured and disorientated they desperately groped about in the impenetrable darkness trying to get their bearings. The two *Morrison's* managed to stay together but *Archibald* and *Bolton* each lost contact with the others.

The men who had been walking towards the pit bottom heard a sharp retort a second before the blast caught them and sent them tumbling and rolling to the ground. Most of the 30 men underground were hit by the blast, but the miners who suffered the most serious injuries from the burning searing flash were the ones who were "*farthest ben.*"

Up on the surface, the managing director's son *John J. Ure* was standing at the door of the smithy when a boy ran forward and told him that "*something had fallen down the shaft of No. 1 pit.*" Ure didn't believe the boy but thought he better go over and question the pithead man. As they were talking, the cage arrived at the surface and four miners stepped out with their hair and whiskers burned.

Realising that there had been an explosion *John Ure* and firemen *Edward Torley* and *James Strachan** entered the cage to go down into the workings. The first thing they noticed at the pit bottom was that the ventilation system had been dangerously damaged by the explosion. Undaunted, they took a chance and pushed on towards the site of the accident which was about a quarter of a mile from the pit bottom.

At about five stoops length or 100 yards from the scene of the explosion the air became extremely dangerous forcing the three men to turn and head back.

In the meantime, oversman *John Bolton,* exhausted and suffering from serious burning injuries, had managed to negotiate his way through the labyrinth of passages and reached the safety of the pit head, but there was no sign of the manager or the *Morrison's.*

Enlisting the assistance of firemen *Thomas Paterson* and *Archibald Muir*, the three men once more descended the pit and set about repairing the bratticing in an attempt to restore the ventilation. They reached the face where the damage was the greatest between six and seven o'clock and it was there they found the bodies of *Charles Morrison* and his son *William.*

Two hours later and some distance from where the rescue team found the Morrison's they found the body of *William Archibald.* All three bodies were relatively free from burns and were laying face down pointing in the direction of the pit bottom. Having survived the initial explosion they had died from the effects of after-damp poisoning while attempting to make their escape.

The survivors, who were suffering from the effects of after-damp and a variety of injuries, were treated by *Dr Robertson* the colliery doctor and *Dr Grant* a Blantyre doctor highly experienced in treating after-damp poisoning. The most seriously injured was oversman *John Bolton* from Udston Rows, who was severely burned about his arms face and neck and *David Coutts* who had burns to his face, sides of head and hands. *Donald Mathie* age 31, Gladstone Street, Burnbank, was burned on the face and neck and he had also sustained injuries to his side and legs when he was thrown down by the force of the explosion. His son *James Mathie* was injured about the face and neck. *Felix Tierney,* 7 New Street, Burnbank received burns to his face, hands, arms and neck as well as being injured on the body by being blown over. His son *James Tierney* was burned on the face, hands and arms. *Robert Marshall,* age 16, 13 Ann Street, Burnbank, was burned about the face, back and hands. His 8 year old sister Susan who had been the cause of his father's early finish, died from tuberculosis the following day.

This explosion, the first in Udston Colliery was an ominous warning of the fiery nature of the mine. Five years later on 28th May 1887 an explosion of fire-damp triggered off multiple dust explosions killing 73 men and boys. *Edward Torley* and *Archibald Muir** two of the firemen involved in the 1882 rescue, had a remarkable escape from death in the 1887 explosion when the cage in which they were ascending the shaft was almost wrecked by the blast. *Archibald Muir* had an arm broken in three places; he was severely burned and shocked. The force of the explosion was so great that 17 year old James McGourty who had been travelling with them was projected up through the cage and killed when he struck the winding gear forty feet above the pit head.

James Strachan is known to have been among the rescue parties at another two major explosions, the 1877 Blantyre disaster which claimed approximately 216 victims and the 1887 Udston disaster.

Archibald Muir started working underground at the age of 10 years and in total worked 63 years in the mines. He was a hero and survivor of the Home Farm Colliery disaster in 1887 when with another fireman he warned the men of the flooding and was responsible for saving many lives with this action. For 43 of the 63 years that he worked underground he was an employee of the Udston Coal Company. During his time working in the pits he was a miner, roadsman, and fireman and also became an oversman after gaining his undermanagers certificate. He died on the 26th June 1923 age 76 years.

This photograph is the only one known to be in existence showing Udston Rows. The angle of the building suggests that it has been affected by underground workings. The football team was known as the Udston Football Club and the names of a few of the men are known. Back row, 5th left Freddie Reardon, 2nd right Willie Rogers, end of row unnamed manager. Front row 1st left John Sharp (trainer) seated next to him is Harry Dorricot, c. 1930. Photograph courtesy of Mary Fleming

UDSTON ROWS

Work commenced on the sinking of Udston Colliery during the summer of 1872 and while the colliery was at the planning and marking out stage a coin of *"one of the Georges"* was found beneath one of the pins being set to mark off the site of the pit. This coin was taken as a sign of good fortune and this prediction seemed to be reinforced by the fact that on the 17th February 1875, the contractor *James Barrowman* reached a five foot seam of fine soft coal at a depth of 125 fathoms (755 feet) some time before several other coal and ironstone pits which were being sunk in the locality at the same time. The coal was found to be of an excellent quality when submitted for independent testing.

To house the miners, the Udston Coal Company built with the cheapest of materials and without any thought for the mining families who would be herded into them a village consisting of 38 single ends, 11 room and kitchens, 1 two rooms and kitchen, and 1 four roomed house; a total of 51 houses. Concrete blocks were used for the front of the houses and the gables and back were built of brick. There were no gardens, back doors, washhouses or sculleries. Outside sinks were provided with four families being allocated the use of one sink and the washing of clothes was done outside, with the water being heated in a cast iron pot supported by the bricks which surrounded the open fir; or inside the homes in a wooden bine (tub) with the water being heated over the domestic fire.

There was no running water in the houses; all water had to be carried from one of the two standpipes provided at the end of the rows. There were no cooking facilities other than a swee which swung over the black cast iron fire or two metal bars which were placed horizontally above the burning coal and the pots were placed upon them. All meals had to be cooked over this fire and all water for laundry or personal care was heated in the same way. To the left of the fire was a small oven under which a fire was lit and this was used for baking. Once a pot was boiling it would be placed on one of two hobs which were attached to each side of the fire. There was no electricity or gas, paraffin lamps were used to light the houses.

Only two dry privies were provided for the houses and each privy was partitioned in the middle and consisted of a plank of wood over an open hole in the ground. There was one at each end of the rows and they had no doors for privacy. The men used them but the women and children used a pail in the small loby (hall) of their home, making sure that the door was locked before they started. Urine was emptied into a drain and the pail washed out at the stand pipe, anything else was emptied into the privy which stunk and was infested with flies. They were emptied by a man called Dickson who would arrive with a horse and cart. After filling his cart he would set off leaving a train of liquid faeces and urine trailing behind him. In 1914 a Royal Commission into the conditions of miners houses described the toilets as disgraceful - indescribable. The rent at that time was 1/6d (7 _ p) and 2/6d (16p) per week.

The pub and a large shop selling everything including butcher meat and paraffin were owned by the Hamilton family, there were also three small shops in the homes of Mrs McKinven and Mrs White (top of the row) and Mrs Jen Patrick at Dunn's Laun' (Land). There was a hall with an earth floor and known as the "houf" in one of the buildings and it was here that socials and dancing took place. Several of the families living at Udston were musically gifted and they supplied fiddle and accordion music.

With no effective birth control available large families were the norm; during the 1920's- 30's babies were delivered by Mrs Colquhoun a midwife who lived in the rows. In the 1901 census there were a total of 247 people listed as living at Udston Rows and this included 109 children up to the age of 14; Udston Primary School was built close to the village the same year. It had two classrooms and a small room for the headmistress. The census also shows that there were families of seven to eight members living in single ends. In 1928 almost 200 children were on the roll of this small school and older children had to walk to Burnbank three miles away for secondary education. In the winter the Udston children were allowed to leave the school one hour earlier than the rest of the children so they could get home before darkness fell as the road was unlit. By February 1938 most the inhabitants of this small village had been rehoused at Eddlewood, Hamilton and there were only 4 pupils left at the village school which closed when the village was demolished.

Udston Colliery was the site of the second largest mining disaster in Scotland. On the 28th May 1887 an explosion of fire damp ignited coal dust which set off a chain of explosions in the Splint seam resulting in the deaths of 73 men and boys. Thirty one women were left widows and 103 children left without fathers. Many of the dead came from Udston Rows. The Udston Coal Company paid for the funerals but unless the families already had a lair or could afford one the victims were buried in unmarked `paupers' graves …..and most of them were. Udston colliery closed in 1922 and the miners found employment at local collieries.

Much of the information about life at Udston Rows was given to me by Mrs Mary Fleming nee Swinburn of Eddlewood seen in the photograph opposite with her brothers John left and Hugh right. The photograph was taken approximately 1924 at the door of Udston School.

The Swinburn family consisted of four girls and five boys, in order of birth Jean, Meg, Nan, Bob, Allan, John, Ben, Mary and Hughie. They lived in a room and kitchen at Udston Rows. Mrs Agnes Swinburn, nee Douglas was up at 5.30 am to light the fire to make cooked breakfasts for her husband Jack before he left for the pit and also for her nine children before they went to school. The photograph opposite shows three of her spotlessly clean children who are a credit to her and a testimony to her hard work. Mary the little girl in the photograph was a beautiful child and today at the age of 91 she is still a very beautiful lady with a mind as sharp as a tack. I am indebted to her for sharing her memories with me.
Photograph courtesy of Mary Fleming.

Above Earnock Colliery, below Earnock Hall and reading room and middle row (Albert Buildings) the front row (Argyle Buildings) which was built of stone can be seen in background. Photographs courtesy of Sir Simon Watson Bt. of Earnock.

EARNOCK COLLIERY

Number 1 and 2 pitheads at Earnock Colliery, Hamilton. The small single story building behind the two men was the ambulance room. The brick building to the right was the engineroom. Circa 1904 Identified by Miss Jessie Whitehouse daughter of William Whitehouse, cashier at Earnock Colliery Photograph from Ballantyne Collection courtesy of Hamilton Natural History Society.

MINERS' WIVES

*An Earnock granny
with new baby in plaid
c.1930's
Earnock Rows in the
background*

*Photograph courtesy of
Andy Bain*

We have borne good sons to broken men,
  Nurtured them on our hungry breast,
And given them to our masters when
  Their day of life was at its best.

We have dried their clammy clothes by the fire,
  Solaced them, cheered them, tended them well,
Watched the wheels raising them from the mire,
  Watched the wheels lowering them to Hell.

We have prayed for them in a Godless way
  (We never could fathom the ways of God)
We have sung with them on their wedding day,
  Knowing the journey and the road.

We have stood through the naked night to watch
  The silent wheels that raised the dead;
We have gone before to raise the latch,
  And lay the pillow beneath their head.

We have done all this for our masters' sake,
  Did it in rags and did not mind;
What more do they want? What more can they take?
  Unless our eyes to leave us blind.

Joe Corrie. (1894—1968

EARNOCK COLLIERY
September-December 1937

Earnock Colliery was developed by *John Watson* coalmaster, in a field behind Hillhouse Farm. The farm formed part of Watson's large Hamilton Estate.

It took 2 _ years from cutting the first turf until the Ell coal was reached and production commenced. During the development of the colliery there were several minor but no fatal accidents.

John Watson was one of the better coal masters investing in the latest safety equipment. Because of this his mines never experienced any of the major disasters so common in the Scottish coal field. Nevertheless, many men and boys died working in his coalmines.

Earnock Colliery has 75 known deaths and there were certainly more, but unfortunately the method of recording the deaths of miners involved in accidents and who died after being brought up the pit, makes it almost impossible to identify them.

The death certificates record only the place of death and the Record of Corrected Entries which records the results of the Fatal Accident Inquiry normally fails to document the name of the colliery where the accident took place and unless local newspapers report on the death it is impossible to find out in which colliery the accident happened.

The following stories tell of how four Earnock miners lost their lives during a four month period in 1937.

ARCHIBALD CAMPBELL

On the 10th September 1937 three miners *Archibald Campbell,* Main Street, High Blantyre, *James Russell.* 22 Waverly Street, Burnbank and *John Gaffney* 33 Kennilworth Crescent, Burnbank, were moving a conveyer machine when a large stone weighing a ton fell trapping them in a 30 inch high section of the workings.

Miners rushed to help from other parts of the workings but it took them nearly two hours crawling on their stomachs before they could extricate their trapped workmates.

Archibald Campbell, a married man with one child appeared to have been killed instantly, but *James Russell* and *John Gaffney* survived and were taken to the Glasgow Royal Infirmary where it was found that *Russell* had sustained a fractured left arm and body injuries and *Gaffney* had injuries to his right side and thigh. Another man *James Walsh* (25) of Purdie Street Burnbank was slightly injured by the fall.

THOMAS WILSON

Three months later at 8 a.m. on the 27th November 1937 in the Splint coal seam of No. 3 Pit three miners, fireman *William McLean* (50) *Walter Winning* (40) and *Thomas Wilson* (30) were standing discussing their work when the wooden pit props suddenly gave way and *Thomas Wilson* of 2 Kennilworth Crescent, Burnbank was trapped by the timber and a ton of debris. *William McLean* of Earnock Rows and *Walter Winning* of Ulva Place Station Road, Blantyre were caught by the edge of the fall and both sustained injuries to their legs. Despite strenuous efforts it was an hour before *Thomas Wilson* was released and the married father of one was found to be dead.

AN UNDERGROUND INFERNO

Less than three weeks later, at half-past five on Christmas Eve in the haulage road of the Humph Section of No. 1 Pit, chain runner *Archibald Riddell* was going down the heading with a rake of loaded

hutches when one of them went off the road. He signalled to the motor man to stop the haulage and while they were attempting to ease the hutch upright it was set on fire by a flash and flames from a damaged electric cable. Despite heroic attempts by *Archie Riddell, Daniel Nelson, William McKinley* and *Adam Smith*, the flames spread to other hutches and the haulage road was soon a raging inferno.
Archibald Riddell some hours after being rescued.
A hero he refused to leave elderly miner.

William McKinlay an elderly men, was first to be overcome by the deadly fumes and *Archie Riddell* and *Adam Smith* attempted to remove him from the danger zone while *Danny Nelson* was sent to raise the alarm. *William McKinlay* knew the men were too badly affected by gas to carry him out and he pleaded with them to leave him, but they refused and continued in their attempts to drag him to safety until they collapsed unconscious. All three survived after being brought out by rescue teams.

When the alarm was raised 40 miners who were working in the section were moved away from the danger area. The fire squads, led by manager *James Young* and undermanager *John Lowe* sprayed the section water in an attempt to bring the fire under control. The great clouds of billowing smoke which issued from the fire were carried away along a return airway.

Mr *Arthur Stoker*, Divisional Inspector of Mines for the Western Area and junior inspector Mr *Hoyle* were summoned by telephone and they joined the fire teams underground to advise and keep an eye on the proceedings.

Several hours after the outbreak, *James Young* returned to the surface to attend to other arrangements for dealing with the fire. Unknown to him the smoke which had filled an old working eventually filtered into the fresh air course and then swirled down the haulage road filling it with smoke and deadly white damp fumes.

Within a few minutes 25 men were affected by the white damp and many of them collapsed unconscious in the haulage road. Word was immediately conveyed to the surface and underground, miners who were unaffected by smoke were desperately trying to reach their fallen comrades.

The situation had unexpectedly and dramatically taken a turn for the worse and the lives of all the miners underground were now hanging in the balance.

A telephone call to the Coatbridge Mines Rescue Station brought three rescue teams rushing to the colliery by car bringing with them much needed supplies of oxygen.

Seriously hampered by the flames, fumes and dense smoke, the rescue team made repeated attempts to reach the trapped miners but were driven back. When they finally reached them, seventeen were unconscious. At one point it was feared that seven of the men were dead. Time after time the rescue team entered the inferno and each time returned with an unconscious miner.
John Lowe

Given oxygen underground by Burnbank G.P. *Dr McEwan*, the miners eventually began to recover consciousness. The last man to be rescued was undermanager *John Lowe* who was in a serious condition and despite oxygen and restoratives being applied; he remained unconscious for one and a half hours after being brought out of the pit. The men were all treated in the ambulance room at the pithead and afterwards they either walked or were driven home by car.

At Eddlewood Rows, John Hutton's family knew nothing of the drama until he was brought home and laid on the floor in front of the fire. His health was so badly affected by the fumes he never worked again.

Underground manager *John Lowe* died five days after the fire and three months later, *Alexander Young* also died; his lungs irreversibly damaged by smoke and gas. Both men were married with families.

The following seventeen men were brought out unconscious from the fumes.
ROBERT ALLAN (56) Oncost worker, 34 Bruce Terrace, Blantyre.
JAMES BLAIR (56) Fireman, 76 Albert Buildings, Earnock.
WM. BROWNLIE (60) Fireman, 35 Annsfield Street, Eddlewood.
ANDREW EASTON (59) Oncost worker, 35 Albert Buildings, Earnock.
JOHN HUTTON (56) Fireman, 24 Annsfield Place, Eddlewood.
JOHN LOWE (54) Undermanager, Earnock Cottage, Burnbank.
JAMES MURDOCH (45) Fireman, 12 Guthrie Street, Hamilton.
ROBERT MUNRO (21) Blacksmith, 60 Argyle Buildings, Earnock.
WM. McKINLAY (68) Oncost worker 51 Albert Buildings, Earnock.
HENRY McLEAN (59) Oversman, 29 Chapel Street, Hamilton.
DANIEL NELSON (23) Oncost worker, 76 Eddlewood Rows, Eddlewood.
ARCHD. RIDDELL (34) Chainman,, 9 Annsfield Road, Eddlewood.
WILLIAM SINGER (59) Oversman, 63 Argyle Buildings, Earnock.
ALEX. SINGER (20) Engineer, 12 Gordon Terrace, Burnbank.
ADAM SMITH (23) Chainman, 20 Barrack Street, Hamilton.
CRAWFORD WILSON (24) Oncost worker, 47 Albert Buildings, Earnock.
ALEX. YOUNG (56) Oncost worker, 76 Albert Buildings, Earnock.

James Murdoch, survivor   Alex.Young, died 3 months later   John Hutton, survivor

THE PRICE OF COAL

There are weary* legs on the lowsin'* shift   *tired *finishing
And mony* an auld*, stiff frame   *many *old
Stumbles a wee* in the *lang laigh drift*   *little *long low roadway*
    When the men are *airtin' hame.*   *heading home

Bit, oh! they are gled*, are the *weary chiels*   *glad *exhausted men*
    When the darg* o' the day is by,   *allocated work
To turn their backs on the grimy pits,
    An' gaze at a clear blue sky.

Yet some *gang ben* that never win, but   *go through
    For may be a *rid, wat,* shirt,   *red wet*
A twisted mooth* an' the *een ticht shut*,   *mouth *eyes tight shut*
    Tell o' the grievous hurt.

God help the workers doon* below,   *down
    For naebody seems to care
Whether the coal be clotted or no'
blood   Wi' the bluid o' the toilers there   *John Frew. Hamilton Circa 1921*

Cage at the bottom of one of Earnock Colliery's shafts, c.1904. Note the electric lights. Earnock was first colliery in Scotland to have electric lighting underground and also in case of a major accident taking place, there was a telephone link to the surface. Photograph courtesy of Hamilton Natural History Society and South Lanarkshire Museum.

DON BOYLE'S
TALES FROM EARNOCK ROWS

AN AWFU' TWUST!

Hogmanay, 1929 and my grandfather, Donald Cameron had heroically resisted the half bottle of whisky kept reverently in the top drawer of his cabinet in the bedroom.

At 10 p.m. he had to be at Earnock Pit to see to the horses and nothing could be allowed to intervene between him and his beloved ponies. (In fact if it had been announced on the radio that the world was to end in 20 minutes he would have dropped everything and raced directly up to the pit to make sure the horses were alright!)

It was only a 10 minute walk to the pit but Donal' always insisted on being there an hour before starting time in case anyone thought he was slacking so at 8.30 p.m. off he went up the back row to call at the home of his assistant, Jimmy Smith, who happened to be his brother-in-law and who was known to his own family as "Auld Smith".

He was met at the stair head by his sister-in-law Katie who was terribly upset. "Oh Donal'" she exclaimed "Thank Goad ye're here! Ye better come in quick!" Fearing the worst he hurried inside and went straight through into the solitary bedroom where the teenage Smith sons were standing excitedly at the bed recess calling on their father. Stepping forward expecting to see a corpse he was met by the sight of "Auld Smith" lying so blootered out of his mind with the drink he could not even comprehend what was going on around him—and cared even less!. Donal's heart sunk to his boots; any other night this would be funny, but not tonight because the penalty for not showing up at work on Hogmanay would be instant dismissal and eviction from the house where the family lived. To show up drunk would have similar consequences—but it might be the lesser of two evils.

The ladies of the family were ordered through to the living room while Donal' and the sons tried to drag "Auld Smith" from the bed. His knees buckled beneath him and he flopped in every direction as they tried desperately to get him into pit clothes.

It took all of twenty minutes to finally get his boots on and tied up as best they could. It was only when they were getting his arms into his jacket that they noticed that his trousers were on back to front. Too late! There was no time to start again. He would have to be "oxtered" up to the pit as he was!

Helping him out onto the staircase and down the first few steps from the landing, they let him stand for a moment leaning on the rail at the top of the longer staircase.

As Donal' turned to one of the Smith lads to say something "Auld Smith" suddenly went tumbling headlong down the full length of the staircase and landed in a heep at the bottom. He lay there mesmerised and began to touch himself all over feeling for broken bones—and as he did so- he became aware that his belt buckle was behind him!

They rushed down to help him but "Auld Smith" looked pleadingly up at the three faces staring at him and gasped "haud on the noo Donal'! Ah've gi'en masel' an awfu' twust!!"

Incredibly they managed to get him down the pit where Donal' hid him among the hay and when the fireman (also called Smith) came near, he covered for his brother-in-law by shouting out instructions to him on the pretext that he was busy working. The day was thus saved but more than twenty years after his death our family still laughed at "Auld Smith's "Awfu' twust."

THE DAY I JOINED THE MILE HIGH CLUB

July 1943 and the world was tearing itself apart. In the vast expanses of Russia the Red Army was locked in a life or death struggle with Hitler's Wermacht, while in the Pacific and Far East the Allies were striving desperately to contain the advances of the Imperial Japanese war machine. Just when you imagined things couldn't get any worse they suddenly did just that. The notorious Hill Street gang under their fearless leader "Big Andra'" crossed the Puggy Line and stood boldly at the top of the Front Row. There were more than 20 of them! This was an absolutely intolerable situation and we felt that the future of Earnock was at stake.

Immediately the Fiery Cross was dispatched round the Rows and through the closes and every available able bodied lad in Earnock rushed to the cause…. slungs and clubs in hand.

Half our number rushed through the Front Row closes and took up position halfway up the Row. When big Andra' saw us he sensed victory and lined up to lead an attack, but just at that moment the other half of our gang appeared behind him coming round the top of the Front Row.

The Hill Street boys knew that they were caught in a trap and instantly raced back across the Puggy Line without a shot being fired. Honour had been restored!!!

However our leaders Martin (Big Robbie) Robertson, Joe (Buff) Dick and Davey (Mac) McKinley decided that we should "kick ass" and we crossed the Puggy Line in pursuit.

When they saw us coming the Hill Street lads "took the high ground" and went scrambling up the steep slopes of Earnock bing and kept going until they reached the long flat summit at a height of 200ft plus. (The bing was almost _ of a mile long) and at its far end beyond the pit, it rose yet another hundred feet at the point which was called "the tippers" so that viewed side on from a distance it looked like some monstrous Sphinx. There they stood defiantly on top of the bing screaming insults down at us and daring us to come up after them.

They then threw a hail of stones at us but we were safely out of range standing among the bushes and birches which had grown on the lower slopes and around the foot of the bing through the years and all we could do was to scream insults and taunts back up at them, daring them to come down and fight.

In a moment of sheer madness which I can only attribute to 8 year old bravado – I slipped away from the gang and moved further along the bing to where I knew there was a gully which the rain water had gouged out through the decades and down which, when it rained, the water would come cascading in a great torrent. I crept into the gully unseen and started to climb upwards on the 50 degree slope towards the summit. It took all my energy and a good few minutes of hard climbing but I eventually made it.

Now a good lesson in life is always to have a plan of action ready when you need it most – but sadly I had none!

I appeared suddenly behind some of the Hill Street lads and some of them fearing that the Earnock gang had scaled the impregnable heights took flight down their own side of the bing. Not however "Big Andra')!!

Now some things to understand about "Andra' the Fearless". He was 14 years old – tall for his age and with great physique. He was a great fighter and despite the disadvantage of being both deaf and dumb, had established himself as undisputed leader of one of the toughest gangs in Burnbank – and here I was, an 8 year old nonentity facing him on top of the Earnock bing with all my allies watching from a safe distance 200 feet below.

I had come up behind him but he turned and looked at me incredulously. "Dae ye gi'e in?"* I asked naively, pechin for all I was worth.

Whether Andra' read my lips or was just amused by my appearance I never knew. With a gleeful smile on his face, he grabbed me by an arm and leg and swung me round a few times before launching me off the bing into the skies above Earnock.

I thought I would never reach Earth again but, incredibly, what struck me most was that this was the first time I had been able to see into the pit manager's garden!

I must have fallen at least 40 feet before I hit the side of the bing again and continued to roll, slide and bounce all the way down to where the Earnock gang stood.

They heaped praise on me as they picked me up – but I think it was really meant to be posthumously!

Anyway! I think that that day, I had been initiated into a special version of the Mile High Club! Thank you, Andra'!

Photograph taken in 1964 from top of Earnock bing looking towards junction of Hillhouse Road/Wellhall Road, Hamilton when the bing was being removed.. Courtesy of Hamilton Town House Reference Library.

*Give up/surrender

Earnock bing c. 1964. Photograph courtesy of Hamilton Town House Reference Library.

THE BOYLES OF EARNOCK ROWS

The above Boyles belonged to two separate Earnock families. The Boyles with the bowler hats lived at 35 Albert Buildings and the Boyles with the bunnets at 48 Albert Buildings Earnock Back row l-r Dave, James, Jimmy, Tom, Joe, Tommy, Charlie, John. Middle row, L-r Cuthbert, Andrew, Michael, Joe, front row Patrick and Dan. c. 1900

A NIGHT TO REMEMBER

Friday 14th March 1941 – I was 5 years old and sound asleep in the set-in bed in the living-room at 92 Albert Buildings, Earnock.

I became aware of someone pulling my arm and turned to hear my Grandfather *Donald Cameron* say, "*come on son, we'll need tae go doon the stair*". He then helped me up so that I sat with my legs dangling over the side of the high set-in bed (they were deliberately high to allow storage space below) pulled a jumper over my head and put my socks and 'gutties' on my feet before helping me up onto his back to carry me out of the house.

We went onto the top landing and I was aware of other people on the gravel road below. It was dark but there was a curious red glow touching the clouds which seemed to lend a faint reddish light to the whole of Earnock just allowing us to make out the figures moving below us.

I was aware too of a strange sound filling the night like the noise of a thousand drums beating in the distance (to me it sounded like the sound of heavy laden coal wagons moving slowly on the Puggy line.) Just as we were about to step onto the stairs there was an incredible flash of brilliant white light – like a gigantic flash of lightning over in Forgie's wood. It was so bright that for an instant that it appeared as though Earnock was sitting in bright sunlight. I could even see the colour of the leaves on the trees 150 yards away across the park.

In fact what had happened was that an Ack-Ack (*anti-aircraft gun*) battery in the wood had opened fire at the distant high flying German bombers. I was totally mesmerised at all I was seeing.

The Burnbank bomb site at Earnock railway sidings near Newfield housing scheme.

We went down onto the road to cross to the shelter and there we saw several men standing looking into the sky above the back row. One of them was my pal's dad *Rab McLelland* and he turned to my grandfather and *said "that will be Clydebank that's getting it tonight!"* He was of course correct, although one of the bombers did drop a bomb much closer on the railway sidings in Burnbank behind the place we called Sing-Sing and blew the wheel of a railway wagon through the wall of a house in Gladstone Street and one of my school pals *Willie Carlton* had their house windows blown in.

My grandfather was ushering me into the shelter to join my brother and my other pal wee *Joe Young*. I could see some of the women sitting on the long wooden benches and saw *Jean Stein – Jock Stein's* mother sitting on the seat nearest the door. She had made a huge silver kettle of tea and was dishing it out to all and sundry.

When she saw my grandfather she called out "*come on in Donal*" but my grandfather true to character replied "*naw ah cannae Jean, ah'll need to go back tae bed – ah'm workin' in the mornin*"! That speaks volumes for my "Popps". The world could get on with its masquerade and its pantomime but there were pit ponies to be seen to in the morning and that was what was really important. The rest of us stayed in the shelter for more than an hour gabbing and drinking tea then the "all clear" sounded and we tripped back to our beds. Earnock was at war and it was indeed – a night to remember.

*　　　*　　　*

Don Boyle's stories vividly portray life as seen through the eyes of a child growing up in Earnock Rows and by writing them down, he has recorded part of the life of this little mining village forever. I am indebted to him for letting me include his reminiscences in this book.

Earnock hall derlect and ready for demolition. c. 1964, photograph courtesy of Hamilton Town House Reference Library.

THE EARNOCK SMITHS

Earnock had several families named Smith so they used the old Gaelic practice of giving each family a distinctive prefix to distinguish one family from another.

1.—The Shilley Smiths were the largest family in Earnock with 15 children. They lived in a 2 bed roomed house near the top of the back row (Albert Buildings.) Davy is the sole survivor of that generation and is now living in Hamilton. As a youth Davy was lightening fast on the football field a turn of speed which earned him the nickname of "The Bumbee." He retired a few years ago after a successful career in the house furnishing business.

2. – The "Speedie" Smiths also lived near the top of the back row. There were 3 boys and 1 girl in the family. Sadly all the boys have now passed away and only Ellen is left. Ellen married a nice lad from Larkhall who was Irish and also called Smith. I have not seen Ellen for a good number of years. They got the name because the father Wullie was a fast runner. He was also Scottish Champion Quoits player. The boys in the family were all referred to as Speedie.

3. Riddie Smith (so called because of her flaming red hair) had two sons and they lived upstairs near the foot of the front row (Argyle Buildings) which was commonly called the piano row; probably because the first people to live there were the tradesmen of the pit and were marginally better paid than the "colliers." One son *Sanny Smith* was a fireman at Earnock Pit and thereafter became the well known doorman at the Plaza Cinema in Burnbank. The second son was a very good amateur boxer and used the ring name of "Gunboat." True to the Earnock tradition he was never known as anything other than Gunboat Smith and his family were known as "The Gunboat Smiths." The daughter of the Smith family married *Frank Cassidy*—the famous "Lightening Barber" who had his shop in Glasgow Road opposite the Plaza cinema. They had a son and a daughter.

There were 2 more families called Smith at Earnock —one lived upstairs near the top of front row (Argyle Buildings) and they had a lovely daughter called Margaret. The family moved to Whitehill and Margaret married and emigrated to Canada or America. The other Smith family lived downstairs in the middle row (Albert Buildings.)   *Don Boyle*

EARNOCK'S MARY YOUNG

Mary Young with husband Joe Daly

Remember those days in old Earnock Rows
More precious, more dear, each memory grows
Remember our friends, remember their names
Remember the laughter, remember the games.

Memories of days we knew long ago
The faces of people that we used to know
The sound of their laughter still coming to mind
Memories of people so gentle and kind.

How could a place so humble and plain
Come into mind again and again
Were it not for the people once that we knew
People whose hearts and love were so true.

Out of the past those memories will steal
And in our dreams feeling so real
Faces of friends who now are so few
How wonderful, Mary, speaking with you.

To smile at the life once that was ours
Sharing our memories like garlands of flowers
And I know no song ever was sung
Was half as sweet as Earnock's Mary Young.

Don Boyle. Formerly of Earnock Rows.

JACK

Don Boyle

*Earnock Boys
and lifelong pals*

Jack McLelland

Here's tae ye lad, ma auld pal Jack
'Tis grand this while tae ha'e yer crack
O' bygone days in Earnock ra's
When Jenny skelpit baith oor jaws!

When a' aroon' oor childhood world
The Redskins rode and Mounties whirled
And Robin Hood – that desperate kid
Was often seen ower Castle's wuid!

How oft thro' Forgie's wuid we'd creep
Sae feart that we'd mak' a cheep!
Lest mounted on his muckle dug
The soond wad reach the Wee Man's lug!

Each Sabbath day we'd walk tae Newhoose Mill,
Wi' grub enough a bear tae fill
We'd trek up there like wildebeest awa'
Oor gutties on we'd pech an' blaw.

Mind the fun and fires we made
Campit roon the Auld Stockade
Mind yon hare that thro' the windae loupit
And caused your Bill wi' fear tae coup!

O! names that ring oot frae the past
We mind them a' frae first tae last
Collie, Shug and Jamesie Larkin
Big Legs Eleven—stone mad Martin.

The Wallace boys and Mitchell Pim
Stern at times but never grim
The Shielsie twins we cried "the Binzies"
Frae the middle ra' – beside the Lindsays.

The simplest yins we loved the best
We loved them a' among the rest
Tam Gillespie – that harmless bragger
Wha spoke aboot his "Silent Dagger!"

And frae the middle ra' was Alex Broon
The lad we a' cried "A-Boon"
And wee Joe Young wha threw a fit
When a' folk cried "Josie Posie - sook – a – tit".

The McKinleys, Smiths and Dicks
Unsurpassed for a' their tricks
Wild we were – but never bad
And the gentlest o' us a' wis Jack McNab!

How many memories time unleashes
How many times we begged pit pieces!
And yer Pop was at the pit sawmill
On yon boggie let us play oor fill.

O! Woe the day when Jenny I did meet her
And in her haun' a carpet beater
Richt doon the stairs we made a dive
Wi' baith oor erses flayed alive.

And when oor Brian on leave cam' hame
Doon tae the Plaza we were ta'en!
O! man we felt jist like a toff
As Jack Pacitti' trifles we could scoff.

Like Sawyer Tom and Huckle Finn
The gather steyed thro' thick and thin
Jack a' they years ha'e come and gaen
But you and I hae steyed the same.

For a' the gowd Ah widna' change
Nor wi' a prince ma life exchange
Oor friendship's been beyond a' price
Oan puir man's fare – it's been the spice.

O – Jake Ah wish the best for you
May ye conquer fields anew
May a' yer hopes a' fa' in line
And happy be – as Auld Lang syne!   *Don Boyle*

THE SPIFICATION OF AULD JOCK BROON

Not a whustle* was heard or a bobby in sicht,   *Whistle*
  As they shut up the public-hooses;
An' auld Jock Broon wis chucked out ae nicht
  Frae the pub, whaur he always boozes.

As he stauchered* through the rain an' sleet,   *staggered*
  We couldna contrive what ailed him.
And before he had wauch'led* up the street   *walking in a clumsy ungainly way*
  His lingle legs quite failed him.

Loud we vowed against the drink,
  As we gathered him oot o' the gutter;
An' we wuner't * what his wife would think,
  As we carried him hame on a shutter.

We thocht we heard her flyte* an' howl,   *scold*
  An' in accents shrill upbraid him,
An' we peetied his case, the *puir auld sowl,*   *poor old soul*
  As doon on the flair* we laid him.   *floor*

We rowed* his jacket below his heid,*   *rolled *head*
  An' loused* his knotted laces,   *loosened*
Drew aff his buits*, an' then stood roon'   *boots*
  Wi sad, averted faces;

An' the *droothiest loon* in a' the lot   *thirstiest youth*
  Swore by the stalk of St. Rollox,
That let it be cauld, or let it be hot,
  He'd *gang nae mair* tae Bulloch's.   *go no more*

Slowly an' sadly we turned awa'
  Resolved tae become teetotal,
An frae that nicht we *ane an' a'*   *one and all*
  Ha'e shunned the whusky bottle.

J.M. Earnock Colliery
c. 1894

Earnock House from the lawn circa1887 the home of Sir John Watson Bt. of Earnock, coal master.
Below the great drawing room at Earnock House c. 1888. Photographs courtesy of Sir Simon Watson Bt. of Earnock

Above, Old Neilsland House c.1877. Owned by Sir John Watson Bt. Below the Swiss Cottage in the grounds of Neilsland House c.1877. Photographs courtesy of Sir Simon Watson Bt.

Above Neilsland House previously – Midstonehall, home of Mr T. Watson, son of Sir John Watson Bt
Below the drawing room at Midstonehall /Neilsland House 1893 photograph courtesy of Sir Simon Watson, Bt.

SUPERSTITION
AND
SPOOKS IN THE MINE
By John Henderson
Transcribed from the Hamilton Advertiser 5.1.1924

Superstition is slowly dying, but the death is a lingering one. Among the miners---and amongst men, at that, whom you would never associate with anything superstitious—you hear and see things that astonish you, you are in the twentieth century. Underground, men—sensible enough fellows otherwise—tell you in hushed tones about such and such a road being haunted. The ghost takes various shapes: sometimes the rattle of a chain is heard, sometimes a low moan, sometimes a miner is seen, or his voice heard, long after he leaves this world.

The weirdest story I have heard is the story of the "Ghost Road." This road was the scene –all too common in the annals of mining—of a fatal accident. The story goes that a man was killed by a fall and that out of the debris only part of his arm was seen and the lamp, burning brightly, clasped firmly by his hand. When danger is near in this colliery, it is told, the arm and lamp are seen. I have traversed this old road often and often yet. I never saw the "spook" in fact; the appearance of such might have been a welcome diversion!

I remember telling this story to one whom we will call "Harry." I have never associated this individual with being superstitious, yet his face plainly showed he believed every word of it. Wild horses could not have dragged him into that road by himself after that. When his assistance was asked in the way of "redding*" falls in it, Harry was always very willing to go elsewhere; but into the "Ghost Road" –no! He was twitted at times about being afraid. "I could gang thro' that road frae ae' en' o't tae anither an' never turn a hair," he somewhat rashly said once. As events proved, he "turned" a few hairs and we are not quite sure but his hair was tinged with grey after his experience.

The road in question was an airway and had to be frequently travelled so that any small falls could be cleared and the ventilation not checked in any way. One day Harry was told to go into the air-course and bring out some graith. Harry was reluctant, but since he had no other choice than to obey, he set off in rather a gingerly fashion. Proceeding along the road with his heart in his mouth, suddenly he heard a sound. He stopped. What was that! It was the sound of footsteps! His hair stood on end. Nearer and nearer they came, and suddenly an arm shot out, and in the hand—a lamp. Harry let out an unearthly yell and bolted. He came panting out of the air-course and his face proclaimed that he had seen visions. Soon a thrilling story about this "ghost" was being told. In awestricken tones Harry was describing his feelings on perceiving the apparition, when out of the road popped the "ghost." It was merely an official who had been inspecting the airway, and Harry's imagination had supplied the rest. But would you catch Harry going into that road again? Not he!

Miners should be forgiven much of their superstition however. Their work is not of the ordinary routine. They find their minds, somehow, chastened and subdued by the gloom around them. Probably that is why many of them seek the warmth and cheer of the public house. Gloom and glitter being extremes, they seek the latter for the sake of a little variety in their lives. Maybe! We have known miners who, having dreamed of accidents, firmly told their women-folk they were going to no work that day. Meeting a bareheaded woman in the morning has also been known to turn some of them from going to their work! I have noted that where superstition is met with it is mostly the Celtic type (not the football club) that is susceptible. The vast majority, however, are not superstitious and face their work in a manner which denotes they do not know what is meant by superstition.

*redding –clearing

FAIRHILL COLLIERY

Fairhill Colliery, c. 1904
Photograph courtesy of Hamilton Town House Reference Library.

Situated at what is now Millgate Road, Fairhill, Hamilton, Fairhill Colliery was owned by Archibald Russell and its workings extended for 60 acres. Opened in the late 1880's the colliery employed 250 men and boys underground and 72 on the surface. There were two oblong winding shafts sunk to a depth of 880 feet and three seams were worked at the colliery, The 7 feet thick seam of Ell coal was found at a depth of 740 feet. The Main coal at 816 feet was 4 feet thick and the highly prized Splint coal seam found at 887 feet was 7 feet thick. The coal was worked in the stoop and room system, horses were used for haulage and the output was 1000 tons per day.

The mineral railway which carried the coal from the pit ran the short distance from the pithead to a level crossing at what is now the junction of Mill Road and Millgate Road and then on to join the branch line serving Cadzow Colliery behind what is now Mill Grove.

Fairhill Colliery appears to have been one of the safest collieries in Hamilton Parish having only two recorded deaths.

KNOWN DEATHS AT FAIRHILL COLLIERY

20.10.1894	WILLIAM JACK	45	Roof fall (skull crushed to pulp.)
14.01.1895.	PATRICK KELLS.	16	Roof fall (fractured spine, lived 10 days.)

FAIRHILL COLLIERY
THE CAPPING OF ONE OF THE TWO SHAFTS 1939

Laighstonehall House, once home of Sir John Watson's son and heir John is just visible top left of picture. Top middle shows McCaffer's tomato houses and top right are the last houses in Mill Road before the rugby playing fields. Top right to the front of the houses can be seen a hut which was used as a shop. This site now contains a public house (The Mill Inn) a hairdressing salon and a general store.

SOME MINERS KNOWN TO HAVE WORKED AT FAIRHILL COLLIERY

ROBERT McCULLOCH started working with coal master Archibald Russell Ltd, as a coal miner at the age of eleven years at Muirhouse and Clydesdale Collieries, Wishaw. He then went to Barncluith and Silvertonhill when the two pits were being sunk. Later he went to Fairhill Colliery and was there until the colliery closed. After the closure he worked at Greenfield then Whistleberry Colliery where he was still working in 1920 and at that time had 55 years service with the same firm. He was a fireman at Silvertonhill, Fairhill and Whistleberry Collieries and like many miners he was a keen booler and was a member of the Caledonian Green, Hamilton.

JAMES SALMOND started working underground as a small boy in 1857 at the Old School Pit near Parkhead Cross, Glasgow and he was employed in the coal industry for 62 years. Quick to learn he soon grasped the principals of mining and climbed his way up the colliery promotion ladder. He worked at Westmuir, Mount Vernon, Clydesdale, Uddingston and Netherton collieries. He joined Archibald Russell's company in 1888 as manager of their Barncluith Colliery and then as manager at Fairhill Colliery. He was to finish a 62 year working career as general manager of the company.

James Brown, 30 Portland Place, Hamilton, (1891) …. James Cossar, (1897). Arthur Jack, 179 Glasgow Rd. Burnbank………. Harry, Matt, Alex, John and George Lauder……. John Martin. 4 Portland Place. Hamilton (1903)…….. Matthew Rae, (checkweighman) (1892), Alex. Scott, (Ostler.) 1897 …Dougald Smith (above-ground manager) Haughhead Farm (1890)… Robert Tait …….Tom Vallance (pony driver) ......Robert T. Wallace. Underground Manager… Messrs Davies, Gaffney, Forsyth and William Whysker.

Photograph courtesy of Hamilton Town House Library.

GALA DAY IN EDDLEWOOD ROWS 1911

On Saturday 11th August the children of Eddlewood Rows didn't need any coaxing to get out of their beds. It was gala day and they were up like a shot; this was the one day of the year set aside for the children where they could enjoy themselves and also possibly win a small monetary prize.

By half-past ten two thousand children and adults dressed in their Sunday best were assembled at the Rows ready to leave. As the Quarter Colliery Silver Band struck up a tune, the happy parade marched out of Eddlewood Rows and up the Strathaven Road towards the field in the Muttonhole Road set aside for the Gala by Robert Frame at his Cornhills Farm. This was a great day for youngsters and adults alike. A trip to the farm was like a day at the seaside for them. Life was hard for the children of the Rows.

On their arrival at the field the children were given buns and milk which were consumed with great relish. The highlight of the day was the sports events and here every child was hoping to cross the finishing line first and get their reward. Presiding over the Gala was manager John Blake with Hugh MacFadyen as secretary and William Whitehouse colliery cashier as sports secretary.

The following children won prizes on that warm August day in 1911.
Boys Races   5 years--1st Robert Nicol, 2nd Pat Radigan, 3rd John Maxwell,
 6 years -- 1st Robert Cunningham, 2nd George Summers, 3rd Robert Thomson.
 7 years -- 1st Wm. Fraser, 2nd Robert McKay, 3rd Michael McNamara.
 8 years -- 1st Peter Cunningham, 2nd Chas. Robertson, 3rd Edward McCrum.
 9 years -- 1st Thos. McGraw, 2nd Hugh McLeary, 3rd James Higgins, 4th Michael Radigan.
10 years -- 1st Wm. Wilson, 2nd Henry Dickson, 3rd Thomas Dunn, 4th Robert Brown.
11 years -- 1st Peter Wilson, 2nd Hugh Lyons, 3rd Robert Campbell, 4th Thomas Hamilton.
12 years -- 1st John Oakes, 2nd Wm. Dunn, 3rd Dan Kerr, 4th John Greenhorn.
13 years -- 1st Wm. Fullard, 2nd Wm. Braithwaite, 3rd Andrew Dunn, 4th John Gibson.
14 years -- Patrick Oaks, 2nd Archibald McBeth, 3rd James Wilkie, 4th Wm. Durham.
Candy-barrow race -- (5 to 8 years) – 1st Edward Orr and Alexander Wilson, 2nd James Shaw and Gilbert Thomson, 3rd Alexander Miller and George Summers.

Candy-barrow race -- (9 to 14 years) --- 1st James Wilkie and George Orr, 2nd William Durham and Alex. Thomson, 3rd William Robertson and Hugh Lyons.

Three legged race -- 3 to 8 years ----Thomas McGraw and James Frew, 2nd Allan Wilkie and James Cunningham, 3rd Edward Orr and Alex. Wilson.

Three legged race -- 9-14years ---- 1st Patrick McLuskey and James Scullion, 2nd Michael Shaw and John Oakes. 3rd Robert Campbell and Robert Frew.

Sack race -- 5-8 years, 1st Wm. McKay, 2nd Gilbert Thomson, 3rd George Summers.

Sack race --9-14 years, 1st Wm. Robertson, 2nd Thomas McGraw, 3rd James McGraw.

100 yards handicap -- (boys) 1st Thomas McGraw, 2nd John Oakes, 3rd John Collins.

300 yards relay race -- (boys) -- 1st A. Symons, J. Milligan and J. Hepburn, 2nd M. Shaw, David Kerr and R. Frew.

120 yards Handicap -- 1st Denis Brown, 2nd John Calder, 3rd James Hailey.

440 yards handicap -- 1st William Cochrane, 2nd James Campbell, 3rd James Hailey.

Half mile handicap -- 1st George Lennox, 2nd William Cochrane, 3rd William Campbell.

Tug-of-war -- 1st John Shepherd's team, 2nd J. Callison's team.

Five-a-side football -- 1st J. Brown, J. Murther, Andrew Prossar,* A. Laird and Nat. Hutton. 2nd A. Taylor, F. Durham, J. Kyle, James Brown and H. Gillard.

Pillow fight -- James Owens. Old men's handicap—1st Peter McLuskey, 2nd Owen McQuade. 3rd William McKay.

Girl's Races -- 5 years -- 1st Nellie Cunningham, 2nd Mary O'Neil, 3rd Katie Ramsey. 4th Sarah McGuire.

 6 years -- 1st Agnes Rodney, 2nd Jeanie Hamilton, 3rd Maggie Wilson, 4th Nellie Donaldson.

 7 years -- 1st Maggie Higgins, Jeanie Brownlie, 3rd Margaret Calder, 4th Susan Ross.

 8 years -- 1st Rebecca Brownlie, 2nd Maggie Thomson, 3rd Janet Shepherd, 4th Jeanie Gardiner.

 9 years -- 1st Jeanie Campbell, 2nd Jeanie Donaldson, 3rd Mary Marshall, 4th Maggie McKenna.

10 years -- 1st Maggie Donaldson, 2nd Agnes Wilson, 3rd Lizzie Thomson, 4th Mary Thomson.

11 years -- 1st Lizzie Lyons, 2nd Alice Cunningham. 3rd Janet Dykes, 4th Martha Campbell.

12 years -- 1st Mary O'Neil, 2nd Daisy Gallacher, 3rd Maggie Meikle, 4th Marion Forrest.

13 years -- 1st Maggie Dickson, 2nd Maggie Berry, 3rd Mary Cunningham, 4th Maggie Whitten.

14 years -- 1st Janet Rankin 2nd Janet Houston.

Skipping rope race age 3 to 7 -- 1st Maggie Bender, 2nd Margaret Calder, 3rd Maggie Wilson, 4th Eva Bender.

Skipping-rope race -- 8 to 14---1st Maggie Dickson, 2nd Lizzie Lyons 3rd Maggie Whitten, 4th Kate Maxwell.

Married ladies race-- 1st Mrs Young, 2nd Mrs Stewart, 3rd Mrs Kerr

*Andrew Prossar a coal-cutting machineman enlisted in the Cameronians and fought during the First World War. On demob he returned to Quarter Collieries where in 1919 his back was broken in an accident at the coal face. He died several months later aged 31 leaving a wife and four small children, the youngest Jean aged only 3months.

Eddlewood Colliery stables now converted to private homes c. 2007.
Photograph courtesy of Wullie Kerr

. THE WEANS O' EDDLEWOOD "RAWS"

C. 1924 Photograph courtesy of William McDowell. Top L—. Dennis Brown, 5th top row Peter Wilson, Boy with pram Tom McCrum. Front Row 3rd from left Solly Calder, far right sitting boy William McDowell.

THE WINNER!!

Archie Torrance   *Wullie Kerr*

This rocking horse was used by a street photographer in 1948 and the photographer must have left half the local weans screaming in a broken hearted protest when they were lifted off for the next child to have their photograph taken. Both the boys were the sons and grandsons of miners and had they been born 20 years earlier they would have had no choice; they too would have worked down the pit.

THE FOLK O' EDDLEWOOD "RAWS"

THE ROBERTSONS

Front L- r Martha Robertson nee Gold, James Harkness
Philip Robertson, Back Helen G. Harkness, nee Robertson

THE KERRS (THE MIDDLE ROW)

William and Catherine Kerr with l-r   Jean, Katie and Mary.

THE McNAB FAMILY (THE BACK ROW)

Back row. L-r Janet (Jen) Richard (Dick) Mary, Hugh, Ann. Front row L-r William (Bill) Mrs Euphemia McNab,
John (Jock) Margaret (Meg). Thomas (Tom) Mr George Coutts McNab, Martha (Mattie or Mat) George C. McNab
a brushing contractor eventually moved to Earnock Colliery and from there this family of 12 emigrated to
Australia. He came back on two visits but eventually settled in Australia. Photograph courtesy of the Walter family
New Zealand,   direct descendants of Martha McNab who was born in Eddlewood Back Row and who left Australia
and settled in New Zealand.

THE KYLE FAMILY

Back row L-R Katie, John, Lizzie and Nettie front row L-r Andrew, Helen, Tommy, Pat, James and James Jnr. Circa 1918. Photograph courtesy of Mary Neilan.

THE McADAMS (THE BACK ROW)

Margaret   Jack   Isabella, Bernard (fireman) Tom   Mary,   John   Jim.
Photograph courtesy of Mary McGurk (McAdams)

MINERS' WIVES

THE McADAMS TWINS

*L-r Mary Riddell, Unknown, Bella Rae, Mrs Reid.
Photograph courtesy of Archie Torrance.*

*The McAdams twins Mary and Tom being held by
their twin siblings Jack and Margaret circa
1941.Eddlewood Back Row can be seen in background.
Photograph courtesy of Mary McGurk.*

THE WILKIES (THE BACK ROW)

*Back l-r Isa, Allan Wilkie (coal miner) Allan (Lally) Baby Helen on her father's knee.
Front l-r Walter Kerr, Cathy and Susan Wilkie. Photograph taken up Eddlewood bing*

Eddlewood workers carpet bowls team, winners of the Lanarkshire League Cup April 1929. Picture taken at Neilsland Colliery. Back row---left. James Baird. Photograph courtesy of Liz Baird.

*   *   *

Oversman

In memory of our dear departed comrade, Alexander Forrest, Eddlewood Rows.

Another of our comrades, a man beloved by all;
Has left this world behind him and answered to the call,
He was a whiles a wee bit crabit if things did not go right,
But fine we kent that Sandy's bark wis aye worse than his bite.

At Eddlewood the boolers will miss wee San'y sair,
For there's nae mistake aboot it, he was an earnest player;
If yince he saw an openin', ye can tak' this tip frae me,
He could slip in his bool between it and land it richt on the tee.

To them that's near and dear to him this must be an awfu'
blow,
But we hope they come round to realise it's the road we all
must go.
A few short years upon this earth, then we're laid beneath the
sod.
This should be a warning to us a', "prepare to meet thy God."

There was one thing with wee San'y, he didna keep up spite,
He could lecture in the mornin' and shake your haun' at night,
'Tis sad to think that we shall never see this face again,
But we hope he's in a better land, that's our earnest prayer,
Amen.   *Willie Gray, Low Waters. 7.3.1931.*

THE FOLK OF
EDDLEWOOD ROWS 1930-1950'S
By
Elaine Dickie. (Hutton)

ANNESFIELD ROAD.

(FRONT) ---No. (2) Bulloch, (4) Proudfoot, (6) O'Neil, (8) Pollock, (10) David Shaw Jnr. / Lizzie Rodger, (12) Harry Shaw Snr. (14) Dixon, (16) Malloy, (18) Boag, (20) Dick, (22) Johnstone, (24) Cairns.

(BACK) --- (2a) Kane, (4a) Dobinson, (6a) Hamilton) (8a) Maxwell, (10a) McKenna, (12a) Fred Dobinson, (14a) Fletcher Dobinson, (16a) McInnes, (18a) Selfridge, (20a) unknown, (22a) Anderson, (24a) Alex. (Sanny) Hutton.

UPSTAIRS. --- (2B) Anderson, (4b) O'Neil, (6b) Brown, (8b) Donaldson, (10b) Harry Shaw, (12b) Reilly, (14b) Gillespie, (16b) Laird, (18b) Stevenson, (20b) McGuire, (22b) Gibson, (24b) John Hutton Snr.

ANNSFIELD ROAD --- shop buildings. 3 shops + 3 houses owned by Alex. Davidson. Paper shop---Fotheringham's, Chip Shop--- Johnny, Grocer shop---Davidson's. TENNANTS--- Annie Hamilton, (cobbler with shop next to Ranch public house.) Wilson Family (John Wilson Snr. Who looked after the local football team.) McDonald Family.

Further down street another shop building and 3 houses. Grocer Tam Whitehouse (lived at Meikle Earnock) Tenants unknown.

Building facing Tam Whitehouse. --- Cuthbertson, Pollock, Baird, Brownlie, Johnstone, (3 names unknown) Rogan, Landsbourgh, Dalton.

BACK ROW. --- Park, Hanlon, Hepburn, Hailstones, Wilkie, McGurk, Riddle, Thomson, McLinden, Airlie, Wynn, Maxwell, Torrance, Kerr, Henderson, Allan, O'Neil, Neil, Cairns, Martin, Connay, Forbes, Robertson, Calder, Coyle, Fitzpatrick, Cameron, Brown, Nelson, McAdams.

STRATHAVEN ROAD BUILDING

FRONT STREET, No. (80) Forbes /McSeveney, (78) Hutton/Collington, (76) McGill, (74) Kirk, (72) Napier, (70) Frew / Nicol, (68) Mr Boag (overseer, repairs to houses) (66) Affleck, (64) unknown, (62) Frew, (60) McNaught, (58) unknown.

Upstairs—(round back) (80a) Wm. Hamilton, (78a) Fleming, (76a) Baird, (74a) Brownlie, (72a) Wilson, (70a) Brown, (68a) McGuire, (66a) unknown, (64a) Hillis, (62a) Miller, (60a) unknown, (58a) Young.

The numbers of the Strathaven Road building were changed when new shops were built. Each number had 8 numbers added on e.g. 80 became 88.

SOME SURNAMES FROM EDDLEWOOD ROWS. Brindon, Campbell, Cook, Dickson, Duncan, Dunn, Foley, Gebbie, Hawkins, Kenny, Kent, Kerr (Wm) Kerr (Dan), Mackay, McCartney, McCrum, McKinnon, McLuskey, McQuade, Radigan, Reid, Riddle.

EDDLEWOOD "RAWS"

Eddlewood Rows showing the hall and the Middle Row and washhouses. Back Row can be seen behind Middle Row. Illustration courtesy of Wullie Kerr.

WULLIE KERR'S MEMORIES OF A CHILDHOOD IN EDDLEWOOD "RAWS" 1950-58

As we get older we have a tendency to let our thoughts wander back to the "old days" and many different types of memories and experiences resurface from deep within our minds. Good memories and not so good memories but every memory contributing colours of differing hues to the tapestry which has been our lives. Foremost and most vivid among them, are the memories of our families and the people we knew as children and who added so much to the quality of our childhood.

In recalling life in Eddlewood "Raws," memories of so many families come rushing back bringing with them mixed feelings of joy for being part of this unique mining community and regret for the loss for a society and way of life which no longer exists. It was these families, the Duncan's, Kerr's, Nelsons, Maxwells, Rogan's, Robertson's, Wilkie's and many others, who provided so much from so little for us the children growing up as part of this small mining village.

Here we were all poor together. Most of us lived in overcrowded houses where many slept six to a bed and everyone called you "son" and the lassies "hen" and kindness and responsibility for the safety and wellbeing of your neighbour's children was part and parcel of life, and we knew and felt we belonged.

Today, society is so very different and children do not have the same freedom to roam unaccompanied by adults and this is so very sad, as they never experience the joy of setting off on the road to establishing their independence by being allowed to wander the countryside as we did.

"*Nothing tae dae*" was just not in our vocabulary. There were never enough hours in our day to do all that we wanted. The bings were a major attraction for boys and girls alike; they were our adventure playgrounds and we spent hours sliding down them on pieces of salvaged linoleum, corrugated iron, shovels and anything else which we thought would provide us with a fast journey from the top to the bottom. We excavated holes and from these "dug outs" we played "sodgers," threw hand grenades and fought and beat the Germans and Japanese in hand to hand combat on a regular basis. Another haunt was the old wages office where my mother paid her 2/6d (15 _ p) fortnightly rent to J. Watson & Co. Ltd. When hunger drove me home my mother would take one look at me and say *"you have been sliding down that bing"* and I would swear I had never been near it. Then she would point out the holes in the seat of my trousers where I had come off the linoleum and I knew then that the game was up and I was for it.

In the spring we spent hours searching every hedgerow and tree looking for birds nests. We played at "dokies" a kind of follow the leader over burns, (streams) up banking's (earthen banks) swinging on the branches of trees, climbing rocks and cliffs. We dammed the burn and paddled in the water, we caught baggies and felt like big game hunters when we caught a "rid breester" (a small fish with a red breast). We ran the streets for miles pushing a girr and cleek in front of us, played cowboys and Indians, cops and robbers, tig, rounders, football and bools (marbles) in the sheuch. When dusk came it was time for hide and seek, kick the can and chap doors run fast.

The girls joined in many of our games but they also had their own games which few of the boys if any joined in. Ropes (normally played in the winter) being one which comes under that category, being judged too sissy for us "macho" men. They also "stotted" balls against the walls of the houses chanting rhymes as they bounced a ball with one hand and caught one with the other. Beds or peever (hopscotch) was another popular game. The small girls used to play at "hooses" where they marked off areas of ground approximately 2 x 2 metres with stones and then divided up the "house" into sections (rooms) where they would entertain, offer invisible cups of tea and sell sweeties (small stones) in cone shaped pokes made from small squares of newspaper taken from the lavatory where it was used as toilet paper. The key was imagination and there was no lack of that as children improvised with what they had to have a good time.

Like boys the world over we also got up to mischief and on more than one dark Friday night I hid up a close with brothers *Dan* and *Rab Nelson* waiting on *Archie Struthers* from Meikle Earnock dairy coming round selling fresh milk. There were few vans then; *Archie* done his round with a horse and cart and Friday was the night he collected his week's milk money. Just before he got to his last two customers he would buy a fish supper from *Annie Forrests* which he would then hide in a secret compartment beneath his seat while he went to the doors for payment.

Annie Forrest's chip shop

The middle shop was Johnny the Tally's

Like gangsters we watched his every movement, but we were not there to ambush the milkman……. it was his fish supper we were after. The minute he was out of sight, we ran out of the close, jumped up on the cart and stole some chips and a bit of fish, and then ran for our lives before he saw us. Another of our tricks was to climb rone (conductor) pipes at night, dazzle the nesting sparrows with a torch, and then grab them. We would take them to "*Johnny the tally's*" chip shop, open the door, throw them into the shop and then watch helpless with laughter as he tried to catch the birds with the chip basket.

Our mothers had hard lives and on hindsight we must have made it harder with some of the things we got up to. They cooked, cleaned, baked and carried out household tasks from break of day till bedtime. Washing had to be done outside in the washhouse and many a winters' morning they must have been blue with the cold until the washhouse fire caught. The tasks were endless; grates had to be cleaned and black leaded with Zebo, socks had to be darned, clothes made and patched, shoes polished. There were no ready made meals then. Everything we ate was prepared by our mothers.

Our fathers had their doos, whippets, greyhounds, plots (allotments) and not a few of them liked "the tossin" on a Sunday afternoon; but for many of the families Sunday morning was church or chapel first, then a walk up the five parks, up the Strathaven Road and round the Muttonhole Road. The more ambitious walked much further than this.

On a Sunday night we would head for the house of *Dan* and *Chrissie Maxwell* who showed films on a 16mm projector, charging 1d for the kids and 3d for the mothers with the donations going to charity. As the time for the film to start got nearer, the excitement among the children approached fever pitch and peace would be restored by a roar from Margaret Wilson calling for order because the film was about to begin. At the interval the mothers got tea and biscuits and the kids a glass of lemonade.

When Neilsland Colliery closed on August 1st 1932, some of the combined Eddlewood/Neilsland Colliery miners were transferred to Earnock Colliery, but Earnock was within a decade of closing down and could not employ all of the miners. Of the men who lost their jobs, few found employment at Hamilton due to the worldwide depression and the exhaustion of the local coal seams. Men travelled miles to work at pits outside Hamilton. Some moved to Fife, others left the industry and many were forced to apply for parish relief to keep their families.

The grinding poverty of the miner's family was echoed by the equally grinding poverty of unemployment and the struggle to make each penny do the work of two. To heat their houses, many of the men resorted to searching for wood or going up the bing to collect "pan dough" (coal dust gum found at the foot of the bings which when dried into briquettes burned well.) The men felt so ashamed at having to resort to this, they often went in the dark.

By the mid 1950's all the pits had closed and although there were three small drift mines at Quarter they employed few men. In the now crumbling colliery rows, stories of the darkness of the mine were still being handed down by our fathers and grandfathers who enthralled the younger generations by recalling their lives working down in the bowels of the earth. When the *"big chair"* was drawn closer to the fire and the *"faither"* settled down and began his story with the words *"I remember when"* he spoke and it was as if he still got up to go to work at the pit every morning. The children held their breath as they heard stories of pit ponies, cave in's, explosions and strange happenings 1000 feet under the earth. It was from their lips that they also learned of the camaraderie and loyalty among the miners. Previous generations had also been raised on these stories and because of them, most of the young boys could not wait to join their fathers and grandfathers in that mysterious underground world; but this way of life was no more and even the "Raws" themselves were soon to vanish as the inhabitants were rehoused in new houses with 2 and 3 bedrooms, electric light, baths and hot water; luxuries their mothers and grandmothers had never dreamt of.

To say that life in Eddlewood "Raws" was all sweetness and light would be wrong. Life is not like that; neither in the "Raws" nor in any society from the richest to the poorest. There were sinners among the saints as there always are, but it was a caring society where people looked out for each other and everyone was poor together. There was an abundance of laughter and joy as well as sorrow and the sinners as well as the saints added to that rich kaleidoscope which contributed so many colours into the lives of the children growing up in Eddlewood "Raws".

I am greatly indebted to Wullie Kerr for the wonderful contribution he has made to this book. Wullie through his sketches, photographs and reminiscences has documented for posterity, a way of life which has long gone.

WILLIAM KERR, COAL MINER

William Kerr's family originated in Newton, Midlothian and he was almost certainly descended from bonded colliers or slaves. Between the years 1845-1881 the population of the Parish halved when there was a mass exodus of coal mining families from this area as the pits became worked out. Among these families were the Kerr's who moved to Craigneuk before settling in the Hamilton area. Wullie started work at Barncluith Colliery when he was 13 and later went to Eddlewood Colliery.

Wullie and his family were among the miners living at Eddlewood Rows who were targeted for eviction during a strike at Eddlewood and Neilsland Collieries in 1897. Wullie, described by the newspapers covering the story as "one of the most highly respected men in the district" had a wife Kate (nee Bulloch) with heart disease and before he would see her put out into the street he barricaded his house and prepared to fight the sheriff's officers. He was left in the house after the look on his face told them that he meant to fight for his right to a roof over his head.

Wullie and Kate had nine children Katie, Mary, Lizzie, Maggie, Hunter, Alexander, David and Fergie. Tragically Kate died giving birth to Fergie and with no mother to care for the baby and Wullie having to work to support his family, he very reluctantly had to give him up for adoption to a relative. Remarrying some years later Wullie and his second wife Nellie Cochrane had a son called Walter.

Wullie Kerr worked underground as a hewer until 1932 when Neilsland and Eddlewood Collieries closed. A coal miner and proud of it, he was forced because of the industrial depression to look elsewhere for employment and eventually found work at the Clyde brickworks, retiring from there at 80. He died aged 84 in 1962 and he has many descendents still living in the Hamilton area.

The Strathaven Road with its panoramic view of Hamilton and the Clyde Valley

I REMEMBER HAMILTON

A young Scot's lad I remember, took a walk one day,
Frae the miners' Raws in Eddlewood, up Meikle Earnock Brae,
The fields stretched far on every side, the grass sae bonny green,
And his heart was light as he travelled the hawthorn hedge between.

Up past the Station, the Common, where the "Cushy" used tae rise,
Past the Beechfields sleepy village, neath the scudding, cloudy skies,
The lark sang sweet upon the wing, as the lad trod Scotia's Road,
And in his heart was a happy song, as he walked there with God.

Up tae the Crossroads and then turn left alang the Muttonhole,
Past the big dam and the Cornhills, straight on ower the Knoll,
Till the road that came frae Strathaven met him at Limekilnburn,
Twas then, back hame tae Hamilton, did he let his footsteps turn.

A narrow sidewalk beckoned, where twa could barely pass,
Just room enough to accommodate a wincher and his lass,
The young laddies eyes wi' wonder while walking gazed aroon',
On his right loomed lofty Tinto, on his left lay Glesca toon.

The Mausoleum, lay in a' its grandeur and there the lovely Clyde,
Was like a ribbon cutting its course thru the countryside,
Motherwell's steelwork stacks stood smoking in far off Lofty Raw,
And his eyes could see the valley of the River Avon braw.

Past Eddlewood Toll tae Cadzow Brig', Low Waters, Burnblea Street,
Past Portland Square and the Gas Works, he went on tacketed feet,
Tae the Auld Vic Picture Hoose, the Station, they a' were his that day,
And, as he turned at the Auld Cross, he travelled a carefree way.

Hamilton tis half a century gone, since that lad I knew,
With a proud song in his heart, trod your byways thru and thru,
Yet still he takes that "daunner" in his memories far awa',
For that young lad back there, was me, I was born in Eddlewood Raw.

Samuel (Scotty) Kent

THE EDDLEWOOD "TOSSIN'" SCHOOL

Illustration courtesy of Wullie Kerr

Gambling was popular among the miners and the game of pitch and toss *"the tossin"* as it was known, had its many regular punters. Because it was illegal, these *"tossin' schools"* were, like the street bookies, an easy target for the local police who raided them on a regular basis.

Eddlewood *"tossin' school"* was held on a Sunday afternoon at the site of an old loading wall at the disused mineral line almost directly opposite the Eddlewood Bowling Club.

Wullie Kerr son and grandson of Eddlewood miners, whose family had lived at the "Raws" for sixty years, moved into No. 16 Eddlewood Rows when he was 7 years old and this was to be his home until he was 14. Gifted with excellent recall of the life in the "Raws," he described how as a wee boy he used to sit on the loading wall and watch fascinated at the crowd of men four and five deep circling *"the tosser"* (the banker and who also as his name suggests, tossed the two coins sitting on a stick heads up into the air) and a couple of *"babar's"* the men who took the bets from the gamblers. The men standing in the circle would lay bets on the result of whither the pennies would land heads or tails up when they landed on the ground.

At the heart stopping moment when the coins were tossed in the air, adrenalin levels surged and the punters held their breath until they hit the ground. If the coins fell as they had predicted, two heads or two tails they won money from the tosser but if not, they lost what they had bet against the toss. If the toss resulted in a head and a tail then the coins were tossed again.

The atmosphere at the moment of tossing was electric and even as a child Wullie Kerr was able to recognise this. Unable to see what was going on because of the *"sea of large flat bunnets"* in front of him, he would slowly move down the wall as the game progressed getting closer and closer to the men. At the end, when the money was being counted, he would help the "babars' " pick up the coins and for this he would receive a handful of pennies.

For most of the men the *"tossin'"* was a pastime when they had a few pence, but some were addicted to the adrenalin surge and would have bet their shirts on the toss of the coins and this was bad news for their families who at times were left destitute when a week's hard earned wages left with the "Tosser." The change in the gambling laws and the opening of betting shops seems to have been the major influence for the disappearance of *"tossin' schools"* at some time during the early 1970's.

Above Eddlewood Reading Hall and Middle Row.
Below Meikle Earnock Village 1877, photographs courtesy of Sir Simon Watson Bt.

CADZOW COLLIERY OFFICIALS

Front row 2nd left William Walker oversman circa 1900. Photograph courtesy of Hamilton Town House Reference Library. Below The Ranche Public house, Cadzow photograph courtesy of Myra Murdoch.

BOOM TOWN!!!
CADZOW COLLIERY
1876-1877

In April 1872, Messrs Austine & Co. the proprietors of Allanton Colliery Ferniegair obtained the lease on the minerals lying almost 900 feet under 600 acres of the Duke of Hamilton's High Parks. The area where the colliery buildings were to be sited was just outside the boundary of the Dukes land and on 13 acres owned by Mr Glaude Brownlie. Six weeks later the development of the colliery began when the first sod for No. 1 shaft was cut by Mr Austine with Mrs Austine cutting the first sod for No. 2 shaft. With the opening of Cadzow Colliery, the sleepy little hamlet of Low Waters turned into a bustling hive of industry with miners arriving from all over the country.

The sinking of the shafts presented Cadzow Colliery Company with a series of complex problems. The coal wasn't easy to win and the developers had to fight flooding from underground wells, fire and great blowers of dangerous gas which roared from fissures in the coal face. On 2nd December 1876 work on the colliery was brought to a standstill after miners working with naked lights at the bottom of No.1 shaft set fire to one of these blowers.

Up until then, it had been thought impossible for any ignition of gas to take place because of the air current produced by the massive 40 feet diameter by 12 feet broad ventilation fan installed by the colliery company. However, they were wrong and the air current only fed the fire with oxygen. Despite a desperate battle to bring it under control the men were eventually forced to ascend the shaft as the fire rapidly took hold and spread along the whole airway and up the upcast shaft.

In an attempt to drown out the flames, water was poured down the shaft but the gas rose to the surface of the water and continued to burn. Explosives used in the shaft also failed. Water was then pumped down by the massive Cornish engine but with no success.

The air in the vicinity of the shaft was by now heavily impregnated with dangerously explosive methane gas and it was decided to cover the mouth of the shaft with planks of wood and then seal it with puddle clay to starve the fire of oxygen. To achieve this every available pair of hands, miners, officials and management were used in this incredibly dangerous job. The whole process from the start of the fire took twenty hours.

The colliery was closed for approximately three weeks and then it re-opened. Special rules had been introduced and the use of open lights were prohibited, from now on only safety lamps were permitted underground to prevent the danger of explosion.

Some seven months later on the evening of Tuesday 26th June in the Splint seam of No. 1 Pit, ten men were hard at work. Two of the colliers; one undermining the coal and the other filling a hutch were working at the coal face some forty feet from the pit bottom and twelve feet away from them were the two firemen in charge of the nightshift.

Five feet from the coal face the miners' Davy lamps were hanging on a "horse" (a cross piece of timber) which had been nailed to the bratticing (material for directing the air flow). Suddenly without any warning a loud hiss was heard and gas shot out from a fissure, igniting as it forced its way through the mesh of a Davy lamp. The blower was now a high powered jet of flame and almost immediately the workings became an inferno.

Miraculously only one man, *Jim Sillars* was injured and he only had slight burns to his right forearm. All forty men who had been underground were evacuated to the pit head with their "graith" and the five pit ponies were wound to the surface. Had the gas accumulated before ignition then the men would surely have been killed.

Managing director *Colonel Austine*, manager *Hamilton Smith, Ralph Moore* inspector of mines for the district and *George McCreath* mining engineer were hastily summoned and the race was on to save the pit.

A brick wall was erected to seal off the affected area but it was no sooner up when it was destroyed by an explosion of firedamp. It was decided then to close Nos. 1 and 3 pits because of the danger of the fire spreading due through the statutory connection between them.

In an attempt to prevent the air getting to the fire, 250 men with twelve horses and carts and many wheelbarrows ferried large quantities of waste material from the bing to the shaft. The intention was to fill the bottom of the shafts with waste up to a height of 25 feet above the doorway cutting off the air supply, but this was made extremely dangerous by the frequent explosions which took place as gas accumulated and ignited. However, by Thursday the great volumes of steam which blew out of Nos. 1 and 3 shafts between explosions ceased and it was then thought that the fire was under control and soon mining operations in No.2 Pit would be able to continue. To ascertain the condition of this pit, Hamilton Smith and a fireman went down the shaft to have a look about the workings and came back up satisfied with their observations.

Their hopes however were short lived; within two hours of their returning to the surface it became apparent that gas had found its way into No.2 Pit, when a violent explosion shot debris from the mouth of the shaft. For the next 3 _ hours at intervals of approximately 10 to 20 minutes, a fresh explosion rocked the neighbourhood. It was reported that the sound which could be heard for miles, was like that of "*a big gun battle taking place on the heights at Low Waters.*" A decision was then taken to attempt to seal the shafts. During the interval between the blasts, men attempted to seal the shafts with planks of wood and puddle clay but they repeatedly saw their work destroyed as explosion followed explosion. One blast not only destroyed the wooden planks covering the shaft, it blew the roof off the fan house, depositing it 150 feet away.

It was nothing short of miraculous that only one man was injured; *Adam Murray* a colliery fireman had his wrist broken when an explosion shot up the shaft. The courage displayed by the Cadzow miners and management was unbelievable as time and again they returned to the job after being "*thrown on their backs and cast about like nine pins*" by the force of the concussion from an explosion shooting from the mouth of a shaft. Eventually the explosions ceased when the shafts and an air tunnel were finally sealed. It had taken four days to bring the inferno under control and now it would be left to nature to fill the workings with water and extinguish all traces of the underground fire.

Three months later on Tuesday 9th October Cadzow colliery re-opened. The Splint seam where the massive gas blowers had originated was being was worked not only in Cadzow Colliery, but in numerous collieries throughout the area. Less than two weeks after Cadzow Colliery re-opened the worst disaster in Scottish mining history occurred in the same seam at Blantyre Collieries, High Blantyre, killing approximately 216 men and boys.

The Inquiry which was held into the cause of the Blantyre disaster included this ominous warning in its report about the dangers of large quantities of gas in the Splint coal seam. "*The most alarming part of the evidence is that which shows that within a radius of two miles of Hamilton West Railway Station (in which Blantyre Colliery is situated) 14 new collieries, with 32 pits, varying from 120 to 180 fathoms in depth, are either being sunk or the coal being worked under the same system of stoop and room as at Blantyre, and that all of them give off fire-damp. One of these collieries, situated at Cadzow, has opened the same seam as that in which the explosion took place at Blantyre, and the issue of gas has at present caused the working to be discontinued.*

Ten years later, again in the Splint seam and this time at Udston Colliery, a massive explosion cost the lives of 73 men and boys. The deadly fire-damp was to cost the mining industry many lives.

THE FIRST CADZOW MINERS - 1881 CENSUS

WILSON TERRACE
01. James, Snr. James Jnr, and John Galbraith.
02. Pat. Kean, Michael Grady, James Kennedy.
03. Peter McCabe.
04. William Sharp
05. Alex. Connell (Gen. lab.)
06. Robert Gibb.. (Engine driver)
07. William Silver, Robert Right.
08. John Connor, (General labourer) George Dillworth, Thomas Whelan, James McLaughlin.
09. Thomas Murray (Underground labourer) Samuel Brown, Robert Jackson.
10. Robert Kelly, Lorrance Kelly.
11. George Bell, David Thornton.
12. Robert Anderson.
13. William Mitchell Snr. William Mitchell Jnr.
14. Robert Mathieson. Arthur Mathieson (Roadsman) John Mathieson (Boggie Driver)
15. Arthur Rumgay. (Gasfitter)
16. Gavin Miller. (Blacksmith)
17. James Simpson. (Colliery fireman)
18. John Murray. (Safety lamp trimmer) William Murray (Pony driver) Matthew Vance John Coulter (Roadsman)
19. William Collins, Solomon Collins (labourer)
20. Andrew Findlay. (Gen. lab.)
21. William Walker. (Colliery fireman)
22. William McFederies. (Oversman)
22. William McFederies. (Oversman).

MOORE STREET.
03. Hugh McKinlay.
05-35 (Uninhabited.).
37. Thomas Ferguson. (Ironstone miner).
39. John Downie.
41. Uninhabited.
43. John Aitkinson, James Aitkinson.
45. Matthew Keith.
47. James Orr, John Twaddle.
49. John Clarkson. Michael Clarkson.
02. Uninhabited.
04. Michael McGinty, James and Michael Dollan.
6-8 Uninhabited
10. John Armour. (General labourer)
12. Thomas Whitehouse. Andrew Whitehouse.
14. John Balls, Robert Pescoe.
16. Robert McFarlane.
18. William McInnis.
20. Benjamin Richards. (Blacksmith).
22. Uninhabited.
24. Robert Gray. Joseph Angwin.
--- Edward and George Burns.

AUSTINE STREET.
04. Dennis Hobbin.
06. Robert Mathieson.
08-12. Uninhabited.
14. John Farrell, (Gen. lab) James Campbell.
16. James, Patrick, John, Wm. Cameron
18. James McLachlan, Wm. McDonald.
20-24 Uninhabited.
26. Archibald and James Burns.
28. Benjamin and James Wild.
30. James and Robert Hogg.
32. John and Robert Paterson. Alex. Paterson. (Pony driver)
36. Uninhabited
38. Frederick and Robert Cain. Thomas Thomson.
40. John, Samuel and Michael Dugan.
42. Henry Ayre.
44. Thomas Muir, (Gen. lab.) Joseph Selfridge.
46. James Gallacher. .
48. Gilbert Thomson, Gilbert, James and William Thomson.(Pony drivers)
50. Terrance and Edward Murphy. Hugh Murphy (Pony driver)
52. James Kenny. Michael and

05. Alex. Pennel. (Joiner & carpenter) John Caldwell, Thomas McDuff.
07. Ritchie and Robert Rodger
09. Gavin and James Taylor. James Rogan.
11. Henry Mullen.
13. James and George Walker
15-17 Uninhabited.
19. James Waddell. Enginekeeper.
21. Bernard Gormley. Thomas Murphy.
23 Robert Crawford.
25. James Ford. William Dalton.
27. Michael and Patrick Lenard. .

McCREATH STREET.
02. Charles Boyle.
04. Thomas Boyle Snr. Thomas Boyle Jnr. Michael Duey.
6-10 Uninhabited.
12. Michael and Thomas Hassan
14. Bernard McGrorie.
16. Jas.Feannie, Wm.Cairns, Daniel Donnelly.
18-20 Uninhabited.
22. James Taylor. (Enginekeeper)

McCREATH STREET.
24. Charles Brown. (Engineman)
26. John Gibson. (Pitheadman)
28. John and Felix O'Brine.

AITKEN STREET.
01. Mark Stewart.
03. Uninhabited.
05. Denis McMenemy.
07 Uninhabited.
09. James Fitzpatrick.
11. William Fleming.
13. James Orr. (Bottomer)
15. Joseph Crawford. John Davis.
17. Martin Higgins.
19. Stewart Fleming.
21. Duncan McNaught, Henry Green.
23. Hugh Cherry.

LANDALE STREET.
03. Neil Reilly, John Clark.
05. John Hay.
07. Samuel McMullan.
09-13. Uninhabited.
15. Angus McMillan.
17-19. Uninhabited.

SIMPSON STREET.
02- Uninhabited.
04. Andrew Paterson. (Gen. Lab.)
06.08.10.12.14. 18.20.22. Uninhabited.
16. Edward Mhon.
24. Thomas Majick. (Colliery Fireman)

LANDALE STREET.
02.-04. Uninhabited.
06. James Mullen Snr and James Mullen Jnr,
    Daniel McCallum, Joseph Mullen.
08. John Telford (Gen. Lab.) John Telford,
    George Telford (Lamp cleaner)
10-12. Uninhabited.
14. Hugh and John McGregor.
16. James Monaghan.
18. James King.
20. John King.
22. Robert Henry.
24. ---------

BISHOP STREET.
03. Robert McCrum, William McFarlane.
05. Charles, John and William Menzies.
07. Charles McLauchlan.
11. William Clarke, Rbt. Clark Blacksmith
13. Uninhabited.
15. Stephen Toole.
17. Uninhabited.
19. Patrick McKay. Patrick and David McKay.
    Bottomers.
21. John Price.
2.4.6.8.10.12.14.16.18.20.22.23 Uninhabited
24. Thomas Brown.

SMITHY ROW. John Lindsay, (joiner) Jas. Brownlie, Jas. Cornish (engineman) Jas. and Wm. Gray, John Johnstone, Thos, and Wm. Kelly, Jas. Cowan, (underground fireman) Rbt. Dick Snr. Rbt. Dick Jnr. Thos. Brunton (Plasterer) John Brunton, John Watson. (Gen. Lab) John Robison. (Engine Fireman.)

The above men were listed as living at Cadzow Rows in April 1881 and no doubt many of them would be present during the attempts to bring the explosions under control. Unless otherwise stated the men were employed as coalminers and the spelling of a name depended on the enumerator writing down the information. There are obvious mistakes e.g. Robert Right instead of Wright but I have left them as they are documented.

Many of the men had travelled hundreds of miles to work at Cadzow Colliery and I have noted some Cadzow miners working at Ferniegair or Quarter Collieries in earlier census records. In 1872 engineer James Cornish from Redruth in Cornwall accompanied the massive Cornish pumping engine on the sea journey which brought it to the Broomilaw, Glasgow. The engine was transferred to Cadzow Colliery in carts drawn by teams of Clydesdale horses. One hundred horses were needed to pull the carts. After he assembled the engine he was asked to take charge of it and he settled at Cadzow. He has descendents still living in Hamilton.

A lot of families took in relatives and boarders, resulting in gross overcrowding of the small houses. Stirling man James Cowan and his wife Agnes (from Bothwell) lived in a one bedroomed house at Smithy Row with their seven children and Agnes's' father and brother. Next door in another one bedroomed house lived Peebles man Thomas Brunton with his wife Christina (from Fyfe) their nine children and one boarder (also from Fyfe.)

EXPLOSION

The workings at Cadzow Colliery were known to have the potential to throw out huge blowers of gas and special rules for the colliery stipulated that only safety lamps were in use and it was absolutely prohibited to take tobacco or matches underground.

In the 1920's it was generally recognised that Cadzow Colliery was also one of the safest pits in Scotland and this reputation was due to safety policy of manager Hamilton Smith. Any fireman who wanted a permanent job at Cadzow had first to prove to Smith that he was a "*fire-damp sleuth*" and that all safety rules were strictly adhered to. However, despite this vigilance, sudden and unexpected accidents involving gas still occurred.

One of these tragedies took place at half past nine on the evening of Sunday 17th October 1928 while four face workers James Brooks, James Rodden and John Kane (all coal-cutting machinemen) and miner Thomas Paton were at work in the Kiltongue section of the colliery.

The coal-cutting machine had been idle since Friday when the men had finished their work for the weekend and James Brooks who was preparing the machine for work had already inserted a number of new blades. Finished, he pulled the switch to set it in motion and instantly there was a noise like hissing steam and sparks appeared from the vicinity of the coal-cutter followed by a blinding explosion and three of the men James Brooks, James Rodden and Thomas Paton received dreadful burns to their bodies and almost overcome by deadly afterdamp; John Kane of 20 McGhie Street and some other men who had been further away from the scene of the blast escaped with minor injuries and singeing.

The alarm was raised and immediately men started converging on the site of the explosion among them was brusher Harry Creechan who gently covered a shivering shocked man with his jacket. Up on the surface the sound of the pit horn booming out the news that there had been an accident brought men, women and children running to the colliery. At first it was rumoured that there was a major disaster unfolding underground but this was soon proved to be wrong as word began to reach the surface.

Despite their appalling injuries, the three men managed to give their relatives and workmates a cheery greeting when they were brought to the surface where their injuries were treated by Dr Stewart and then they were put onto the ambulance waggon to be transferred to the Glasgow Royal Infirmary where their condition was later described as critical.

Thomas Paton and James Rodden survived for two days before succumbing to their injuries. Thomas Paton 104 Low Waters had worked in the mines since he left school with the exception of the years he spent on active service with his regiment The Cameron Highlanders during W.W.1. He fought with distinction throughout the war and was awarded four medals including the Military Medal and the 1914 Star. He was a quite reserved man with a reputation as a hard worker and a good father to his four children two boys and two girls.

James Rodden (32) 168 Low Waters had been born in Cadzow and had always been a miner. He had only been working as a machineman for two weeks and was taking the place of a man who had been injured. After the blast, James, despite his horrendous injuries and the effects of after-damp managed to drag himself along the pavement of the mine to remove a switch and cut off the electricity supply, making the area safe for the rescue party. He was an amateur footballer playing with Cadzow St. Ann's and Blantyre Celtic. He had four wee girls the oldest only ten. His father also James was killed at Neilsland Colliery in January 1921.

James Brooks (39) Downie Street, Low Waters, was the only survivor. Married with six children he had served with The Dublin Fusiliers throughout the war and had been so badly shell shocked at the Battle of the Somme that he suffered from total loss of memory for nine months. He had worked as a machineman at Cadzow Colliery for most of his working life with the exception of a short spell at Bent Colliery.

Still suffering from the effects of his dreadful injuries James was the chief witness at the Fatal Accident Inquiry held at Hamilton Sheriff Court almost two months later. In his evidence, he told of how before they had started their work, he had made a preliminary test of the section but had found no trace of gas. He was of the opinion that gas had accumulated under the machine over the weekend and it had been ignited by sparks from the mechanism.

David Nimmo, colliery fireman also gave evidence that he had tested twice that day for gas and found no trace of any. One of his inspections had been only an hour-and-a-half before the explosion and he stated that the safety lamps the miners had been using were found by the Government authorities to be in perfect working order. The jury returned a formal verdict.

James and Jane Brooks with their children L-r Margaret, James and Edward

Less than one year later, on the 10th October, 1929, three miners, John Whitton, Robinson Foster and Robert Massie lost their lives when they were gassed while working in the same seam. The dangers of gas were always present on 2nd October 1938 just six years before the pit closed, Wm. Frew, Neilsland Drive, James Johnstone, Eddlewood, Hugh Loney, Wylie Street, and Walter Parkinson, Dechmont Street all Hamilton were overcome by gas and had to be rescued by fireman John Logan and the Lanarkshire Miners Rescue Brigade.

Austine Street, Cadzow "Raws" circa 1900. Photograph by kind permission of Guthrie Hutton
Note the remains of a fire used for the washing and also the wooden washing bine (tub) on pavement.

THE WEANS O' CADZOW "RAWS"

This photograph of some of the children of Cadzow Rows was taken by a street photographer in the 1930's.
Photograph courtesy of Sally Dowdell ne' McGilvray back row 4th from left.
Front stair. L-r. ---- Robertson, Andrew Moffat, Peter Moffat, James McGilvary, John Thomson
2nd row. L-r unknown-, unknown, unknown, unknown, Alice Archibald. 3rd row L-r unknown, Jean Walker, Charlie
Lenie, Alda Munro, Joanne Stewart, Jim Pollock. 4th row L-r Janie McLeavy, Mary Harkins, Sally McGilvray,
unknown, unknown , Annie Harkins, Ella Murray, Mary Murray. John Harkins. Top row. L---r. unknown, Lizzie
Robb. Girls standing left Agnes Pollock. Right, Lizzie Murray

Miner John Carracher developed a great interest in politics and eventually became secretary of the local branch of the Labour Party. A local activist he was invited in the early1950's to lead Cadzow Tenants Defence Association in the fight against the appalling conditions people were living in at Cadzow Rows.

Despite promises from various politicians nothing was done about the plight of the tenants and John Carracher, Pat Murray and a number of women went to a council meeting at Lanarkshire House, Glasgow to protest and they refused to leave until they found out when the residents were being rehoused. Eventually they had to be removed by the police.

The plight of the tenants was now in the public eye and this resulted in new houses being built at Quarter Road end for the families of Cadzow Rows

CADZOW MINERS
Circa 1920/21 left John Carracher age 15-16, right--- unknown

CADZOW FOLK

THE GEBBIE FAMILY
Front row l-r Liz, Peg, Mrs Agnes Gebbie, Wee Jean, Jimmy, Mr William Gebbie, Isa (front) Nan, Archie, Back Row l-r, William, Helen, Polly, Andrew. The Gebbie family were among the families who were threatened with eviction from their home at 49 Moore Street, Cadzow Rows during the strike of 1900 William Gebbie was an underground fireman. Photograph courtesy of Janette Evans.

THE NEILAN FAMILY

Back row, L – r William, Patrick and James. Middle Row, Maggie, Thomas, Sarah and Nellie.
Front Row, John and Henry. Sitting in between Thomas and Sarah Neilan is baby Mary. The family were
among the people threatened with eviction by Cadzow Coal Company during the 1900 strike. Mrs Neilan was
in labour with Thomas while the sheriff's officers were at the door trying to serve them with an eviction
notice. A crowd of miners kept them away but were later fined for obstruction. The family were highly
respected in the district.

THE KANE FAMILY

Top row l-r John, Frank, James. Front l-r Mary Ann, (baby Tommy), Tec, Ann, Arthur, John Snr.
c. 1916. Photograph courtesy of Joe Cassidy.

ROBERT McCRUM
CADZOW COAL MINER

Robert McCrum's grandparents Robert and Isabella (nee O'Hara) had been among the influx of Irish refugees fleeing the horrors of the potato famine in the middle of the nineteenth century. His grandfather came from Armagh and his grandmother belonged to Dingle, one of the remotest spots in Ireland. When Robert was born at Udston Rows in May 1892 his father also called Robert was working underground at Udston Colliery. When the shift was finished he returned to the surface to find out that he had a son after seven daughters. The miners were so delighted for him they lifted him shoulder high and singing at the top of their voices in celebration of the birth, carried him home at to see his new son.

Five years before baby Robert's birth, his father was among the miners working underground when the Splint seam exploded at Udston Colliery killing 73 men and boys. Robert McCrum and other miners who survived the explosion were responsible for saving the lives of numerous men who had been injured or overcome by lethal after-damp gas. He also went back down with the rescue teams after being rescued himself. Unfortunately he was kicked on the head by a pit pony he was escorting in the cage and sustained a serious head injury. Just after Robert Jnr. was born his father's health had deteriorated so much that he was hospitalised until he died in 1894.

To feed and clothe her eight children, Jane McCrum (nee Walker) had to work in the fields of local farms. Taking baby Robert with her, she would leave him lying at the foot of a haystack where she could see him.

Front row L-r Robert McCrum, Isabella and John
Back row L-r Ella George, Robert and May.

Robert fought during W.W.1 and received abdominal injuries from shrapnel. He met and married a Borders girl Isabella Sutherland when he was stationed at Hawick and on demob, he started work at Cadzow Colliery and they lived in a colliery owned house at 1 Field Street.

Robert and Isa had ten children: Margaret, Jane, Margaret Jane, Robert, John, Wullie, George, Tom, Ella and May. Margaret, Jane and Margaret Jane died in infancy, Tom died age six. Living in a single end, the McCrums were grossly overcrowded, but houses were very hard to come by. When the family through the wall from them moved out, the Cadzow Coal Company had their single end converted to a room and kitchen by making a door through to the empty house. While the work was in progress they could see down into the foundations which were flooded with dirty water. The houses were running with damp and a breeding ground for infectious diseases which struck down young children no matter how careful their parents were. In 1936 almost out of her mind with worry over two of her children who were ill in Udston Hospital, Isa McCrum went to the Hamilton Burgh factor's office in Brandon Street and begged him for one of the new houses being built at Mill Road. When he asked her why she thought should get one and she said to him *"Mr, if you don't give me a house I will have nae weans left."* Seeing her distress, he gave her a 3 bedroomed house.

Robert McCrum was buried for 15 hours by a roof fall at Cadzow Colliery. His back was badly injured and he never went down a pit again. He worked for years as a lamplighter with Hamilton Burgh. Their three sons Robert, George and Wullie fought during W.W.2. Wullie was killed in Burma. Wonderful, warm, caring people, the McCrums took in a family who had lost everything in the Clydebank blitz. Their daughter May McTaggart still lives with her husband Joe in the same house in Mill Road.

Above, Joe Cassidy age 5, c. 1950 with McCreath Street, Cadzow Rows in the background.
L--Anne Hughes who worked sorting coal from the waste at the screes (picking tables) at Cadzow Colliery. Her father was a Cadzow miner. c. 1924

Helen Brown out the back door of 237 Low Waters Road (Gaffers Row.) Cadzow Colliery can be seen in the background. Helen was the daughter of William Brown undermanager at Cadzow Colliery. Photograph courtesy of Robin Davidson.(son)

HARRY CREECHAN, COAL MINER

Harry (Henry) Creechan was born at Quarter and started working underground in Quarter Pit at the age of 14. During W.W.1 he was a private in the Cameron Highlanders and fought at the Battle of the Somme. When he was demobbed he returned to work at Quarter Collieries. Eventually he obtained employment as a brusher at Cadzow Colliery and moved to a room and kitchen at 8 School Street. Harry and his wife Margaret had eleven children: James, Alice, Harry, John, (died age 6 with diphtheria) Sadie, Mary, Margaret, John (2nd) Pat, Joe and Danny.

Harry worked at Cadzow Colliery until the coal in his section became exhausted and was closed down, he then went to Earnock Colliery and when it closed in 1942 he went to Bardykes Colliery on the outskirts of Blantyre. After Bardykes he travelled by bus to Denny in Stirling, returning home all those miles, soaked to the skin from working in wet conditions. Eventually he finished his working life at a Coalburn Colliery retiring at the age of 65 years.

Harry Creechan photographed with his wife Margaret (Murray) just as he was just leaving to start his shift at Earnock Colliery. Photograph courtesy of Alice Mitchell (daughter)

THE CORNISH FAMILY

Top row. L-r Charles, Mary and James. Front row Thomas, Charles (father) Rachael (mother) and Andrew. This family were descended from James Cornish the engineer who installed the largest Cornish pumping engine in the country at Cadzow Colliery c. 1915

Photograph courtesy of James Cornish (grandson)

CADZOW BOWLING CLUB 1900

Cadzow Bowling Club looking towards Neilsland Colliery (the stack or chimney of which can be seen in distance). Three large country mansions can be seen, the one in the foreground is Fairview, home of Thomas Thomson manager at Eddlewood/Neilsland Collieries. Behind Fairview can be seen Oakenshaw house and faintly through trees top right can be seen Hollandbush House/South Church manse. These were the large country houses of city merchants and lawyers until the coal mines opened and the miners moved next door. Photographs courtesy of Mary Neilan.

Cadzow Bowling Club which was situated on what is now Graham Avenue and John Smith Court sheltered housing complex. The spire of the Ranche pub can just be seen behind the chimney in centre of picture. John Alston owner of the Ranche dug and laid out the bowling club with his own bare hands because he refused to pay what he considered the extortionate rate of £2000 quoted by contractors

LOW WATERS PRIMARY SCHOOL, c.1953, *photograph courtesy of Mary Leighton nee Manson*
The children in this class photograph were born between 1943/44 and most of them had fathers or grandfathers who were coalminers. Back row l-r Ian Hamilton, Terry Dickson, David Fleming, Hammy Riddell, Jim Freeburn, Tony Yates, George French, Douglas Reid, David Gibson, Freddie Cunningham, David Cape, John Bolton.
3rd row l-r Lillian Allan, Janette Docherty , Margaret Louden, Betty Gemmill, Elizabeth Brannan, Ruby Barr, Jean McKie, Mary Manson, June Cooper, Marjorie Laird, Bessie Scott, Isobel Ralston, Margaret McPherson, Moira Hendry.
2nd row. L-r Jean Fleming, Eileen Brand ,Margaret Riddell, Betty King, Margaret Hendry, Jessie McNab, Isobel Ralton, Mary Moore, Wilma Russell, Martha Gibson, Margaret Martin.
Front l-r Kenneth Watson, Neil Craw, John Campbell, Archie Torrance, Colin Henderson, Ian Munro, Jim Robertson.

ST. ANN'S PRIMARY SCHOOL, c.1948 *photograph courtesy of May Stewart.*
Like the above photograph most of these children come from mining families. Top row l-r Hugh McCabe, unknown, Andy Corns, John Coyle, Wullie Gormley, Wullie Adams, John McGonnagle, John King, John Kane Unknown, Wullie Doyle, Wullie Maxwell, Tommy Walker, John Tierney. Middle Row l-r Barbara McSorley, Maureen Dalton, May Stewart, Catherine Kyle, Anne McKinley, Anne Mayo, Ann Stewart, Unknown, May Murray, Alice Shearer, Mary Irvine. Front row l-r John Boyle, Pat Cunningham, Tommy Feenie, John Dick, Pat Vance, Unknown, Pat Oliver, John Teirney, Unknown, Tommy Kane.

A TANNER DOUBLE
STREET BOOKIES

James Canning, 17 School Street, Low Waters was a coal miner but he was also an illegal bookie on the side. With no betting shops the only way the working man could place a bet on the horses was with a street bookie. Easy targets for the local police, raids were common despite lookouts being posted. In August 1925 while James was taking bets from punters at Low Waters, he was "lifted" by two plain clothes police officers. Instead of putting his hands up and accepting his capture, he refused to walk towards Hamilton and demanded a bus to take him down to the Burgh Police station at the Top Cross.

The officers got a struggling and arguing James as far as Downie Street, but a large hostile crowd had joined on and they were also giving the police a hard time. Not one to miss a chance, James wrestled one arm free from the vicelike grip of the officer and punched *Sergeant Brown* right on the chin.

Watching the arrest was *William Turner* a miner from 26 Eddlewood Rows and when he saw Canning hit the sergeant, he jumped on *Constable Dobie's* back and *Michael McKay* another miner of 125 Low Waters Road joined in, kicking him on the leg and throwing a tin can at Sergeant Brown.

With great difficulty the officers managed to get Canning down as far as Burnblea Street where to their relief, they managed to get him on a bus for the short journey to Hamilton Police Station. There he was charged with having loitered for the purpose of betting and receiving bets, striking a police officer and committing a breach of the peace. In court Canning was defended by Mr *John Cassells*, solicitor but Police-Judge Anderson found him guilty of bookmaking and a breach of the peace and fined him £10 or 60 days. *William Turner* and *Michael McKay* were each fined £5 or 30 days.

In Cadzow the police were not the only ones local gamblers had to keep a look out for. One of the Roman Catholic priests had a hatred of gambling and used to raid the "tossin" schools chasing and hitting members of his flock with his walking stick.

*   *   *

Burnbank newsagent *Guy Lang* also done a bit of bookmaking on the side and he suspected that another two bookies *Jimmy Lyon* and *Mick Mitchell* appeared to be getting tips from the local police station and it was not tips about horses. Their runners were never "lifted" when they were standing at their usual pitches taking bets but his were. He decided to put one of his runners, his brother-in-law miner *Bertie Smith* at his usual stand, but without pencil or paper the recognised tools of the trade and see what the reaction of the police would be.

Bertie Smith, 50 years a face worker at Bardykes Colliery

It wasn't long before the law appeared on the scene. Bertie was lifted and charged with loitering for the purpose of betting and receiving bets. The usual procedure when a runner was lifted was to plead guilty and the "bookie" paid the fine; but not this time, the police had no evidence. Bertie was kept in the cells overnight and appeared before Justice of the Peace Sanny Hunter who, despite the lack of evidence promptly found him guilty; *Guy Lang* paid the fine.

Miner Jimmy Russell

Another of Guy's runners was miner *Jimmy Russell.* One Saturday he was at his usual close in Burnbank taking bets from punters. The street was busy with people bustling about and among the crowd Jimmy spotted a workman dressed in old clothes, bunnet and scarf. The man was shuffling along pushing a wheel barrow and Jimmy didn't pay him much attention; but soon he wished he had, for he dropped his barrow when he passed Jimmy, grabbed him and said "*sorry Russell you're booked*". It was his pal local police officer *Arthur Mackie* who had been sent to lift him. Jimmy was fined, *Guy Lang* paid up and *Arthur Mackie* who eventually reached the rank of inspector was to remain a lifelong pal of Jimmy's with no hard feelings; they laughed about it many a time.

LOCAL RECIPIENTS OF
THE EDWARD MEDAL
(THE VICTORIA CROSS OF THE COAL MINES)
JAMES KENNEDY,
EARNOCK COLLIERY HAMILTON.

At Earnock Colliery, Hamilton, on June 2nd 1914, miners Neil McKillop and James Kennedy were taking down the head coal and the coal face, when a sudden fall of coal trapped Neil McKillop. James Kennedy immediately went to his aid and desperately tried to release the trapped man but another two falls came down completely covering him. This didn't deter James Kennedy; he continued in his rescue attempt and eventually he managed to excavate a hole big enough to allow him to breath.

Kennedy was then joined by two repairers, Andrew Nicol, 50 Lorne Street, Burnbank and William Houldsworth, 101 Stonefield Road, Blantyre and they worked flat out to clear away the debris. When the finally cleared away the fall they found to their horror that Neil McKillop's foot was trapped under a large piece of coal. James Kennedy, desperate to release him crawled under the coal and attempted to lever it up with his back while Nicol and Houldsworth took hold of McKillop's arms and shoulders and tried to pull him out. Before they got him free there was another roof fall and the men were forced to retreat. It was three hours before Neil McKillop was released and he was found to be dead.

John Kennedy's attempt to hold the coal up with his back was an act of extreme bravery carried out in unbelievably dangerous conditions, and for this he was awarded the Edward Medal Second Class. He was also presented with the Carnegie Award for his heroism as were Andrew Nicol and William Houldsworth.

JOSEPH CAMPBELL AND ALEXANDER FARQUHARSON, SWINNHILL COLLIERY, LARKHALL.

On the 7th February 1913 a firedamp explosion occurred at Swinnhill Colliery. Walter Lott (36) a fireman was known to be in the vicinity and on hearing of the explosion fireman Joseph Campbell and miner Alexander Farquharson rushed to the spot in the hope that they could get him out before he succumbed to afterdamp gas.

Both the men attempted to penetrate into the roadway but were driven back by gas. Joseph Campbell made repeated attempts to get through but without success. Desperate to get the fireman out he suddenly remembered that a line of compressed air pipes led in to the affected roadway and that there was a blank flange on the end of them some distance away. The two men then crawled to the blank flange and unscrewed the bolts holding it in position.

Joseph Campbell's hands and legs became numb from the affects of the afterdamp which was lying thick in the roadway, but he stuck to his work until the flange was removed. A length of hosepipe was passed through to the two men and the air was passed through the pipes to clear away the gas. Campbell then ran forward with the free end of the hose where the fireman was supposed to be. At this point he was overcome by gas and collapsed and was carried out unconscious by other men present. When the fireman was reached he was found to have died from the effects of afterdamp poisoning. Joseph Campbell was awarded the Albert Medal first class and Alexander Farquharson second class medals for outstanding bravery under the extremely dangerous conditions present at the time of the accident.

THE COLLIERS LASS

There lee'vd a lass in yonder toun,
And she was neither black nor brown,
In limb and lung the lass was soun',
   Her dearie was a collier
The collier's teens were hardly gane,
His wardly gear was next tae nane,
But she was simple, young and fain,
  And dearly lo'ed the collier.

Her mither warn'd her aft and lang,
Wi' psalms and scraps o' Scottish sang,
And tell't her hoo she wad be wrang,
  If e'er she wed the collier.
For though he was a strappin' cheil,
And vow'd a love as true as steel,
And might be honest, warm and leal—
   Yet still he was a collier.

But mothers shoudna fecht we' Fate—
The lassie had her ain conceit:----
She widna change her min', ner wait,
  What though he was a collier.
There wisna ane in a' the share,
Nor maybe in a hun'er mair,
She could wi' winsome Tam compare—
   In short, she wed the collier.

I needna tell hoo blithe they were,
Hoo love and hope excluded care,
Hoo heaps o' future wealth seem'd sure,
    A' won by him, the collier.
His wages were a crown a day,
Wi' fortnight's pays and uplifts tae;
Wrights, smiths and cobblers, what were they
  Compare'd tae Nelly's collier.

Their days flew bye wi lichtnin' flicht,
Twas hardly mornin' till twas nicht,
There ne'er was woman's heart sae licht,
  Nor sic a happy collier.
Aft in her sleeve sweet Nelly laugh'd,
The while her cup o' joy she quaff'd,
And won'ert folk could be sae daft
  As wish her bye a collier.

But bairns cam' hame an stauns cam' roun'
A' trade depressed brang wages doon,
Till misery an' the bare half-croun,
  Owertook her wi' her collier,
Then debts increased, arrestments cam'
An' recklessness took haud o' Tam
By hook or crook he'd hae his dram,
  They said twas like a collier.

Then sighs were frequent ---tears were seen,
At times in Nelly's hazel een,
And whyles she won'ert hoo twad been
  If she had missed her collier,
In misery's mire they deeper sank,
Their life o' joy was noo a blank,
Ah! Maidens ye the Lord should thank,
  That guides ye bye a collier.

See Nelly courin'* ower her fire,   *cowering
The 'sloven writ ower her attire,
Nae heegher* noo she daurs aspire   *higher
  Than tae her worthless collier,
And hear her speak---Alas! She swears,
And curses even amid her tears,
And kicks and cuffs the duddy* dears, *ragged
  Whas daddy is the collier.

    David Wingate,
    Circa 1860.

When David Wingate wrote this poem he was an extremely unpopular man. The vast majority of miners were decent sober hard working men. Wingate was an underground fireman at Quarter.

"JUST KEEP THE HEID"
CLYDE COLLIERY
19/5/1905

At five o'clock on the afternoon of Friday 19th May 1905, a fire broke out in the haulage engine room near the pit bottom of No. 2 Pit, Clyde Colliery and the air intake carried the smoke through into the underground workings.

In No.3 Pit, fifteen miners were hard at work and when the smell of smoke was first noticed nobody paid particular attention to it. However, when thick smoke started to appear in the roadways the men working nearest to the pit bottom made their way to the cage and signalled to be taken to the surface. It was only after they started arriving at the pit head suffering from the effects of heat and smoke inhalation that the alarm was raised.

Serious fears were then expressed for the safety of the five men and two boys working underground in sections beyond the fire, as the smoke from the burning engine-house would be carried towards them by the air current.

A rescue party of twenty five miners was formed led by the manager Robert Hepburn and oversman James Boyd. Their greatest fear was that the men trapped underground,, might try to make their way to the surface through the main roadway. The rescuers knew that the chances of the men surviving there were very low.

Five of the miners, David Gibson, Peter Daly, James McKillop, Alexander McKillop and Henry Nicol jun. were known to be working in the Pyotshaw seam while John Sharkey and Robert Dickson were thought to be in the Main coal seam.

No one knew the underground workings of the colliery any better than David Gibson, one of the trapped men who had been employed at Clyde since 1877 when he moved from Ayrshire to Hamilton. He was working back shift that day in the north dook of the Pyotshaw seam with a young lad called Peter Daly.

At ten past five the pony driver Harry Nicol had approached him and said that "there was so much smoke in the lye he could not see." Gibson joking with him said he must have set fire to some hay. Harry Nicol then returned to his work, but within a few minutes, he was back saying that an inspection had better be made. Seeing that he was concerned, David Gibson left his work to have a look round about and he had hardly reached the lye when he realised that the pit was on fire. Peter Daly, who at this point appeared from the face with some loaded hutches, was quickly dispatched to get their clothing, while Gibson ran and warned the McKillop brothers who had been working some distance away from them.

When he returned with the McKillop's, he found Daly standing with Nicol. David Gibson knew better than go near the smoke-filled roadway and by using his intricate knowledge of the workings took the lead and instructed the men to follow him to a back air course in the main lye, where he knew there was a hole they could drop through to the Pyotshaw and the Main coal. From this seam they tried to get to the pit bottom, but after travelling only 200 yards they were halted by the smoke which was getting thicker by the minute.

By this time the men were beginning to feel the effects of the smoke and James McKillop in particular was greatly affected by it. He became agitated and disorientated and appeared to give up hope. David Gibson, who kept trying to encourage and reassure the entombed miners, suggested that they retrace their steps to an air shaft he had sunk in the Main coal lye the previous year.

They reached this shaft about half-past five but found there was no rope ladder or any other means of descending the drop of 72 feet down to the Splint seam; so all five men huddled together in a small recess by the side of the shaft, where they managed to escape the worst of the rolling smoke.

Some time later Gibson looked at his watch and remarking that it was half-past seven, said as cheerily as he could "Boys, we have been here nearly two hours." They were discussing how long it would before they were found when Alex. McKillop, who was only a boy, collapsed and started to show signs of losing consciousness. David Gibson, who was seriously concerned about his condition kept the boy by his side and attempted to keep him awake by patting him on the cheek and constantly talking to him.

From the start of the emergency Gibson had assumed the role of leader, making all the decisions and now, realising that rescue might be some hours away he instructed the men to put their lights out, keeping on only James McKillop's and his own. James McKillop's condition was also deteriorating and he was very confused and agitated. He was hyper anxious about the safety of his young brother and seemed to be blaming himself for bringing him down the pit. Despite David Gibson's attempts to calm him down he couldn't be consoled and shortly after this Gibson himself lost consciousness.

Up on the surface crowds of people were standing waiting on news of the missing men. Fearing a disaster six local doctors had arrived at the colliery to offer their assistance.

About half-past ten at night, to the delighted surprise of everyone at the surface, one of the missing miners Robert Dickson stepped out of the cage at the pit-head. He said he had attempted to make his way up by No. 3 Pit but had been almost overcome by smoke and had returned to No. 2. John Sharkey he said was quite safe; he had left him only twenty minutes before coming up. A few moments later John Sharkey also appeared uninjured at the surface.

The rescue team by this time had managed to bring the fire under control and by diverting the smoke into another air course and concentrating the air flow into the main coal seam, had cleared the roadways just enough to start their search for the missing men.

It was the manager Robert Hepburn who first spotted the unconscious men huddled together. His cry of "Here they are" roused Gibson and the others. To the manager's query of how many men there were, David Gibson answered five, but unknown to him, while he had been unconscious, James McKillop, overcome and disorientated by smoke and fumes, had wandered away from the group and had been killed instantly when he fell down the air shaft.

David Campbell a member of the rescue party was sent up to the surface to fetch the doctors and he broke the news to the waiting crowd that four men were alive but seriously affected by smoke. Drs Lees, Graham and Crawford volunteered to go underground into the workings to give them medical attention and soon afterwards the miners were brought to the surface.

The four miners made a good recovery although Peter Daly and David Gibson both relapsed several days after the incident and had to return to their beds.

James McKillop left a widow and four small children, the oldest only six years and the youngest three months. His funeral took place from Holyrood Street, Burnbank the following Tuesday and between fifty and sixty mourners walked behind the hearse as it made its way to Hamilton West Cemetery. The route from his home to his final resting place was lined with large crowds of people.

Among the mourners were his two brothers, Alexander who had survived the accident and John who lived in England and who had been devastated to read of his brother's death in an English Saturday morning newspaper two hours before he received a telegram containing the bad news.

The survival of the four miners was acknowledged to be entirely due to David Gibson's leadership. David Gibson had been among the rescue parties at the carnage of the Udston Explosion in 1887 when

73 men died. He had been responsible for bringing out alive, James Lang, a Burnbank miner and one of only two survivors from the total of 71 men who had been working in the Splint coal seam. His brother John Gibson, Whitehill Road, Burnbank also took part in the rescue work at Udston and he was also underground with the rescue teams at the two Blantyre mining disasters in 1877 and 1878.

NAMES OF THE SURVIVORS

THE FIRST MEN UP THE PIT SUFFERING FROM SMOKE INHALATION

John Henderson, Windsor Street Burnbank. Edward Faloon, Blantyre Village. William Hamilton, 103 Beckford Street Hamilton. John McBride, Muir Street Hamilton. James Semple, 93 Windsor Street, Burnbank.

BRUSHERS IN THE PYOTSHAW SEAM

John Sharkey, Burnbank and Robert Dickson Beckford Street, Hamilton.

TRAPPED IN THE MAIN COAL SEAM

David Gibson, (45) Park Place, Burnbank Road, Hamilton. Peter Daly, 3 Grammar School Square. Hamilton, Alexander McKillop, boy driver, Holyrood Street, Burnbank. James McKillop, Holyrood Street Burnbank. Henry Nicol Jun., Holyrood Street. Burnbank.

Burnbank Toll. This very early photograph shows what is thought to be Burnbank Road and Ann Street.
Photograph courtesy of Hamilton Town House Reference Library.

THE 1926 MINERS' STRIKE SOUP KITCHEN AT
"THE PAWN BACK" POLLOCK STREET, BURNBANK CROSS

Outside the washhouse door. L-r Nan Wilson, Mary Copland, Ellen (Nell) Mungall, Mrs Malone, Mrs Wyper, kneeling Mary McClelland and Sarah Miller. Photographs courtesy of Helen Jacono (ne Dell,) Delaware U.S.A.

Photo taken outside Mrs Anderson's house.. L-r lady at close mouth unknown, Nell Mungall, Daisy Jack (nee Yodel), Nan Wilson, Agnes Anderson holding bell and spoon, Unknown, Mary McClelland.

OUR MINERS
BY A SCOTTISH COLLIERY MANAGER
Transcribed from the Hamilton Advertiser of 25.11.1939

More and more managers are paying tributes to the miners. It is the Welfare spirit and long may it continue. This writer can only add to the tributes already paid to them.

Their work is difficult, dangerous and often poorly paid. They may grouse at times when things are not going too well with them; but even their bitterest enemies will recognise that at times they have room for their complaints.

They are but human and very, very human at that. Their heroism is beyond dispute. It is sad at times to read of some disaster which sweeps a fine body of men into eternity. The only glimmer of light we have when a disaster does happen is the spirit of self-sacrifice which the miner shows. They do not advertise their bravery. They cheerfully take risks because they feel it is their duty to do all they can to rescue their brothers who have been embroiled in the horrors of a mine disaster.

There are miners walking the streets today—plain, unassuming chaps—who are walking epics of the highest type of heroism. They did not wait to ask whom they had to help in the dark hours. No, somewhere, there in the darkness of the mine they knew a brother was in need and it mattered not to them what creed or political faith the men belonged to.

The writer is the son of a miner and is proud of it. The pride is chastened by the fact that I never knew my father; he was killed when I was only an infant. He lies in a cemetery with not even a stone to mark his grave; a poor reward, surely, for his endeavour to wrest from nature a livelihood for his wife.

Not only was he killed, but indirectly the stone which killed him ruined the health of my mother. She seemed to droop and fade away and I at an early age was left to face the world alone, so that I know what the bereaved feel like, for I have come through the ordeal.

Oh, ye scoffers who think the miner is continually grumbling at his lot think what he has to face; and, if you could face the same trying experiences as he had and with the same spirit which he shows, then you would be entitled to call yourselves men.

During my thirty years' experience in the mines, I have come across some fine men. You will not find their names in any "Who's Who," and I doubt if they would consider it a compliment if their names were inscribed in such a book.

Many of my mining friends are deeply religious. They have wrestled with nature for a bare living and in that wrestling with nature they have come very close to Him who made this earth. They realise how unfair it is for a man to usurp, for his own purposes and for his own selfishness, what does not belong to him, but should be the heritage of all.

Often I have got into hot water for my views on this subject. I cannot see for the life of me why some should amass wealth from the mines who never dirtied their hands and others who have given all their health and strength and are now waiting when death shall release them from their ill-health. Make no mistake about it, many managers think as I do, but they place their jobs first, carry on and hope for the best!-----

There will be a storm of indignation among a section of our managers as for my next observation. But I care not. I know I am going to speak the truth and I don't care who reviles me for doing so. Were many of them honest they would speak out as I intend to do so, I hold, and, believe me, I do not come to my conclusions hastily, that if more care were taken by all concerned in and about our mines, many men who have been lost would now be alive. Far too many have been offered up as a sacrifice on the alter of a damnable greed, which can only be equalled by the militaristic mind which is prepared to shed blood so long as that blood shed is not their own blood.

We have science now, understood in a way which was never understood before. We have safety devices which should eliminate many of the dangers in mining. Why is it that disaster after disaster occurs and we know more clearly now than ever the cause of such disasters. It is because our mineowners think more of the expense of installing these safety devices than they do of the awful effects which occur because these devices have not been installed.

Mines are getting deeper. The increased temperature increases the molecular activity in the gasses with the result that when an accident happens, the explosion is intensified because of the higher molecular activity.

We have travelled a good distance since the days of Sir Humphrey Davy and the immortal John Buddle. We no longer walk into a danger zone without knowing just what danger there is. But are we fully equipped to meet the increased dangers! Look at the record of our mining disasters and that will supply the answer.

Remember, ye citizens of Great Britain, the debt we owe to our miners! Remember what Earl Haig said about them as soldiers as hard and as unyielding as the rock with which they wrestled in civilian life they stood against the waves of the field grey. And the battle was intensified only, if you will remember, that on the German side the men who also came so determinedly on were also miners! And what use did it do us? None, absolutely none, except to give us an insight into how good human material was sacrificed through the lack of brotherly love which was absent and without which the world cannot exist in peace.

Many of the shareholders in our mines, when a disaster does come, are the first to put their hands in their pockets for the relief of the victims. Oh, but had they the same degree of foresight! Do they go to their company meetings and ask what steps have been taken to make the mines safer from which they are drawing their dividends? Do they deplore the high accident rate? No; what concerns them most is what they are getting in return for the money they have invested.

It must not be understood that the writer is really caring for the political aspects of the case. I so far have mixed but little in politics; but I do say any scheme for the welfare of the miner not only in his hours of leisure, but during his working hours, should have all our wholehearted support, no matter what particular faith or creed we hold.

This is not a tirade against our colliery managers. Many of them have too great a responsibility and often it is the unexpected to them which does happen.

The article is at once meant to be in praise of the miner and in his defence. It is about time he was recognised not as a nut in the industrial machine but as a citizen who should have all the rights a citizen should have. And it is also the duty of one class of citizen to see that another class of citizen should not unduly suffer.

WILLIAM LAWSON
A HERO OF THE UDSTON COLLIERY DISASTER
28th MAY   1887

FIVE GENERATIONS
Front row l-r William Lawson, daughter Kate Davies, great great-granddaughter
Janet Jones. Back Row granddaughter Janet Neilson, great granddaughter Margaret
Jones. Photograph courtesy of Margaret McTaggart, granddaughter.

When the news that there had been a disastrous explosion at Udston Colliery Hamilton began to reach the other collieries in the area, it is said that the back roads were crowded with miners hurrying to the colliery to volunteer to go underground with the rescue teams. Among these men was William Lawson a miner at Allanshaw Colliery and he was chosen to go underground.

The rescue work was carried out under the most primitive conditions with no electricity, breathing apparatus, or any of the specialist equipment available today. All that was used in the desperate race to reach the trapped men was picks, spades, their bare hands and brute strength. William injured his hand during the rescue work and it developed into blood poisoning, forcing to return home; he was off work for 3 weeks.

William Lawson worked underground for almost 73 years; he was only seven years old when he started working in the coal mines of Lanarkshire and he continued to work until he was nearly 80. He remained an active man up until a few days before he died in January 1945 in his 99th year.

ALLANSHAW COLLIERY

KNOWN FATALITIES AT ALLANSHAW COLLIERY

DATE	NAME	AGE	CAUSE OF DEATH
31.12.1875	EDWARD CONNOR	26	Fell down shaft (multiple fractures.)
29.03.1876	JAS. PATERSON	38	Shaft accident (multiple injuries)
24.07.1876	DAVID DUNN	35	Fell 360 feet down shaft 360 (body cut through middle)
10.02.1879	HUGH BROWNLIE	35	Hit on head by cage at pithead.
10.02.1889	ROBERT KELSO	24	Fall of coal (3 tons) at face (multiple injuries)
31.08.1884	ROBERT McGUIRE	28	Roof fall (both legs broken, gangrene)
07.10.1884	NEIL REILLY	28	Roof fall 8 cwt.
14.01.1890	GEORGE BINNIE	65	Hit by hutch (survived 6 days, chest infection)
21.01.1890	THOMAS McCALL	51	Roof Fall (multiple injuries)
15.11.1899	JOSEPH MURRAY	35	Roof fall (fractured spine)
14.04.1904	PATRICK HARRISON	60	Explosion
14.04.1904	EDWARD HARRISON	20	Explosion
16.07.1911	JOHN ESPIE	43	Accident in haulage road (multiple injuries)

Names of men known to have worked at Allanshaw Colliery
James Brownlie (1879) *James Dunn,* Hope Street, Hamilton, *James Forsyth,* Church Street, Hamilton
(1879) *Thomas Inglis* (1887) *Allan Livingston,* Burnbank (1884) *Joseph Park,* manager (1887)
William Paterson, Back Row, Hamilton, (1892) *John and Joseph McCaig,* Windsor Street, Burnbank
(1894) *Antony Strain,* Quarry Road, Hamilton, *Graham Stevenson* (1887) *David Wilson, Young* Street,
Hamilton, *W.W.P. Wilson*, Manager, (1909) *John Young*, High Patrick Street, Hamilton. (1875)

*　　　*　　　*

THE KERR FAMILY
*This photograph of Barncluith Colliery miner David Kerr and his wife Jane was taken c. 1899. In the 1891
census the Kerr's were listed as having 9 children: John (17) Mary (15) William (13) David (11) Andrew (8)
Marion C. (6) Jane (4) Elizabeth (2) George (3mths). By 1901 they are living at Co-operative Buildings
Cadzow and there are another two children listed. Maggie (7) and James C. Kerr age 6. Photograph
courtesy of Wullie Kerr.*
By coincidence the photograph on the opposite page is of Mrs Jane Kerr's brother Walter Fleming.

BARNCLUITH COLLIERY

Front row great-great grandparents Mr and Mrs Walter Fleming. Back row L-r Annie Akesson, (Mother) Fanny Akesson (15 months) Fanny Stoddart (Grandmother) and Annie Devonport (great-grandmother.) c.1944 Walter Fleming started working down a coalmine when he was nine years of age. He moved to Barncluith Colliery and was there for 31 years until it closed. H e went on to work in several of the Hamilton Collieries after the closure and retired in 1932 age 73 years. He had been a miner for a total of 64 years. He died in 1945 aged 84 years.

Barncluith colliery was developed simultaneously with Silvertonhill Colliery by Archibald Russell. The two shafts were situated quite close to one another and the mines were interconnected. Between them the collieries annual output was 120,000 tons per year.

MEN KNOWN TO HAVE WORKED AT BARNCLUITH COLLIERY

Samuel Baird, Alexander Blair, James Cather, James Craig, James Dunn, John Dunnachie, Andrew Fleming, John McGuire, Thomas Scoular and Andrew Wilson, (1878) Thomas Docherty, Castle Street Hamilton, (1883) Duncan Hutton, (15) 35 Low Patrick Street, Hamilton, (1889) Robert Muir, Hugh Muir, (Contractors) Alexander Salmond, (1883) John Wilson, Low Patrick Street, (1893) Alexander Black, William Dobbie, Robert Jack, David Kerr, George Kerr, John Kerr, William McLuskey, James Moffat, James Paterson, James Ross, Dawson Smith, David Smith and James Wardrope (1896)

KNOWN DEATHS AT BARNCLUITH COLLIERY

DATE	NAME	AGE	CAUSE OF DEATH
14.06.1879	William Kerr	14	Run down by wagons (fractured thigh)
19.05.1883	John Robertson	37	Crushed to death by 1 ton of stones falling down shaft
28.01.1890	James McKay	32	Roof fall (fractured spine and head injuries).
10.09.1891	Abraham Dargue	44	Roof fall (severe injuries, ribs driven into lungs)
10.01.1893	Pat Clark	24	Roof fall (severe crushing injuries, fractured spine)
10.01.1893	John Wilson	28	Roof fall (internal injuries)
01.08.1895	Henry Burns	27	Roof fall (head injuries)
02.10.1898	Daniel Woodhead	51	Roof fall (no details)

KNOWN DEATHS AT SILVERTONHILL COLLIERY

10.06.1898 William Fleming 16 Fall of coal from face (fractured skull and spine.) William, his father and a man named Dempsey were undermining at the face and had reached 18 inches below the coal when it suddenly collapsed on top of him. His father and Dempsey frantically dug him out but he was dead. His parents were Walter and Fanny Fleming in the above photograph.

THE MINER AT HOME

Transcribed from Hamilton Advertiser of 20.6.1903

Of all the trades or professions, none are more interesting than that of the miner. When a child they were my bogie men. As I grew older, I lost my fear of them and would run to meet them coming from their daily toil and would sit for hours drinking in greedily the words that fell from their lips as they recounted the thrilling scenes, the hairbreadth escapes and the thousand and one things that were continually transpiring away down in the mine.

These stories fairly carried me into another world…….a world full of startling adventures, where every person was a great hero. To my boyish mind it seemed a glorious life, the idea of being hundreds of fathoms down in the bowels of the earth, away from God's precious sunlight, away out of the world as it seemed, appealed to me with a strange fascination.

The miner to me was a great being, a man to be looked up to and respected. But alas! Little did I ever dream what the poor, weary miner really was. I have passed my childhood days and left my boyish imaginations far behind and, (much against my parent's will) I have tasted the glorious, romantic life of the poor unfortunate miner and as I pause now and look back to the time when I made my foolish resolve to become a miner it is with bitter feelings of regret. Though hardly so either, for it has taught me many things that I had never dreamt of. It has shown me what trials and dangers bestrew the path of the luckless miner and my sole prayer to God is that the time may be not far distant when those who have the power, will take some interest in him and raise him up to a level with his fellow-beings.

Some people say "O they are never content; they are always grumbling" But God knows he has cause to grumble. Let us look at him, not as he is spoken of by his friendly enemies who are always on the alert for a chance to still crush him further down in the mire, but as men who have suffered as he has suffered, as men who have tasted the very bitter life of the miner. We will take him under five headings……His Personality, His Work, His Dangers, His Wages, and His Enemies.

Firstly………..His Personality.
In all my dealings with him, I have always found him (apart from his work) a quiet, contented, well-living man, who after his daily task is o'er, spends his evening at his own fireside mesmerising his family by telling them fairy tales concerning his work in the mines; generally honest and straightforward with friends and enemies alike; one who if taken in the right spirit, would share his last crust; one who while possessing a keen sense of wit, is brave hearted kind and true. On the whole despite the many stories we hear daily to the contrary, a straight-forward quiet living man, and the public would do well to investigate into the character of the many troubles that arise from the mines before they so harshly condemn the unheard miner.

Secondly-----His Work...
Well I can't go into particulars about his work because it is not a thing that is easily explained, so I will deal sparingly with it. In the first place it varies greatly. Sometimes he is working places as high as six or seven feet; at other times as low as eighteen inches. But no matter where he is working, you can always be certain he has to work as hard as he can. He generally goes down the pit between six and seven o'clock in the morning, and comes up again between three and four in the afternoon, running about nine hours per day. True he is in a much better condition now than he was a few years ago. Then he went to work between four and five o'clock in the morning and did not stop till about five and six o'clock at night, his day consisted of about thirteen or fourteen hours; but still though, he has a shorter day. His labour is much the same when we take into consideration the many improvements that have been made in machinery, the more enlightened times, and the little better food that the miner receives.

Thirdly………….His Dangers.
Of all the trades or professions there are none more fraught with danger to life and limb than that of

the miner. From the first minute when he goes down the mine to the last when he is leaving it life is not worth a moment's purchase. Some great authority, after reckoning up for years, stated that the death rate of the coal mines in Britain equals one third of the death rate of the battlefield, a fact, which I for one would readily believe. But he is only giving the numbers that are killed outright. He does not take into consideration those who, after working for ten or fifteen years down a filthy mine and swallowing poisonous gasses at every breath, throw up work when they are unable to follow it and after lingering for a year or two in a half-dead state, die old men at the age of thirty-five to forty years, the time when other men, who have taken better care of themselves, are only ripening into their prime.

But to his dangers. Let us commence with his descent in the cage. He has always the chance of falling off it, to be picked up a mangled corpse at the bottom. Perhaps something goes wrong with the machinery, which causes his instant destruction. Perhaps it may be the engineman loses control of his engine. A thousand and one ways to show how he may lose his life, while only descending to his work in the cage. But to proceed. After whirling through hundreds of feet of space, he reaches the bottom at last, but here his dangers are only beginning. He may perhaps have to walk a mile or so before he reaches the place where he works, which leaves him ample opportunities to leave this weary world. Maybe a stone falls from the roof killing him instantly. Perhaps a train of hutches comes along and before he has time to reach a manhole, passes over him crushing out his unhappy life. Truly his life is in danger even while only travelling to his working-place. At last he reaches his place safe and sound, but here he finds death lurking in every square foot. What dangers there are here it is impossible for me to describe, but I will name a few of the easily recognised ones.

Fourth-----Fire.

Now what is fire? It is generally understood among the miners to be poisonous gases which come out of the minerals. They accumulate in the old workings (parts of the mine that have been finished) and then move up and down the mine. Sometime they are at one end, sometimes at the other. They move very quickly too, having been known to travel about two miles in less than an hour. These gases are very dangerous and at one time it was impossible to work in the mines where there were any signs of them; but some time ago a new lamp was invented which was safe enough (the inventor boasted) to work in a gas tank and even went the length of trying it in one. Now by using this lamp in place of the naked light, it is possible to work among these gases, but great care must be taken that no matches or pipes are taken down the mine. For this reason a by-law was made by the coal companies where they found it necessarily to use these lamps, to the effect that any person found taking pipes or matches down the pit would be prosecuted by the proper authorities, but despite the care taken and the heavy fines imposed some men still take down their pipes and matches with them and it is never found out until we see in the newspapers an account of a dreadful colliery explosion resulting in the loss of many lives, the accident caused by someone lighting his pipe. The miner when looking over his evening paper and on noticing these frequent disasters, shakes his head solemnly and murmurs " God save them, poor fellows," for he knows full well within his own heart, that the same thing may happen to him at any moment. Everything that can be done to remove these gases has been tried but without avail, so the poor miner has still to run this great risk. The fire, if only in a small quantity, after it has been ignited or "kennelled" as the miners say ---will travel a considerable distance against the current of air, keeping close to the roof, until the air beats it back, so that the miner has a chance of saving his life by lying down on the road or pavement and covering his head and face with his coat while the fire passes harmlessly over him. This however is only in cases where the gases are in small quantities. If in a large solid mass, then God help them, for there is no escape. Those who are not instantly killed by the explosion are choked by the Black Damp (the explosion blowing all the air out of the place). Then even if he does escape all these dangers he still has the good chance to quit this mortal coil. A fall of coal or a bad roof would give a very sufficient excuse at the inquest. At last he comes through it all, and, very tired and weary, he treads his way home, where his anxious wife is patiently waiting his return, and as with weary feet and heavy heart he enters his poverty stricken home, he mutters a fervent prayer to god that he has been spared to see his dear ones once again.

Fifthly-----His Wages,

And what does he receive for all this hardship? A fortune? No! Wealth? No! Nothing but a miserable pittance sufficient to keep body and soul together. There has been and still is a great deal of misunderstanding as to the real wages that the miner receives, but let us look at them together. Seams from 1 _ feet thick to 2 feet .thick, rate per ton 2s 10d to 3s per ton. He is supposed to fill two tons per day making his wages about 5s 10d per day. From 2 feet to 3 feet seams rate per ton 2s 5d to 2s 6d. supposed to fill 2 _ tons per day making his wages about 6s per day. Seams from 5feet to 7 feet rate per ton 1s 4d supposed to fill 4 tons to 4.1/2 tons per day making his wages from 5s.4d to 6s per day.. Now we see how it goes. The larger the coal the smaller the tonnage rate, hence those in larger seams have just to work as hard as those in the small because they have to fill in some cases nearly double the quantity of coals to make the same wage. Thus we see that the benefits of large seams all go to the master. The above prices are as near as I can come in. There may be a little discrepancies in some cases but it is certainly not much, so that looking at these prices we can easily guess what kind of wage the miner receives. Average then at 5s 6d per day and five days per week; that gives us the sum of 27s 6d per week--- and a very princely salary for a man who has to run so many risks But even if it was that it would not be quite so bad, but I can honestly swear that out of the many thousands of miners in Scotland at the present time the bigger portion of them are not making the small sum of £1 per week and then, if coals turn a little dearer and the chance of a rise in wages comes to the miner, our friends turn round and tell us that we are to blame for it and refuse to buy the coals until they come down in price again and so ends our harvest and our little chance of better wages passes away as if it had never been.

Lastly---His Enemies.

Well I can say for one who is in such poor circumstances he can boast of an unlimited number of enemies. We will first take his enemies in the mines. Damp is a very dangerous enemy towards him and it is to blame for a great many of the bodily troubles that the miner is subjected to. You can easily tell it on him by the white cheek, the heavy eyes, the drawn up back and the racking cough which he is continuously troubled with. It begins to act on him firstly by making him a heavy sleeper and being always very tired in the morning. It goes on until he is unable to take his food, black rings appear under his eyes, his cough gets worse and so on until after a few years he finds himself unable to follow his employment. He stops work and after lingering about in a half dead state for a month or two, dies an old man at the age of from thirty to forty years, another victim of this dreadful thing called damp.

His Personal Enemies

Strange to say, in looking thoroughly into this matter we find among his most dangerous enemies men who are paid by him to look after his interests; men who at one time were miners themselves, who, while pretending to befriend him and lead him on the straight road, are simply fooling him, as has been proved over and over again. They tell him to do this and they tell him to do that and they are all the time working to their own interests, while he, poor fool, is going from bad to worse simply by taking their advice. I think I hear some of you asking, "Why don't you change your leaders?" But what difference would it make? Put the old leaders off and install new ones in their places and what would happen? Nothing; things would go on just the same. The old, old story, man sell thy brother. Burns said once that "man's inhumanity to man, makes countless thousands mourn," and I think at that time he must have been thinking of the miners and their leaders---at any rate, it suits them, to a tee.

Next, his Master--- the miner's greatest enemy.

Of all the grumbling that we hear from the miners, the cause can be easily traced to the master. He it is who, even if the miners would be content, will not let them alone, but must always be nagging at them, dog and cat style, always seeking for a chance to drag him deeper into the mire. He it is who is never content unless he is getting forty to fifty percent for his capital. He it is who must have his large profits even if he has to grind the very life and soul out of his workers. There is never any real harmony between this master and men. When the prices are high and there is a ready sale for the coals, the miner has the pull to a certain extent; but when the prices begin to go down and the markets begin to get overcrowded, then it is the masters who have the power and they do not forget to use it, forcing their workers to run a thousand risks, to breath impure air and to sacrifice their lives in the struggle to earn their daily bread while they, the masters, live on the fat of the land, get their every whim gratified, go to church every Sunday and try to quieten the prickings of their guilty consciences by giving large sums of money to this and to that --- money that rightly belongs to the hard-working slaves who are daily risking life and limb to secure a miserable existence. I have known these same gentlemen, who are looked upon as the leading lights of this very dark world by the people who do not know them, to bribe two or three hungry miners with a bottle of whisky in order to betray their fellow men and sad though it be to say, they can always boast that a few shillings could buy any of us any day. Then these people will say he is only a drunken miner; but what else is left for him to do, cast down by friends and foe alike, every shilling that he earns is having to go for bread for his starving wife and children, whose life is one long struggle for existence, looked upon by his master as little better than a dog, whose very soul is dead within him by the cruel irony of fate, whose faith in his fellow-being is killed by the treachery of his master. The above is the true honest life of the Scottish miner, and then we sing "Britons never shall be slaves!" But what better is the poor luckless miner?

THE SINGLE END

Left, the fireplace, middle shelves and window, to the right two set in beds
15ft by 10 ft including space for beds or 11 ft. 9 ft not including bed space.

Home for the miner was usually a tied house close to the colliery. This illustration of "a single end" depicts the type of housing stock built to accommodate coal miners and their families. There was no running water, sink or toilet; food was cooked on the domestic fire. Water had to be carried from a stand pipe very often some distance away. Many of the "Rows" had no washhouses and clothes were washed outside in the open and dried in a pulley above the fire when it was raining. Dirty pit clothes were hung over winter dykes or chairs until dry and then they were "dodded" (hit) off the outside wall to remove the dirt and dust for the start of the shift in the morning. In this one room the miner and his large family lived and slept, breathing in the noxious fumes from the drying pit clothes.

Ablutions took place in full view of the other occupants and privacy was an unknown luxury. Miners, returning home from the pit covered from head to toe in dirt and coal dust washed in a large portable tin bath placed in front of the fire with the women of the house attending to them. The water for the bath had to be heated either outside over a fire or over the domestic fire.

James C. Welsh Member of Parliament for Bothwell, in his maiden speech to Parliament in1923 spoke of how he had witnessed in a miners' row of about four or five hundred single ends, the sight of an injured miner lying writhing and groaning in agony in one of the two set in beds. On the other bed lay the body of a dead child and at night time during the period of waiting between death and burial, the dead child had to be lifted out to allow the living to get in. This he said was the reality of the miners' row.

PIT VETERANS WORKING IN 1944

In 1944 Lord Traprain, Regional Controller of the Ministry of Power, wrote to pit managers asking them to forward the names of men who had *"outstanding attendances and long service at their work."* The men who were chosen each received a certificate bearing the illustration of a pithead, the recipients name and a signed message of thanks from Lord Traprain.

The following 14 men were chosen from the Collieries of the County of Lanarkshire by the Pit Production Committee's of their respective pits. The yardstick for choosing them was the length of years in the industry and their general steadfastness in carrying on their duties. Between the fourteen men they had achieved a staggering 747 _ years working in the coal mines of Lanarkshire.

1. JOHN BURNS (47) West Machan Colliery started work at the coalface at the age of 14 years. Later he passed his colliery manager's examination by attending evening classes. He worked seven days a week and had not been absent from the colliery except for two day's holidays since the outbreak of war. The colliery has high average output.

2. DUNCAN CAMERON worked at Blantyreferme Colliery for 42 years except for a break during the First World War.

3. ROBERT CRAIG (72) Cornsilloch Colliery had a 41 _ years service and had only been absent for one day to attend a funeral.

4. JOHN DUFFY (76) Calderhead Colliery started work at 9 years of age and worked at the coal face from the age of fourteen. For 67 years he worked for the same firm.

5. ROBERT GALLOWAY (66) Ross Colliery was engaged at every grade of work at Ross Colliery over a period of 57 years.

6. ALEX. HENDERSON (70) Canderrigg Colliery had worked in the mines since the age of 13.

7. ROBERT HULSTON (76) Douglas Colliery had been in the mining industry for 65 years and had an almost perfect attendance record at Douglas for 46 years.

8. SAM LOVE Parkneuk and Coursington had been 50 years in coal mining. He became undermanager in 1907 and was appointed manager in 1916.

9. JOHN ROCKS (80) Tannochside Colliery had worked there for 60 years. He had been underground till 1941 and then started work on the surface.

10. JAMES RODNEY (69) Ferniegair Colliery started work in the colliery at the age of 12. He had a total of 57 _ years in the same colliery and was oversman for 36 years.

11. THOMAS SIMPSON (69) Ardencraig Colliery worked in the pits of Airdrie for 59 years. He started work at the age of 10 years.

12. WILLIAM SWAN (70) Hirstrigg Colliery commenced work at the age of 11 years. He became the manager at Hirstrigg Colliery in 1916.

13. JAMES SNEDDON (74) Broomside Colliery. Worked at Broomside for 64 Years.

14. WM. WILSON (67) Bankend Colliery started age 10 years in 1887 with 10 years underground at Fence Pit Tillietudlem.

THE LAST TON OF COAL
HAMILTON

COLLIERY	OPENED	CLOSED
Allanshaw Colliery	Approx. 1875	11th November 1912.
Allanton Colliery	Approx. 1862	February 1929
Avonbank Mine	1824	1857
Avonbraes Mine	1950	1964
Barncluith Colliery	1876	1914 or 1926*
Bent Colliery	1876	1930
Bog Colliery	Unknown	16th December 1927
Cadzow Colliery	1876	29th December 1944
Clyde Colliery	1873	November 1933
Dykehead/Summerlee	1855	10th February 1940
Earnock Colliery	1876	18th April 1942
Eddlewood Colliery	1875 Linked with Neilsland	1st August 1932
Fairhill Colliery	1891	1932
Ferniegair Colliery	1859	27th February 1947
Greenfield Colliery	1863	February 1935
Hamilton Palace Colliery*	1884	May 1959
Home Farm Colliery	Approx 1864	16th December 1927
Haughhead Colliery	1867 Merged with Ross Colliery in 1898	
Knowetop Mine	Early 1950's	1966
Merryton Colliery	Approx. 1860	Approx. 1904
Neilsland Colliery	1893	1st August 1932
Ross Colliery	1883	13th July 1945
Silvertonhill	1876	1914 or 1926
Quarter Collieries	Early 1800's	1959
Thinacre Mine	1950's	1963
Udston Colliery	1875	March 1922
Wellhall Colliery	1883	1908
Whitehill Colliery	1886 Linked with Greenfield.	Unknown

It has been very difficult to obtain the exact dates when individual collieries closed. For some reason much of this information has not been documented.

I have had to rely on clues contained in local newspaper archives and sometimes this only gives an approximate date e.g when an obituary states that a man worked in a certain colliery until it closed in 1932.

*Barncluith and Silvertonhill Collieries are documented by one researcher as having closed in 1914 but in 1926 the Hamilton Advertiser published a poem called Closing of Barncluith Colliery. This poem suggested that the colliery had closed recently.

*Hamilton Palace Colliery. Although situated inside Bothwell Parish the land where the coal was extracted lay under Hamilton Parish.

BLANTYRE

Never forgotten, the memorial service on the125[th] anniversary of the Blantyre disaster October 2002 photograph courtesy of George Hay

THE MINERS' MEMORIAL WINDOW ST. JOSEPHS R.C. CHURCH BLANTYRE

St. Joseph the carpenter.   The coal miner.

This beautiful coloured stained glass panel was jointly designed and made by designer and illustrator Andrew Foley a Blantyre man and his wife Fiona a gifted stained glass craftswoman. It is situated above the door to the interior of the church.

THE PRICE OF COAL

The sound of heavy pit boots marchin' up the street
Wis better than ony alarm cloc' tae git me oan ma feet
Anither day is startit an' little did a ken
The sorrow this day wid bring, afore the cloc' struck ten.

The weans a' ready fur the school oan this wet an' windy morn
A went tae the door tae see them awa' when I heard the dreaded horn
Ma mither rushed oot past me, her face wis filled wi' fear
The horn wis blastin' louder, blood wis rushin' in ma ear.

Rushin' tae the pit-heid, trippin o'er the stanes
Everybody runnin,' some trailin' alang their weans
Silence when we reached it, a tear at every e'e
Wringin' hauns an' prayiin,' "God please hear wur plea".

They're bringin' up mair boadies, the number's noo a hunner an' ten
Everybody's watchin', hopin' the faces they'll no ken
Don't let it be my faither or ma wee brither Drew
He never wantit tae go doon the pit, bit joabs they wur few.

Through the crowd a heard a soun' o' ma mither sorely cryin'
A pushed an' shoved tae reach her, through the deid an' dyin'
Ma faither wis lyin' lifeless, never tae speak again
He must have suffered terrible, bit noo he's free frae pain.

We didna hive tae wait long afore we goat mair news
They've noo brocht up ma brither, recognised by his shoes
Oh God ye wurna listenin' an' a feel sick wi' rage'
Oor Drew wis only a wean—thirteen years of age.

Wull someone tell me why, whit happened doon that pit
Some bloody thing went bang, wull someone tell me whit
An' whit of a' the boadies still doon in that black hole
Whit a price we've hud tae pey the day, whit a bloody price fur coal.

Etta Morrison. (Gray)
Born at 1 Dixon Street
Dixon's Rows
Blantyre

In memory of Thomas White (37) and his son Andrew (13) who both died in the Dixon's explosion on 22nd October 1877 and who were listed as bodies Nos. 110 and 129 on the list of recovered bodies. Also dedicated to the memory of all the men and boys who lost their lives that day; an estimated 216 in total.

*   *   *

The definitive number of Blantyre miners who died working in local collieries and also others outwith Blantyre will never be known. The names of 690 men and boys and 2 young girls have been researched and recorded by myself and Blantyre Heritage Group and can be seen in Blantyre Library and Hamilton Town House Reference Library.

THE WILSON FAMILY

During my research into the local mining industry I have read thousands of accident reports and have noticed that time and again the same families: fathers, sons, grandsons, uncles and cousins appear in reports of accidents or fatalities. The Bolton, Callison, McKillop and Wilson families were particularly unlucky. One woman, Elizabeth Auchterlonie of Kirkton, Blantyre lost her first husband James Nelson in the 1877 Blantyre disaster and 10 years later on 28th May 1887 death struck again when her second husband Hugh Auchterlonie and her two sons James (16) and John Nelson (14) were among the 73 men and boys killed in the Udston Colliery disaster. The suffering endured by these families and countless others must have been indescribable as time after time their world fell apart. The following story of the Wilson family of Blantyre beggars belief but nonetheless it is true.

*   *   *

Coal miner Thomas Wilson lived at Larkfield with his wife Rebecca (Welsh) and their family of seven sons and two daughters. Their house had been provided free to the family by Thomas Wilson's uncle, farmer Thomas Scott who owned the estate and farm of Priestfield.

On the 13th May 1877 one of their sons John (14) was caught in the haulage machinery in Greenfield Colliery sustaining such serious leg injuries that he died five days later in Glasgow Royal Infirmary. Five and a half months later on Monday October 22nd Thomas Wilson (45) and two of his sons Thomas (21) and James (17) lost their lives when a series of explosions swept through No 2 and 3 pits at Blantyre Collieries. Had it not been for a quirk of fate another son Walter (11) would also have lost his life. The previous week he had been involved in a quarrel at the colliery with members of a family called Russell from Greenfield, Burnbank and unknown to his father he obtained employment at Greenfield Foundry. On the morning of the disaster, he left the house to start his new job before his father was awake.

The Russell family involved in the quarrel (a father and two sons) had also left Blantyre Collieries and had obtained work at Greenfield Colliery starting the day of the disaster. The result of this quarrel between a boy and three workmates meant that all four had unwittingly avoided being killed in the explosion.

Although Walter was only 11 years old, he helped to support his three younger siblings, Robert (10) and Rebecca and David aged 6 years. The three younger children were sent to an industrial school until they reached the age of 13 years when they went out into the world to earn their living with Walter helping them to obtain employment.

Disaster however was still stalking the family and on 13th January, 1879 at Auchinraith Colliery Blantyre, another brother Francis (Frank) Wilson was seriously injured when a 4 ton piece of coal fell on him. Frank died two years later and his death was directly attributed to the injuries he had received at the pit.

Eleven years later William, twin brother of Francis, was killed outright by a roof fall at Dechmont Colliery Cambuslang. Six years after that David who had been only a child when his father was killed also lost his life at Dechmont Colliery when he was caught by a fall of stone from the roof.

Out of this family of eight sons and two daughters (one daughter Elizabeth died as a child) there were now only Walter, Robert and Rebecca left. Walter and Robert went to Callendar Colliery, Falkirk to work; but death followed them. Robert obtained serious head injuries when a steel splinter flew out of position and struck him on the head. He never really recovered from the injury and died as a result of it. In total from this one Blantyre family there were eight deaths directly attributed to underground accidents. The only male member of the family to survive to old age was Walter Wilson who in 1939 was living at Graham's Buildings, Halfway, Cambuslang.

CRAIGHEAD COLLIERY MINERS

Top row first on right James McGilligan, 11 Hardie Street, Blantyre. Photographs courtesy of Betty Longmuir nee McGilligan

THE NEXT GENERATION OF MINERS

Saint Josephs School Blantyre, c.1930 top left James McGilligan grandson of James McGilligan in above photograph.

JOHN WOTHERSPOON
COAL MINER
A BLANTYRE HERO

Photograph c. early 1900 courtesy of Jean Robertson (granddaughter.)

John Wotherspoon was born into a Baillieston mining family on 2nd December 1855. His parents were Hugh and Ann Wotherspoon. In 1877 John aged 22, was living at Larkfield and working at Blantyre Collieries when the catastrophic explosion in Nos, 2 and 3 pits claimed the lives of approximately 216 miners. He immediately volunteered as an explorer and was in the first kettle to descend one of the wrecked shafts after the explosion.

Ten years later John Wotherspoon again volunteered and was among the rescuers who entered the pit after an explosion raced through the Splint seam of the Udston Colliery half a mile from Blantyre killing 73 men and boys.

A miner all his working life, John lived with his wife and family for many years at 10 Priestfield Terrace High Blantyre. When he died in December 1945 aged 90 years, his passing marked one of the last links with Dixon's mining disaster.

DUNCAN McDOUGALL
COAL MINER
A HERO OF THE BLANTYRE DISASTER

Middle of front row ----Catherine and Duncan McDougall, photograph courtesy of Mary Wood, (great granddaughter)

Duncan McDougall was born at Shettleston, the son of Duncan McDougall a coal hewer and his wife Mary Spiers. Catherine Livingston his wife was born at Govan, her father Neil Livingston was a coal hewer and her mother was Elizabeth Cochrane; both moved to Blantyre with their parents when they were children. They were married in the E.U. Congregational Church in 1878 and the above picture shows them on the occasion of their diamond wedding in 1938. Duncan was 81 years and they lived at 17 Glasgow Road, Blantyre. They had seventeen children — twelve daughters and five sons—but only six of the daughters (all married) were alive when this photograph was taken. Two of their sons James and Neil were killed in action during World War One and another son Duncan died as the result of war wounds. Present at the diamond wedding celebrations were their six daughters and three of Mr McDougall's brothers—one of whom George, was best man at the wedding. The McDougall's had 46 grand children and 21 great-grand children.

When Duncan McDougall was 20 years of age he was working as a coal hewer at Dixon's Blantyre Collieries but on the morning of 22nd October 1877 he had for an unknown reason failed to go his work and this undoubtedly saved his life. He was among the men who after the explosion volunteered to go down underground into scenes of indescribable carnage and devastation. He worked with the rescue teams and assisted in bringing the bodies to the surface. At the time the photograph was taken he still had in his possession a pony driver's whip which he found in the pit after the explosion. He stopped working underground in 1914 and was working at Earnock Colliery when he retired in 1927. He died in 1942 aged 85 years.

UNSUNG HEROES

I sing of deeds unknown to fame,
By heroes worthy of the name—
The hardy miners, doomed to toil
Long fathoms deep beneath the soil;
Where deadly air and poisonous damp
But scarce sustain their flickering lamp.

No cheering rays of heaven illume
The darkness of their living tomb,
Where, buried from the light of day,
With brawny arms they cleave their way
Thro' stubborn walls of coal and rock;
'Midst blinding dust and stifling smoke,
That sap the life and clog the breath,
And doom them to an early death.

Yet, all undaunted in the strife
While brightly burns the lamp of life,
From day to day, with ready click,
They ply the hammer and the pick;
Or wield the ponderous sledge of steel,
Till nerves and sinews tingling reel;
Till arms grow numb, and down their cheeks
The grimy sweat, in channelled streaks,
Proclaim the glowing open pores,
And smartly nip their bleeding sores.

Mark yonder toiler, sore beset,
With sodden garments, reeking wet,
With precious sweat, that slowly glides
Adown his breast and heaving sides;
With swinging swish of heavy pick,
His blows are falling fast and thick
Upon the hard, unyielding rock
That all his efforts seem to mock
And bar his way to precious bread
By which his little ones are fed.

In stooping posture, bending low,
See how he swings him to and fro;
Till rocks in splinters flies around
And burning sparks, with hissing sound
Dart here and there, like meteors bright,
Athwart the gloomy face of night.
Enshrouded, 'midst the dust and haze,
His smoky lamp seems all ablaze;
Its crusted wick and lengthened flame
All unmistakably proclaim
The lack of pure and healthy air
That silently the lungs impair.

Anon, he wipes his grimy face
And snatches just a breathing space
To stretch his limbs and quickly eat
His morning's meal, made double sweet
By hours of toiling on his might
That whet and spur the appetite.
His cap and lamp are laid aside;
His printed 'kerchief, well supplied
With bread and butter, cake and cheese,
Is spread across his grimy knees.
No rich repast. No dainties there,
But plain and honest homely fare,
Washed down with milk or tepid tea,
Renews his lost vitality
And fits him further in the strife
To battle for the means of life.

With anxious care he looks around
With ears alert for every sound-----
The snapping props, the rumbling din
Of falling rocks, that hem him in;
The deadly gases snakelike hiss
From open seams and crevices;
The beaded damps, that pattering drop
From fungus-bearded roof and prop;
Or volley's blast, with distant boom,
Re-echoing from room to room.

But hark! What sound is that he hears,
That fans to flame his smouldering fears?
It bursts amidst the gloom
Like thunderbolt of doom,
And hurls him, with the shock
Against the jagged rock.
He struggles to his feet,
But ere he can retreat,
A rush of air and dust
A fearful, whizzing gust
Comes sweeping up the track,
And whirls him on his back.

In agony and pain
He rallies once again
And runs, with frantic speed,
To meet the wild stampede
Of miners, half attired.
"Oh God! the pit has fired,"
He shrieks in wild dismay,
And hurries on his way,
In breathless, eager haste,
Thro' ruin wild and waste,
O'er twisted, riven rails
And broken brattice deals
That, littered, lie around.
He clears them with a bound
And ploughs his way across
Great wreaths of drifted dross
.

On hands and knees he creeps
O'er rugged, rocky heaps,
Thro' water, slush, and mud,
All bruised, and sore distressed,
With wildly heaving breast,
Still groping all the way,
At last the light of day
Appears upon his sight,
Where men in woeful plight
And helpless youths are found
All wildly crowding round,
With agonising cry,
"O God, and must we die"

Awhile in abject dread and fear
All herded close, like stricken deer
They stand benumbed and stupefied;
Till dauntless Courage, close allied
To craven fear, resumes her sway
Triumphant o'er the trembling clay,
Then heroes, minus cap or lamp,
Rush bravely thro' the after-damp
To rescue those who, haply, may
Have fallen helpless by the way.

There fathers go to seek their sons
And swell the list of missing ones;
And sons their fathers seek in vain;
While shrieks and groans and cries of pain
Around on every side are heard
From men, with faces scorched and scarred;
With hair all singed from off their heads,
And tattered skin that hangs in shreds,
Like tissue paper, limp and wet,
From arms and limbs as black as jet.

From lamps and flasks is handed round
The ready oil to bath each wound
And woollen jackets, scarfs and caps,
Are temporised to serve as haps*,   *covers
To shield them from the frosty air
Till loving hands, with kindly care,
Shall woo them back to health and strength;
Or hap*, to linger on at length   *perhaps
In agony till kindly Death
Relieves them of their troubled breath.

O thou, that breath'st the air of heaven
To whom the blessed light is given
The birds, the sunshine and the flowers
To sheer thee thro' thy waking hours--
If ere compassion's kindly ray
Illume they breast, and points the way
To Mercy; then in Mercy's name,
In trumpet tones aloud proclaim
Who toils in caverns, foul and grim
Far down the deep, dark-throated mine,
Debasing soul and form divine.

'Tis not the struggle of a day,
Nor glory won in single fray
But silent valour of a life
That marks the hero in the strife.
'Tis he who battles bravely on,
When life and hope are almost gone
With Mother Earth until she yields
The treasures of her mines and fields,
To keep in comfort and in life
His brother fainting in the strife.

Then honour to whom honour's due--
The brave, the valiant and the true
Those men of ruffed, sterling worth
Who disembowel Mother Earth,
And give the product of her womb,
To cheer us through a world of gloom.

George Cunningham. (Pate McPhun,) circa 1912.

181

OLD HIGH BLANTYRE

Above Priestfield Terrace, c. 1957
Photographs courtesy of Jean Robertson

Priestfield Terrace with High Blantyre Parish Church and manse beyond the bridge, c. 1957

Dixon's No. 1 Colliery seen through the white gates, c. 1957

Priestfield Terrace taken from the railway bridge, c. 1957

HIGH BLANTYRE PARISH CHURCH WOMEN'S GUILD

L- to r.. Mrs Ferguson, Isabel McIntyre, Mrs Campbell, Helen McIntyre, Mrs Wotherspoon,
Mrs McLachlan, Mrs McCaskie, Mrs Robertson, Mrs Liddel, Mrs Walsh c. 1950's
Photograph courtesy of Jean Robertson.

High Blantyre Parish Church halls
Photograph courtesy of George Hay

A BLANTYRE MINER'S WIFE

*Maggie Russell with
her eldest son John outside
her home at Glen Cottage
Auchinraith Road, Blantyre
July 1902*

Margaret (Maggie) Russell nee Spiers was born in East Kilbride where her ancestors had lived since the early 1700's. She moved with her parents to Blantyre when her father John Spiers changed his employment from an ironstone miner in East Kilbride to a coal miner at Blantyre. John had gone to America several times but his wife would not go and he gave up trying and came home for good. Maggie was a dressmaker when she married Blantyre coalminer Adam Russell. Adam sailed from the Broomilaw, Glasgow on the Columbia and arrived in America on the 12th September 1904, he was going to pave the way for his wife and children to come over. In 1905 in a letter to her sister Annie who was already in America, Maggie appears quite reluctant to leave Scotland. However she left in 1906 taking her three little boys John, Adam and Willie. A further three children James, Margaret and Gilbert were born in Farmington Illinois, Maggie aged 36 years died in March 1916 after falling and injuring herself while tidying the back yard on Hogmanay. Adam brought the six children back to Burnbank. Willie the child she was so worried about survived and was over six foot tall. He was Chief Constable of St. Boniface Police in Manitoba Canada.

A LETTER TO AMERICA

My Dear Sister,

     I really do not know how to begin to write a letter to you as I feel ashamed for not writing but I have had so much to do and I was always hearing from mother. As you know the children have all had the fever and Willie had diphtheria but they are all better now but Willie and it has left him a poor wee thing, he is so delicate. He has been ill for a fortnight now and he is looking so very ill, he looks like he is going into a decline. I have an awful work with him he is just like a baby but the other two are healthy enough.

Adam Russell

I had a letter from Adam and he wants me to come out with John and Kate but I am waiting on another letter to see what he is going to do. The doctor says that it might be the life of Willie. If I should come I will come your way first along with Kate and John for a few weeks. You might tell me what I should bring for the boys to wear if I do come. Adam seems to be getting on better and for the sake of Willie I would come. Grace had another daughter she is keeping very well and what a great big baby it has a face as big as Maggie's and black hair, it is like my father.

I hope you are all keeping well; I will need to draw to a close I will write again soon and let you know what I am going to do. With love to Jim and yourself and the children I remain your loving sister Maggie.   xxxxx from the children to Jacky and baby.

THE DEPRESSION

Between 1913 and 1929 well over 1,000,000 men and boys were employed in British Collieries but this was to change dramatically as the demand for coal fell. The years between 1928 and 1936 were desperate times for the mining communities with many of the pits idle. It was calculated that 25% of miners were either out of work or working short time. Unemployment was the spectre that hung above the head of every mining family and starvation was always lurking around the corner.

The combined effects of the world economic slump of the nineteen thirties and the exhaustion of the coal seams resulted in the closure of many local collieries, bringing widespread suffering to mining communities throughout the county.

In October 1936, 800 Scotsmen set off on a hunger march to London in protest at the unemployment situation. Among them were the following 24 Blantyre men: Edward McLaughlin, M. McNaught, James Innes, M. Cumminskey, J. Shearer, A. Bell, Wm. McFadyen, W. Marshall, T. Brannan, Edward McGuire, D. Kane, James Keary, J. Higgins, A. Russell, James Anderson, W. Allan, James McVey, D. Kelly, J. Duffy, A. Devlin, J. McLean, G. Flynn, J. Carroll and P. Miller.

THE MINERS' RAW

When clachans are quate*　　　　　　　　*quiet
On a Saturday Nicht,
And black is the grate
Ance* wi' burning coals licht*,　　　　　*once, *light
There's something ado wi' the miners—
An something that's no' very richt.

Nae clatter* and clang　　　　　　　　*loud sharp sounds
Frae the derlect pits;
Nae shutters play bang
Whaur the miners' raw sits;
A *gey missley soond* in the mornin'　　* much missed sound
Is the scuffle* o' tackitty buits.　　　　* noise

Nae mair will the man,　　　　　　　*no more
As he gangs oot tae fen'*　　　　　　　*work
Wi' the door in his haun'
Shout his Guid mornin's ben*,　　　　　*through
Nae mair will his labours be wantit
He's feenish'd*—that's a' he's to ken*　*finished *know.

The mither and wife
Has her *thochts *she maun thol*,　　*thoughts *must put up with
For sherp* as a knife　　　　　　　　*sharp
Stabbin' into her soul,
Is the fear that weans'll gang hungry
And steekless* when "He's" on the dole.　*without meat

Ay! Broken at last
Are the hopes that were bent;
Gey cauld is the blast
When on miner's it's sent;
And daurk* is the cloud that is hinging*　*dark *hanging
Oot owre his wee world o' content.　　*J.F. Circa 1929.*

LITTLE MOTHER
(IN A DEPRESSED AREA)

One at her breast and two at her feet,
Trudging along the dull, squalid street;
Face lined with care but comely and sweet—
   Little mother.

Irksome her labours tending her flock,
Often her day a round of the clock;
Felon in cell! Your comforts but mock
   Little mother.

Often her lot is squalor and want,
Wolf on the doorstep hungry and gaunt;
Cares of the day her fitful dreams haunt
   Little mother.

Same daily struggle, on thro' the years,
Only her courage quelling her fears;
No time for shedding vain, idle tears—
   Little mother.

Sister of ease, your scorning forbear,
She envies not your freedom from care,
Counting her blessings precious and rare—
   Little mother.

You, without daughters! You, without sons!
Think of the trials, the risks that she runs;
Builder of Empires! Feeder of guns!—
   Little mother.

One at her breast and two at her feet—
Symbol of womanhood, noble, complete;
Honour the name—a name ever sweet---
   Little mother.

TOM McEWAN, Circa 1939.

DIGGING THEM OUT
A TRAGEDY OF THE MINE

BEFORE.
How we curse and swear,
At stones we tear
Of the bloodied cenotaph
    Piled up there,
While the moans and groans,
From beneath the stones,
Tell of the crushed
    And mangled bones.
Of the men we know
Whom an hour ago,
Were our mates and comrade
        Here below.

DEATH.
There's the click! clock! cluck!
Of the dripping muck,
As we hew and hack
    Where the timber struck.
There's a tinge of blood
In the slimy mud,
That oozes round like a
    nightmare flood.
There's an eerie feeling
Sets the brain a-reeling,
As though Death's hand's to
    Each man stealing.

Hold thy burden, bear it slowly,
Careful, over rail and rope.
Breathe a curse or prayer holy,
    Caution while there's life, there's hope.
"Gently, brothers, gently ease him."
"Water! Let me hold his head."
"Christ! Can none of us appease him."
"Mighty God! But old Jim's dead!"

AFTER.
There's a torture trail,
Over rope and rail,
There's a mangled body
Crushed and frail.
There are moist eyes red,
As they bow the head,
And mourn their comrade
Newly dead.
There's a parson's goal
For his holy soul,
But we reckon'd the cost
 In the price of coal

If blood be the price
We have paid it twice,
There's an alter red,
 With our sacrifice,
We're a grain of sand,
In the Master's hand,
But there's something wrong,
 If---you understand,
It's not—that we thought
Of the soul God got,
But more of the flesh----
        So cheaply bought.

Will a few tears shed
For our mangled dead,
Provide for a roof
    O'er the children's head?
Will the sleet and snows
When the cold wind blows
Consider their worn and
    Ragged clothes?
Will it ease their woes
Or their benumbed toes
To say you love them?
    Goodness knows!

There's a vacant chair
By a fireside bare,
There's an aged woman
    With silvery hair,
There's a graveyard stone
Where the wild winds moan
There's a wife and child,
 In a cot---Alone.
But—they wonder why
As they sit and sigh,
The fates that decreed that
    He should die.

J HIGGINS,
Circa 1927.

"WHERE ARE YOU LADS?"
A CAVE IN
AT
BARDYKES COLLIERY
21ˢᵗ March 1936

Of all the types of accidents in coal mines the roof fall must be at the top of the table for killing and maiming. Many of these accidents resulted in single deaths but occasionally a number of men were caught by the fall with the result that several of them were killed and such an accident took place at approximately 7.30pm on Saturday 21ˢᵗ March 1936 when seven brushers were at work in "Hawthorne's section" at the Bardykes Colliery situated between Blantyre and Cambuslang.

The section of the roadway that the men were preparing for the miners was 9 feet high and 12 feet broad and the brushers had been working away without any problems when, in the words of *Campbell Hawthorn* one of the survivors:-- "*Suddenly there was a crack from the roof.*" Sensing what was happening he threw himself to the side of the road where caught by falling debris, he lay unconscious for some time. When he came round it was "*pitch dark*" and he could hear stones falling from the roof and the groaning of the pit pony which had also been caught in the fall. As he attempted to drag himself clear of the danger area he was hit several times by debris, but eventually reached safety.

William Evans another member of the team was miraculously uninjured and pulling himself clear of the fall, he rushed down the road returning with a lamp. He could hear shouts and groans of the men trapped under the debris and when he called out "*Where are you lads*"? *Thomas Coulter's* muffled voice replied "*I am here. I am on the left side.*" *Evans* in an attempt to locate him asked if he could see the light, but *Coulter* replied "*my face is covered.*" The sound of *Thomas Coulter's* voice was getting weaker and *William Evans* made a desperate effort to clear a way through to him, but the size of the fall was so great that he made little headway.

Campbell Hawthorne, lying helpless with a back injury could offer no assistance as *William Evans* tore at the rubble with his bare hands to reach *Thomas Coulter.* The trapped man who was getting weaker by the minute knew that the battle was being lost and said to William Evans "*I am done for*" and then there was silence. *Evans* ran to the lamp-lighting station to report the accident and within a short time the first rescuers arrived and took charge.

As the news of the accident reached Blantyre and Cambuslang, large crowds of anxious relatives began arriving by bus and gathered at the pit head. The sight of Father Bernard Keenan, priest at St. Joseph's Roman Catholic Church Blantyre arriving, confirmed to the waiting crowd that a serious accident had taken place.

Underground one mile from the pit bottom, rescuers were working flat out in extremely dangerous conditions to try to release the men who were trapped. A large section of the roof had come down and there was a grave danger that the volunteer rescuer teams themselves could be caught by further falls. The men worked in relays throughout the night but it was eighteen hours before the last trapped miner was reached.

Five men had lost their lives; *George Kirk* (48) 18 Park Street Cambuslang had worked at Bardykes Colliery for 25 years. George should not have been working but had gone out after a phone call from the contractor to say two men were unable to come out. He was married with four children. *Thomas Coulter* 6 Bothwell Street, Cambuslang, was originally from County Armagh and married with eight children. Thomas's daughter Alice was working as a cook at the chapel house of the Sacred Heart at Bridgeton when she found out about the accident. She was serving breakfast to one of the priests when she caught a glimpse of the headlines in his newspaper. Knowing that her father was working at the pit she made enquiries and was horrified to find out that he was one of the trapped men. *Robert Dawson* (52) 32 Church Street, Cambuslang was married with six children under fourteen years and his wife was due a baby any day. Robert had worked at Dechmont colliery for 30 years before moving to Bardykes Colliery. A member of the Salvation Army he also had a son by a former marriage who was living in New Zealand. *Gabriel Roy* of 520 Hamilton Road, Flemington, Cambuslang had worked as a shanker* for many years at Loanend Colliery and had only been at Bardykes for nine months. A quiet and courteous man he had four adult daughters and one son. The fifth victim, Irishman *James Conlan* (47) 72 Glasgow Road, Blantyre was a hard working man always ready to work overtime to provide for his wife and three children: James aged five years, Theresa, age eight and Jane nine months. Resident in Blantyre for fifteen years Jimmy was highly respected. A soldier in the Transport Corps throughout the First World War, he had three brothers in the same regiment who lost their lives.

*   *   *   *a man who sunk and maintained the shafts

John Cornfield

BARDYKES COLLIERY
3rd AUGUST 1938

The first day in a new job brings with it a mixture of excitement and anxiety but for *John Cornfield* (18) his first day underground at Bardykes Colliery was one he was never likely to forget. John of Logan Street, Blantyre was working at the bottom of No. 1 Pit with *Martin Summers*, Udston, Burnbank, *Robert Keir*, Colebrook Street, Cambuslang and *Harry Kerr*, Rosendale Place, Blantyre. Only a short time into their shift the pit bottom was suddenly plunged into darkness followed by a loud rumbling sound. John Colligan shouted "run for your lives boys" just as the 1380 ft. deep shaft began to collapse.

In the pandemonium, the men scattered in all directions and *John Cornfield*, who was unfamiliar with the layout of the pit, became disorientated and got lost in one of the numerous roadways which led off from the pit bottom. In the pitch blackness of the mine it was some time before the other men found him wandering dazed. Miraculously although all four men were suffering from shock, none of them had been hurt. They were eventually led to safety and taken to the surface via another interconnecting shaft.

Almost 1000 men and boys were made idle by the collapse of the shaft and it was to be almost six months before it had been repaired and work was able to be resumed. Despite his experience John Cornfield went back to Bardykes and was to work there for almost twenty years. He then found employment at the steelworks and then went into insurance. Having moved to Cambuslang when he married, he had a very a successful career in local politics, becoming a Glasgow City Baillie and district councillor.

Women who worked at the picking tables sorting coal from waste were called brass pickers. Bothwell Castle Colliery c. 1914. Front row 2nd left Helen Mungall nee Rodger, photograph courtesy of Vicky Shickell (granddaughter)

The Duchess of York opening the bowling green at Blantyre Miners Welfare. The Duke of York can be seen in the background. The bowling club is now closed and about to be demolished to make way for flats..

THE "STAY IN" STRIKE
AT
DIXON'S No. 2 COLLIERY
BLANTYRE
19.9.1936

Blantyre was no stranger to pit strikes and the on at Dixon's No. 2 Pit on Monday 7th September 1936 over the rate of pay for back-stripping appeared to be no different from any other strike. After negotiations with the pit management officials from Lanarkshire Miners' Union recommended that the men return to work on the Thursday morning.

However, when the day-shift miners resumed work, a few of them had ideas different from the official union instructions. Once underground they appear to have put their thoughts forward to the other men, with the result that 54 miners went back on strike; but this time the strike was like no other; they were remaining underground and having a "stay-in".

Although this type of strike had been carried out in Wales, it was a first for the Scottish coal field and it took everyone completely by surprise. Mr McCall the manager of Dixon's reacted by refusing to allow any food to be taken underground and when this news filtered out to the public, thousands of people arrived at the pit to show their support for the striking miners. An ugly situation beginning to develop outside the pit was only averted when information was received from the men underground that despite the official ban, food had reached the men.

Mrs Alex. Richmond waiting for her husband.

The following day, (Friday) pickets were placed at other collieries throughout the district, with the result that every one of them came out in sympathy with their Blantyre comrades. All of the miners, 500 in total at Wm. Dixon's Blantyre No. 1 and No. 2 came out as did 700 at Priory Colliery, 800 at Bardykes Colliery, 500 at Newton Colliery, 600 at Earnock Colliery, 600 at Blantyreferme and 700 at Bothwell Castle Colliery - a total of 4,400 miners.

With the situation escalating hourly there was a real threat that the whole of the Lanarkshire coalfield might become involved in the strike. There was deadlock with McCall, No.2's manager about the question of food being taken underground to the striking miners. Attempts by union officials to persuade the Mines Department and Dr. McCallum Lang interim Medical Officer of Health for the County of Lanark to intervene had been unsuccessful.

A miner suffering from influenza returned to the surface along with three young lads of 15 years of age, but the remaining 49 strikers appeared to be prepared for a long *"stay down."*

A letter from the miners was brought up by a union official and in it the men said that they were prepared to die down the mine rather than abandon their demands. It also pointed out that the manager had been underground twice that day, but had refused to negotiate with the men.

The Richmond family

A rumour then went about that Mr McColl was being held captive at the pit bottom but this he denied this when he returned to the surface. It appears that his delay underground had been due to a broken pump. However, shortly afterwards, everyone, with the exception of colliery management staff was removed from the vicinity of the pithead.

The striking miners kept their spirits up by playing games of dominoes and cards which had been brought down by the men who planed the strike and despite having no food or fresh water, the miners were determined to remain underground until their demands were met.

An unconscious miner being brought up the pit

Late on the Friday night, local doctor George Hutchison accompanied by the Chief Constable descended the mine to medically examine the miners. When he returned to the surface at three o'clock on Saturday morning it was to report that fourteen of the men were showing signs of "definite weakness." He also gave his opinion on the necessity for clean drinking water being taken underground. Dr. Hutchison refused a profession fee for his visit.

Local M.P. Allan Chapman had arrived from London and offered his neutral services to both the miners and management. He spoke to the mine manager on the Saturday and pointed out that he was particularly concerned about the question of drinking water. He returned on the Sunday to talk to Mr Ritchie the managing director of Wm. Dixon's Collieries and was kept waiting for three hours and was seen only after intervention by Chief Constable Keith. Mr Ritchie remained steadfast in his decision not to send down water or food.

Dr Hutchison accompanied by three local councillors

By the early hours of Sunday morning after more than 70 hours underground, only 49 men remained. Robert Swinburn and William Brown had been brought up shortly before midnight in an exhausted condition. At 2 a.m. Alexander McLeod was brought up unconscious. After treatment in the ambulance station he was taken home.

On Sunday afternoon at three o'clock, 15,000 people gathered near the pit and when the managing director's refusal became known, there was an obvious change in the attitude of the crowd which gave fears that riots would take place. As night approached, only the knowledge that Mr Chapman and County Councillors were still negotiating on the question of drinking water prevented the crowd rushing towards the colliery.

The striker's families were becoming increasingly concerned about their health and eventually Thomas Crane and John Miller were allowed down to see them. After an hour underground they returned and were making a report to officials of the Lanarkshire Mineworkers Union when it was announced that the strikers were on their way up to the surface. The 49 men had terminated the underground "*stay in*" and when they arrived at the surface, it was to a tumultuous welcome from the thousands of people waiting at the pithead.

The men who lived locally were able to walk home and others who resides some distance from the pit were taken home by car.

Mrs Wyper with her husband and Thomas Richmond.   *Wm. Keenan receives a refreshment from his wife*

The following day 7000 people attended a meeting at Blantyre Public Park where some of the strikers recounted their experiences during the four day strike. Allegations were made that lights had been extinguished, fans slowed down and the water supply cut off. One of the men jokingly said that they had considered eating one of the pit ponies, but the management had brought them up.

The supporting industrial action at the other collieries was called off, but Dixon's Pits remained on strike for a further week until the men voted to return to work with the cause of the strike still unresolved. One week later a satisfactory agreement was reached between men and management on the rates paid for back-stripping.

REUNITED WITH THEIR FAMILIES

Reunited with their families.

Crowd waiting outside the pit for news.

The following names are of some of the miners who remained underground.
William Adam, 211 Main Street, High Blantyre. James Allan. William Brown, 13 Clyde Row, Auchintibber. Thomas Boyd, (24) William Keenan. Alexander McLeod, 15 Maxwell Cres. Blantyre. Alexander (Kilty) Orr, 207 Main Street, High Blantyre. ----- Paterson. Thomas Richmond. Peter Rooney. Michael Stein. Robert Swinburn, Dunnsland, Udston. Brothers, Samuel and James Weir. John Wildman and ----Wyper

THE WEANS O' BAIRDS ROWS c. 1929-30

Front row boy with ball James McGilligan, photograph courtesy of Betty Longmuir daughter of James McGilligan

Top left the 3 rows of houses are Bairds Rows on a snowy winter's day   *Mrs Brown outside Bairds Rows.*

ANNA'S STORY

Anna Limerick was born in Blantyre on the 22nd of December 1925 the second of the six children. Her parents were coal miner *Thomas Limerick,* a Blantyre man and her mother Annie Keary who came from Flemington. The children *Jack, Anna, May, Samuel, Tom*, and *Betty* lived with their parents in a room and kitchen at Bairds Rows. Jack died from pneumonia aged four.

Life was unbelievably hard for miners' wives; wages were at starvation level and the houses they lived in were either single end's (one room) or room and kitchen (kitchen with bedroom) with outside toilets and washhouses. It was a struggle to make ends meet and one way of clothing the children was to buy second hand clothes off the packwife who arrived from Glasgow by train every Saturday morning. *Annie Limerick* along with many of the other wives from Bairds Row would be up early and away to meet her as she arrived at Blantyre railway station. This way they would get the best of what was in her pack.

The packwife earned a living by selling second hand clothing which she carried on her back wrapped in a sheet and from her, Annie would buy "*knickers and simmits*" for the children. Another way to get clothes was to buy them from "*Johnnie the darkie*" who came round the doors once a week with his case. Anna's mother had a great deal of respect for this traveller and got on well with him.

At that time there were also quite a few tramps and street singers travelling about the country and they could always be sure of a meal at the Limerick house.

Her father *Thomas (Tam) Limerick* worked as a coal cutting machineman at the Priory Colliery. He started there when he was 13 years old. In 1940 Tam had to leave the Priory because years of kneeling had caused serious damage to his knees. He became an ambulance man.

Because he was now no longer employed at the pit, Tam had to vacate the tied house which went with the job. In Lanarkshire at that time, there was such a shortage of houses that it was almost impossible to obtain one, so, to keep a roof over their heads, Anna as the oldest child of the family had to leave her job to work at the picking tables at the Priory Colliery.
.

Anna, a tall attractive girl had left school at 14 and had been working at Richmond Park Laundry, Rutherglen. She was there when many of the uniforms which had been worn by the soldiers evacuated from Dunkirk arrived for cleaning.

On her first day at the pit, she arrived with her face covered in spots from a recent bout of chickenpox. The girls who were to be her workmates eyed her up and down, decided she may be infectious and refused come close to her or share anything with her. It wasn't long however before she was accepted by the girls and was affectionately known as "*big Anna*".

Anna wasn't very impressed by the dark dusty noisy environment when she first started at the pit head and the noise frightened her, but soon got used to it. She had to learn how to work at the "picking" where she sorted out the coal from the waste and she was shown her job by the other girls. There were approximately fifteen to twenty girls who stood at either side of the table.

When the coal came down the tumblers on to the moving table, it very often included huge stone boulders which would get stuck and then Anna or one of the girls would have to climb on to the table and lift them off. These stones and there were many of them, were broken down into a disposable size by the girls wielding picks and hammers.

To get to her work *Anna* would meet *Mary Cowan, Cathy Breslin, Rita Robertson* and *Nellie Cross* who also lived at Bairds Rows and they would set off at 4.45a.m.to walk the 2 miles to the Pit for a 6 o'clock start. Of the girls who worked at the picking tables only six came from the "Rows," the rest including *Kate Callahan, Rose, Alice* and *Lizzie Murray* and *Alice Donnelly* came from Blantyre Village.

On a Monday morning the girls would leave for their work wearing spotlessly clean dungarees and boots so carefully polished they could see their reflection in them. On their heads they had scarfs worn like an "Arab headdress" which covered their hair and neck. The colour of the scarf worn depended on the girl's religion; blue for Protestant and green for Roman Catholic.

Anna recalled how the girls liked to keep themselves as neat and clean as they possibly could and so they took great care with their appearance before they left for their work. However, before they had been 2 minutes at the picking table's, huge thick clouds of coal dust had enveloped everything in sight getting into their mouth, ears and eyes and up their nose. The dust was so thick and their faces so black it was difficult for the girls to recognise who was standing next to them. All that could be made out was white teeth flashing when she smiled. The women who worked at the picking tables were called the "*stoories*" because they were always covered from head to toe in coal dust. Gloves were unheard of and they developed large hacks on their hands.

For Anna, breakfast at the colliery consisted of 4 rolls and bacon made up by her mother and dropped off by her brother on his way to school. Her father had made her a tea can by punching holes in the sides of an empty syrup tin and then attaching a piece of wire for a handle. Tea was made by holding the tin over the coal fire in the bothy until the water boiled. Sometimes it took so long to boil, their break was nearly up. That was how the girls had their breakfast.

There was the luxury of an outside flushing toilet at the pit head that the girls could use, but there was no hand basin or any facility for washing their hands so their breaks were taken with coal black hands.

There were no pit-head baths and when they went home, it was to houses without bathrooms or hot water. Prior to her arrival, Anna's mother would go in and out the washhouses at the "Rows" looking to see if any of the women doing their washing had any *"sapples"*(soapy water used for washing clothes) that they were finished with. If there were any, they would be carried back to the house and Anna used them to wash, if not, then water had to be heated on the fire so she could give herself a wash down. If she was lucky, she bathed in the big portable aluminium bath which would be placed in front of the fire.

Because of the lack of bathing facilities it was extremely difficult to get rid of all the fine coal dust which clung to her hair and skin, no matter how hard Anna scrubbed. Occasionally, she would be sweating at the dancing and coal dust would run down her face from her eyelashes.

Anna worked two shifts, dayshift and backshift and was working backshift on the night of the Clydebank blitz. There was an anti aircraft station in a field at the side of the Pit and the sound of the guns firing on the German bombers was deafening. At the end of the shift the guns were still blazing away and the girls crawled two miles on their hands and knees through bushes at the side of the road in an attempt to avoid the shrapnel which was raining down from the shells exploding above their heads.

Remains of the Ack Ack gun emplacement at the Priory Pit

Anna's father *Thomas Limerick* was trained in first aid and he was among the large convoy of Blantyre personnel who left to assist at Clydebank. It was a week before he came home and it was months before he could eat meat again after witnessing some of the sights he saw at Clydebank.

The miner loved practical jokes and one day Anna was caught out by one played on her by a miner she had spoken to before he went underground. At times when the men came on to start their shift some of the girls would shout over to them asking for a bit of their pit piece, *(packed lunch)* and Anna had asked this man if he had any to spare. He said he would send it up later. True to his word a piece wrapped in paper was sent up tied to a "tree" (pit prop) with a note marked "for big Anna." Delighted Anna opened the paper only to find a dead mouse inside two slices of bread; another time, much worse than the dead mouse came up between two slices of bread, but after the initial shock, the girls found it funny.

Anna's weekly wage of 12/6d was given to her mother and she got 2/- back for her own pocket if her mother could afford it. To supplement her wages she would send her young brother down to the river Clyde to bring home a barrow load of clay. There were three different types of clay, light, medium and dark. Anna would mix the clay and fashion it into balls and then sell it in Glasgow for a shilling a ball. The clay was used by the women for tanning their legs because there were no stockings to be had due to war time shortages. Anna also applied the clay to her legs and then she would pencil in a black heel and seam which made her legs look as though she were wearing stockings.

Anna met her soldier husband *Ernest Keys* when he and three other sergeants appeared instead of the six privates who had been invited to bring in the New Year at her family home. She had never seen any of them before that meeting, but they were far from home and welcome at her parent's house to join in the celebrations. Ernie as he was called, instructed soldiers how to use radar equipment. He had been an apprentice stonemason before enlisting.

That first Hogmanay at Anna's home her mother asked him what his job had been prior to the war. When he said a mason she told her husband. Well! *Tam Limerick* was a free mason and he thought the soldier was one of the brethren and started shaking his hand. Poor Ernie who hadn't a clue what was going on, nearly got his thumb broken by Tam giving him the Masonic handshake.

When the war finished, the men came back to work at the pithead and the "*stoories*" had to give them back their jobs. Anna went to work at the Echo factory at Cambuslang and then several months later her sister got her a job at the Co-operative paper mill at Farm Cross, Rutherglen. Anna married Ernie and left Blantyre to settle in Edinburgh. The day she left home it was as though she was going a thousand miles away; everyone was crying their eyes out, including Anna, who had hardly travelled more than ten miles from Blantyre.

After he was demobbed her husband finished his apprenticeship and then went on to Herriot Watt College and trained to become a builder's estimator. Anna and Ernie had a good marriage, her husband died many years ago. She has one son and three grandchildren.

Anna was plagued for most of her adult life by respiratory problems which had been caused by working among the clouds of coal dust at the picking tables; however she had no regrets about working at the Priory Pit. Summing it up she said that it was hard, hard, backbreaking filthy work, but they had many a good laugh. Anna died peacefully on 30th June 2007 age 83 years. I am indebted to her for sharing her story about the "*stoories*" at the pithead.

Priory Colliery

THE PACK

Ilk Saturday whan it comes nigh,
Packwives frae Glasgow weekly ply
Their wares for Blantyre fouk to buy
　　An bargains tak',
An' loud an' shrill ye'll hear their cry—
　　Hoy, here's the Pack.

Some village fouk still lyin' abed—
The cry, it penetrates the head,
An' senses wauk, as frae the dead,
　　They had come back,
Then up an' aff they rin hauf cled
　　To see the Pack.

'Forenenst "Broon's Pub" they gether roun'
The heap o claes frae Glesga Toon,
Hurdies weel up an' heads weel doon,
　　Like hens whan feedin'.
For twa, three coppers some gey soon
　　Get a' they're needin'.

There's soaks an' bunnets, suits o' claes,
Silk stockin's, knickers, women's stays,
There's buits an' shin', wi' heels an' taes
　　Worn doon an' thro'
An' curtains spread oot to the gaze
　　In green an' blue.

Fine crollys, too, are there an' a',
Berets an' ties, frocks flow'rt an' braw,
A costume too, for shullin's twa,
　　Is yours to keep.
An' saft hats, hard hats, hats o' straw
　　Amang the heap.

Sheets, shirts an' simmits* ye can get,　　*vests
A sixpence buys the weans's a set—
It micht be orange, green or jet,
　　Or somethin' licht--
As lang's it keeps the bairnies het*　　*warm
　　'Twill do a' richt.

Oh jings! It's whiles an afu' tare,
　To hear them wranglin' owre the ware,
　"This shirt," the packwife says, I'm shair
　　Is weel worth thruppence.
"Too dear," an auld wife cries.—"Ach there!
　　I'll gie ye tuppence."

Some things there, whan new, cost notes,
Wee dresses gyms an' petticoats
Wi' troosers, shirts to fit wee tots,
　　An' aulder brithers,
An' blouses, scarves an' skirts an' coats,
　　To suit their mither's.

I aften think, as I gae by
Their affcasts o' the rich and try,
To visualise their mither's joy,
　　The pleasures whan,
She views them on her raggit boy,
　　Or girl or man.

Well pleased she is to see him dress't,
The troosers need a steek, then press't,
An' gif wi' petrol they're carress't,
　　'Twill bricht the blue.
Then no a ane wad e'er ha'e guess't
　　They were'na new.

Whan trade is dull an' siller's sma'
An' *poortith dabs* ye in the raw,　　*poverty hits*
Whan your ain claes ha'e worn awa',
　　Clean aff your back.
Cheer up Blantyre foulks an' wait the ca'
　　Hoy, here's the Pack.

Wm. Sharp.
Circa 1939

AN UGLY PIT BING

Priory Colliery

Wi pleasure I gazed on that quate*, peacefu' scene   *quiet*
When workin' for yince* oot the city,   *once*
An' marvelled to see hoo* each separate green   *how*
Could fashion a picture so pretty.
The many-hued florets, each added their charm,
Full-throated soared the lark in its pride,
While drowsy the noise floated up, frae* the farm   *from*
Half-hid on the banks o' the Clyde.

Historic auld Bothwell lay buried in sleep,
An' yet, where its shadows were cast
It seemed that it cautioned ancient Priory to keep
The secrets they held o' the past.
Still nearer I saw, where the sun's golden rays
Gently lingered mair* tenderly bright   *more*
Aroun' that dear cot—all Africa's praise—
Where Livingston first saw the light.

Even there, midst such splendour sae* restfu' and trim   *so*
Like a hideous cankersome sore,
Rears an ugly pit bing—defiant an' grim
Wi' a green sickly smoke curlin' o'er.
It grieved me to see such a monstrous pile
In the heart o' such grandeur be driven
Like Satan's vile self had tried to despoil
The glory—the Beauty of Heaven.

JAMES MITCHELL.
c 1938.

LIFE IN THE PIT VILLAGE
OF
FIN ME OOT
(CALDERVALE)

Fin me Oot (Caldervale)

Elizabeth (Lizzie) McKnight, nee Guy was 3 years old when her parents moved in 1920 from Parkhead to Fin Me Oot. Lizzie's father was employed at Blantyreferme Colliery as a surface worker transferring pit waste from the pithead to the bing.

Lizzie lived in Fin Me Oot (she said its posh name was Caldervale) for more that 30 years and worked in Blantyreferme Brickworks all her working life.

Her first husband *Richard (Dick) Richardson* also worked in the brickworks. He was conscripted into the army as were Lizzie's two brothers (both miners), at the beginning of the Second World War. All three were killed in action.

When Lizzie was informed of her husband's death her daughter was less than a year old and she was pregnant with her second child, a son.

The following are Lizzie's memories of life in Fin Me Oot.

*   *   *

LIZZIE'S STORY

The Raw was situated in a valley next to the River Calder on the road between Blantyre and Uddingston. The houses, owned by A.G. Moore & Co. were built quite close to the pit and brickworks. Fin Me Oot came under Blantyre Parish. The children went to Newton schools and the women shopped in Uddingston.

The houses consisted of a room, kitchen and scullery. Originally built with dry outside privies, the indoor toilets were added some time before 1920. Coal cellars were at the bottom of the stairs. Both the room and kitchen had two set in beds. The scullery had a sink and cold running water. The gable end houses were called *McNeil's* corner and *McGinty's* corner, after the families who lived there.

There were no wash houses, summer and winter, rain, hail, sleet or snow, the women washed their clothes out the back door. Using nine bricks they would make a nest for a fire and after it was lit they would place a large metal bath filled with water and dirty clothes on top of the bricks. Once the clothes were boiled they would be transferred to a bine (a large wooden bath) to be rinsed and inspected for stains. Any stains would be scrubbed out using soap and a washing board. The women took a pride in their spotless white cotton clothes and after they had been boiled, scrubbed and rinsed, they were wrung out using a wooden hand wringer.

It was a mixed community, but in the 1940's it was mostly Roman Catholic, with 34 Catholic families and 6 Protestant families. There were no problems with religion. Fin Me Oot was a close community where everyone helped each other.

The children had to walk more than a mile to get to school in Newton. The footpath used was not very good. They had to walk round two bings and cross a bridge over the River Calder. Catholic and Protestant children attended different schools.

There were no dustbins. Rubbish was placed in the midden situated directly in the middle of the Raw and approximately 20-25 feet from the building. Originally the midden was closer to the houses. It was emptied twice weekly.

Prior to *Doctor Mitchell* (a lady doctor) setting up practice in Newton, women were attended to during childbirth by their female relatives (mother, grannies and aunts) and usually there was a woman in the community who would help in deliveries. These women were untrained but had years of experience delivering babies. Very often they also laid out the dead.

Large families were the norm. *Harriet Guy,* who delivered many Fin Me Oot babies, gave birth to thirteen babies herself, nine of whom survived. Two sets of twins died at birth. These large families were brought up in the rooms and kitchens.

It was also common for older couples who were childless or with families who had grown and left home to let out their room to young couples with no home of their own. *Lizzie Richardson* and her husband Dick set up home in the room of an older couple called *Wullie* and *Maggie Cairney*. This was Lizzie's home from 1940 to mid 1950's when she moved to Blantyre. The two families shared the scullery and toilet.

There were two wee shops in the Raw. One owned by *Mrs McGarry* and the other by *Mrs McGinty*. The shops sold everything. Originally the shops were the front rooms of the houses, but the *McGarry's* and *McGinty's* set up business in these rooms and lived and slept in the other room, which was the kitchen. *Aggie Walker* came round twice a week selling fruit and vegetables from her horse and cart. The milkman delivered the milk daily at 5 a.m. He also sold bread and scones.

Lizzie's father kept hens and pigeons, as did *Mr McKinnon* and *Mr Nicol.*

Around 1930 a Miners Welfare was built as a meeting place; it was alcohol free. A billiard table was installed at a later date. A swing park was provided for the children at the same time the Welfare was built. There were four swings and a roundabout.

A regular pastime between the miners was bare knuckle fighting. This took place at the end of the Raw.

When Lizzie's father and brothers came home from the pit, their clothes were scraped free of dirt and dried in front of the kitchen fire. After drying the clothes were "doddit" off the outside walls of the house. Her father and brothers would bathe in a large zinc bath in front of the kitchen fire. When the girls bathed they had the privacy of the bedroom.

Although 60 years have passed since Lizzie left Fin Me Oot, her memories of the Raw are still vivid. She was proud to stay there and loved the life of the close community. When interviewed in 2001 Lizzie was living in East Kilbride; prominently placed above her fireplace was a framed photograph of Fin me Oot.

Fin-me-oot can be seen on left, picture courtesy of George Hay.

Gone but not forgotten. Seat made out of old doors etc from Fin-me-oot.

THE BLANTYRE RIOTS

1886 had been a worse year than normal for Lanarkshire's coal miners. For months the price of coal had been dropping and predictably, the coal masters had passed on the loss on to the miners by reducing their wages. By the end of the year the wages being paid were so low that they had gone well below the below the poverty level and a further reduction was being proposed. The miners had had enough and asked for a rise of 6d (2 _p) per day. The refusal by the coal masters to increase their wages led to the miners declaring a strike.

The winter weather had been cold and miserable and mining families were struggling with no money coming in. Christmas and New Year had come and gone and still the miners were holding out. The Union was negotiating with the coal masters and to keep the miners up to date regular meetings were held in Hamilton.

On 7th February, 1887, during one of these mass meetings, the proceedings were interrupted by the sound of music and a band, followed by several hundred men marched in to join the protest. The demonstrators did not impress the miners with their high profile entrance. They were loud, noisy and openly boasting of looting several bread and ginger beer vans en route to the meeting.

The consensus of opinion among the miners present was that these men were troublemakers from the Glasgow area who had no connection with the mining industry. When the meeting was over, the unwelcome guests filed into a public house in Chapel Street and several hours later with their thirst quenched, they staggered out into the street where a police escort was waiting to accompany them to the edge of the Burgh boundary at Stonefield, Blantyre. The Burgh Police Officers sensing that trouble was brewing were relieved when the marchers crossed over the County line and were no longer their responsibility.

The ill timed arrival of a bread van just as the police disappeared out of sight presented an opportunity the marchers could not resist and the van was pillaged with the loaves being used as footballs.

The dye had been cast and before long, some of the local youths, on strike, bored to tears and needing little encouragement were taking part in the football game. A short time later, after the loaves had fallen apart; they lined up to form a mock Salvation Army procession and started marching towards the shops.

On reaching Chapman's grocery store the procession halted and one of the marchers stepped forward to ask the owner if they could come into his shop. His reply that they could come in if they wished appeared to strike the right cord and they moved on without causing any damage.

At the next shop it was a different story. The shop belonged to licensed grocer *John Struthers* and the vision of free alcohol was too much for the marchers. Suddenly, and without any warning, several men ran forward, smashed the plate glass windows and started looting the window display. Only the timely arrival of the owner prevented the looters gaining admission to the inside of the store and reluctantly, they moved on. Half an hour later, the crowd which was increasing in size by the minute and included several women, returned to Chapman's store where the owner, playing for time, tried to reason with them in the desperate hope that police would arrive before they could force their way inside the shop. However the damage to the store was restricted to two broken plate glass windows and the crowd moved on.

With their confidence growing as fast as their thirst the mob were intent on obtaining free alcohol and headed for Dixon's Rows; this time there was no stopping them. The two shops targeted belonged to *Barty McFarlane* and *James Down's* and smashing in the doors and windows the rioters started looting everything in sight.

Barty McFarlane and his son were wine and spirit merchants and they defended their property by every means possible. They fought back with anything they could lay their hands on, including throwing 2lb and 7lb weights at the rioters. During the course of the melee, Barty was struck on the face by a bottle wielding looter and he received a bad wound just above his right eye. Hopelessly outnumbered and covered in blood from their injuries, the two men eventually took to their heels and found refuge in an upstairs flat.

For two hours the looters tore the shop apart and fought over goods and alcohol. By the time the police arrived the shop was an empty shell.

James Downs's licensed grocers shop received the same treatment. Nothing was spared; every item in the shop was pillaged. His substantial stock of whisky, brandy, wine and beer, vanished within minutes as the looters ran down the street rolling the barrels in front of them.

News of the looting was telegraphed to Hamilton County Police Station and two mounted policemen were soon galloping as fast as they could towards Blantyre. The horses were hardly over the town boundary when Constable *John McLuckie* was struck on the mouth with a stone, breaking three teeth and cutting his lip. Unfit for duty he had to be removed from the scene. When Chief Constable *McHardy* was informed of the seriousness of the riots he immediately set off for Blantyre on horseback. He was accompanied by *Mr. J. Clark Forrest,* Honorary Sheriff Substitute and a mounted police officer followed close behind by a brake containing eight police officers.

On reaching Stonefield, the constables dismounted from the brake and lining up behind the three riders, followed them down the street. All was quiet.... too quiet! Expecting trouble they weren't disappointed. Having reached Harts Buildings, they came under attack from a barrage of stones thrown by a crowd who had appeared as if from nowhere. Despite the missiles raining down on top of them, the officers continued walking, until eventually they were forced to halt outside the Public School where, by the dim light of a lantern and for the first time in 25 years, the Riot Act was read in Blantyre.

After it was read Chief Constable McHardy advised the women and children to leave the scene and instructing his men not to touch them, began to disperse the crowd. Within a short space of time the job was done and they moved on towards the foot of Stonefield Road. Here they were advised against proceeding any further as there was a crowd of over a thousand people waiting and it would be dangerous to go on. McHardy however had other ideas and kept on going. On reaching the crowd he informed them that the Riot Act had been read and then proceeded to tell them in no uncertain terms that one way or another, he was going to clear the streets. Appearing to recognise the seriousness of the situation, the crowd, many of whom were only observers, began to break up and move on.

Within a short time further reinforcements had arrived from Hamilton and after several skirmishes, law and order was finally restored.

The next morning the town's shops remained closed, but the peace lasted only until 8am when some young men started staggering out of the houses where drinking parties had been going on all night. Still full of the hard stuff and desperate for more, they were intent on replenishing their supplies, and their chosen target was Dixon's store. Access was gained by using a battering ram to the door and window shutters. The large plate glass windows shattered just as the law appeared on the scene and the police, drawing their batons, charged straight into the crowd of looters, but this did little to control the situation as they just stood their ground and fought back. Vastly outnumbered, the police had to fall back to await reinforcements.

A hastily arranged meeting of Stonefield merchants concluded that the situation had got out of hand and a telegram was sent to Chief Constable McHardy requesting assistance. He arrived one hour later with Sheriff Birnie and an escort of Mounted Policemen.

Turning into Stonefield Road they could hardly believe the scene that met their eyes. Hundreds of looters were in the process of plundering anything they could lay their hands on. The lure of free goods and alcohol had induced a feeling of euphoria among the crowd and caution had been thrown to the wind. Oblivious to everything, their heads were up and the music was playing. Men, women and children were fighting amongst themselves to gain possession of the plunder. Hams, beef, firkins of butter, jam, flour, tea, cheese and eggs were being handed out and taken away. Every conceivable type of carrying utensil, (bottles, jugs, pails, cooking pots and chanty pots) had been commandeered to remove the alcohol being looted from the shop and the situation was completely out of control.

Quickly regrouping, the police officers formed up in a procession led by the Mounted Police who were holding drawn swords. With McHardy at the head wielding a heavy walking stick, the procession moved forward several paces and then halted to allow Sheriff Birnie to read the Riot Act. The crowd, full of bravado stoned the Sheriff as he read, but before he had finished, the Mounted Police using shock tactics, charged straight in amongst them. The plan worked and terror soon replaced euphoria at the sight and sound of swords swinging through the air. The panicking rioters took to their heels and scattered throughout Dixons Rows with some of them still clutching their ill gotten gains as they ran, but most discarding the evidence. Within a short space of time, all was quiet. The rest of the morning passed relatively trouble free, with only the occasional skirmish when stones were thrown at the Constabulary.

Barrels of alcohol hidden during the riots were being sought out and the contents consumed by local youths who were soon back out on the streets looking for trouble. Between one and two o'clock *McCann* the shoemaker's shop was ransacked and a large stock of boots and shoes quickly disappeared. The looters, not content with destroying the shop, entered his house and stole suits of clothing and other articles.

Round about the same time, a crowd of approximately 500 men, including many who appeared to be under the influence of alcohol, surrounded the Craighead Co-operative Society in Bairds Rows. It was a large well stocked shop and *Mr Forsyth* the manager, sensing trouble, had locked up several hours before. Despite the crowd outside shouting for him to open up, he stood his ground and refused to do so. Shortly afterwards, unobserved, he crept out of the back door and headed for the police station some 700 yards away.

By the time he returned with six police officers the shop was being ransacked. Six of the looters were arrested, but a pitched battle broke out between the crowd and the policemen before they could reach the safety of the police station with their prisoners. The crowd viciously attacked the officers, kicking and stoning them about the head and body. Four of the prisoners were dragged from the arms of the law and the police, although badly cut and bruised, managed to transfer the other two to the police station.

The baying crowd surrounded the police station and within minutes every window in the building was smashed. The two prisoners were released by the police after their names had been obtained, but this did not placate the mob who continued to stone the building. The police houses attached to the station also became a target for the rioters and the families of Constables *Kidd* and *Campbell* had to take flight after Constable *Kidd's* small child was hit by a stone while sleeping in a cradle.

Several police officers who had been on guard at the Craighead Co-Operative left to give assistance at the police station and seizing the opportunity, looters once again moved into the store. However the store's shop assistants weren't falling for the same scenario twice. They had a plan of action and were one step ahead of them. Eleven of the rioters entered the cellar looking for alcohol and as they vanished into gloomy darkness the shop assistants trapped them by pushing the door shut and locking it. Their luck continued when they managed to attract the attention of police reinforcements arriving from Hamilton and the unwelcome visitors were soon handcuffed for removal to the police station; but once again the crowd had other ideas. After a pitched battle the prisoners were snatched from police custody and still handcuffed, fled the scene. Some time later they were seen in a field, frantically trying to remove the handcuffs with stones.

Shops were being attacked and looted all over Blantyre and with the approach of night, a state of terror spread throughout the community. Up until then only one private residence had been looted, (*McCann* the shoemaker) but in the forenoon there had been ominous warning signs of the trouble ahead when 200 men had marched up to High Blantyre and threatened to return when it got dark.

At six o'clock the arrival from Maryhill Barracks of 50 mounted soldiers, resplendent in the uniform of the 4th Queen's own Hussars, gave the towns residents hope that the rioting could be contained. The Hussars were followed by 170 Glasgow police officers who had just arrived at Low Blantyre by train.

Stonefield Blantyre circa 1900, Photograph courtesy of Hamilton Reference Library.

Within hours the rioting and looting had been stopped and the town was peaceful once more. The police and soldiers cleared the streets of people and for the rest of the night patrolled the village to prevent any resurgence of violence.

Only one further incident took place and this was at Stonefield Road where once again stones were thrown at the police; but after a mounted charge, several of the ringleaders were captured and removed to the police station. The rest of the rioters vanished into the night.

The Hussars were billeted in Hamilton Barracks where, when they were not patrolling the streets of Blantyre, they were kept on standby in case of any further unrest. Also on standby was a locomotive, kept at the ready to transfer the soldiers to Blantyre at the slightest sign of trouble.

The Roman Catholic school at Stonefield was turned into the temporary police head-quarters. Drs. *Grant* and *Wilson* two Blantyre General Practitioners were kept busy attending the wounded among them ten police officers and six prisoner's, two of whom were very drunk. One of them a Hamilton man called *William Ford* was suffering from acute alcohol poisoning and was lucky to escape with his life.

Late on Tuesday night and during the early hours of Wednesday morning, raids were carried out on houses all over town and 50 people were arrested and charged with having stolen goods, among them were several women. If looted goods were found in a house all the adults present were arrested and charged. Two men were also arrested and charged with a breach of the peace. By six o'clock in the morning the raids were over and the prisoners were in custody. In less than two hours, 40 of them were being moved to Hamilton and extra security precautions were put into force to prevent any of the men being released by a hostile mob. When being led out of the temporary police station each prisoner was handcuffed to a police officer and taken to the waiting transport.

As the brakes left for Hamilton, they were accompanied by a large combined police and military escort. By half past ten all the prisoners had been transferred to either Hamilton County or Burgh jails and the riots were over.

The women who were arrested were released because there were no separate cells for them and, as their husbands were already in custody they were needed at home. Four of the men *John Hannigan, James Wilson, William Aiton* and *William Ford* were also released; 48 men were remanded in custody and transferred to Glasgow's Duke Street prison in a specially commissioned high security train. When they eventually appeared in court the case against many of them was dismissed because they had already been in custody for 9 weeks. The men who had been out on bail and who were found guilty were either admonished or sentenced to 2 weeks to 2 months in jail.

Compensation was granted to all the businesses damaged by the rioters with the largest amount £680 being awarded to licensed grocer *James Downs*. The County eventually paid out £1717 1s 5d in damages to those affected by the riots.

*On the 20th May 1887 *John Feron,* pipeclay salesman, 395 Old Keppochill Road, Glasgow, was one of the men acquitted after spending six weeks in jail accused of assaulting *James Downs* on the night of the riot. He sued Downs alleging that the criminal proceedings were *"instigated wickedly, maliciously and without probable cause"*.

The decent law abiding mining families of Blantyre were stunned at what had taken place. The riots had initially been instigated by trouble makers from outside the town, but once free alcohol had been passed around, the situation had rapidly escalated out of control. With the arrival of the reinforcements from Glasgow, peace again reigned, it was weeks before the town returned to normal and people began to feel safe in their homes once more.

LIST OF PEOPLE ARRESTED AT BLANTYRE RIOTS.

William Aiton,(31) Church St, Hamilton. *James Bolton,* Burnbank. *Michael Bannar,* (35.) Bairds Rows. *William Bannon,* (35) Bairds Rows. *Michael Bannan (33)* Calder Street. *Robert Brown.* (25) Bairds Rows. *James Burton* (27) McAlpine's Building. *Rose Barry,* wife of *James Wilson.* Baird's Row. *John Cairney,* (53) Dixon's Rows. *David Copeland,* (50) *Owen Carroll,* (47) McAlpine's Buildings. *James Colvin,* Greenfield Burnbank. *Michael Connelly,* (32) Bairds Rows. *Wm Connelly,* *Hugh Conner. James Crawford.* Jun, (26.) Bairds Rows. *Thomas Cunningham,* Burnbank. *Henry Darroch. Grace Donnelly* (50) wife of *Patrick Mullen* McAlpine's Buildings. *Daniel Donnelly, (22) Young St. Hamilton. John Dorran.* (19) Hopehall Stonefield. *John Doyle,* (27) 21 Bairds Rows. *Patrick Ferns,* (33) 59 McAlpine's Buildings. *John Feron,* Glasgow. *Wm, Ford,* (40) New Wynd. Hamilton. *John Furrie* (24) Dixon's Rows *Hugh Flynn,* (21) Turners Buildings. *Robert Ferguson,* Craighead Rows. *John Hannaghan* (35) Muirhead, Hamilton. *John Higgins.* (22) McAlpine's Buildings. *Cormick Higgins,* (62). *John Herron,* (37 McAlpine's Buildings. Patrick Higgins, (21) McAlpine's Buildings. *George Howie,* Blantyre Lane. *John King,* (23) Bairds Rows. *Thomas Laird,* (34) McAlpine's Buildings. *Patrick Lawson, (33)* Windsor St. Burnbank. *Edward Laughlan,* (30) Gardiners Terr. High Blantyre. *Wm. Donald Livingstone,* Cambuslang. *Jacob Lindsay,* Burnbank. *Catherine Lynch,* wife of *Owen Carrol,* McAlpine's Buildings. Isabella Mooney, wife of *John Weatherall,* McAlpine's Buildings. *James McGeachy,* (33) Craighead Rows. *Charles McCallum,* (50) Bairds Rows. *James McGovern,* (19) Bruce's Buildings. *Peter McGuinnes,* (21) Dixon's Rows. *John McAulay,* (21) McAlpine's *Buildings. James McGuire. Rodger McGuire,* (17) Hart's Buildings. *Patrick McGuire,* (40) McAlpine's Buildings. *James Mormon,* Burnbank. *James Mullen,* (46) McAlpine's Buildings. *Patrick Mullen,* (18) *Hugh McMahon,* (18) Young's Building. *Edward McGuire* (17) Watson's Building, Larkfield. *James McGuire,* (50) Hart's Building. *Patrick Nimmo,* (50) Turners Buildings. John *Rafferty,* (25) Turner's Buildings. *Archd. Robertson,* (51) McAlpine's Buildings. *James Scullion,* (22) Hart's Land. *Samuel Smith,* Burnbank. *Wm Tonner,* (21) Cemetery Walk. *William Watson,* Blantyre. *Henry Wilson,* (25) Whitehill Terr. Burnbank. *James Wilson,* (40) Bairds Rows. *John Wetherall,* (38) McAlpine's Buildings.

* Unless otherwise stated above addresses are Blantyre.

BOTHWELLHAUGH
THE "PAILIS"

Bothwellhaugh with bing looming behind it

Hamilton Girls Training Corps. ready to go underground at Hamilton Palace Colliery, c. 1945Photograph courtesy of Miss Jessie Whitehouse.

Hamilton Palace miners

KNOWN FATALITIES AT HAMILTON PALACE COLLIERY

DATE.	NAME.	AGE.	CAUSE.
04.10.1887	WILLIAM McNAIR	28	Roof fall (2 tons)
28.12.1890	ALEXANDER OGILVIE	21	Roof fall (1 cwt)
14.02.1891	ROBERT MOONEY	32	Roof fall (3 tons)
01.08.1891	SAMUEL DICKSON	29	Fall of coal at face (2 tons)
07.10.1892	PAT. CUNNINGHAM	35	Roof fall (3 tons)
20.03.1893	THOMAS CONNELLY	47	Run down by wagon
13.04.1893	SAM. WARMINGTON	28	Roof fall
15.11.1893	JOHN WILSON	27	Fall of coal at face
14.10.1895	ELIZABETH FINDLAY	33	Crushed by machinery (multiple injuries)
15.11.1895	JAMES WILSON	28	Crushed in shaft
19.08.1896	JOHN LYNAS	44	Roof fall 4-5 cwt
06.11.1896	JAMES CONNELLY	37	Roof fall
20.10.1897	JOHN McGROARTY	17	Run down by hutch
06.12.1898	HUGH NEILSON	35	Crushed to death by machinery
10.10.1899	WILLIAM ARMOUR	14	Explosion
28.12.1899	WILLIAM BRUNTON	31	Multiple injuries
13.02.1900	JOHN BUCHAN	34	Roof fall
26.12.1901	ALEXANDER OGILVIE	22	Fall of coal at face
01.06.1900	JOE. CHERESKEWSKI	26	Fall of coal at face
12.04.1902	WILLIAM J. NEILL	34	Struck by broken cuddie tree while lowering hutch
09.06.1903	PETER SIME	22	Roof fall (asphyxia)
09.06.1903	PETER WILSON	29	Roof fall (fractures of pelvis and thigh)
--12. 1903	ADAM SIMPSON/STADDON	--	No details
24.06.1904	JOHN COOK	19	Roof fall (fractured skull)
20.10.1904	WILLIAM MEEK	23	Collapse of underground brick arch
15.03.1905	JOHN FERGUSSON	24	Fell down a blind pit
13.08.1906	EDWARD McCORMACK	29	Fall of coal at face
10.12.1906	ADAM CUMMING	24	Roof fall
04.06.1907	JAMES McKEAN	19	Head injuries
07.05.1908	JAMES RUSSELL	67	Crushed by buffer
19.09.1908	JOHN TINLIN	21	Caught in machinery (crushed right arm, broken ribs)
31.03.1909	ARTHUR DICKSON	32	Runaway hutch (fractured pelvis)

Date	Name	Age	Cause
18.10.1909	JOHN GALLACHER	50	Roof fall (neck dislocated)
15.05.1910	WILLIAM BULLER	40	Roof fall (multiple injuries)
02.10.1910	ALEX. WALLACE	47	Roof fall (fractured femur, septicaemia)
04.10.1911	ADAM BARR	73	Cage fell down shaft (fractured limbs/internal injuries)
10.11.1911	CHARLES CLARK	34	Roof fall (fractured skull)
09.12.1911	THOMAS NICHOLLS	33	Roof fall (traumatic asphyxia)
14.05.1912	ALEXANDER RANKINE	34	Roof fall
12.08.1912	JOHN BELL	54	Roof fall (9-10 tons (traumatic asphyxia)
13.08.1912	WILLIAM AIRD	51	Run down by hutches (fracture and dislocation of spine)
26.10.1912	ROBERT FULTON	22	No details (fractures of thigh and pelvis)
04.03.1913	----TYRELL	--	No details
23.09.1913	JOHN SMITH	47	Hit by pit prop (internal injuries/peritonitis)
25.12.1913	CHARLES McMANUS	51	No details (septic cut of scalp/erysipelas)
02/10/1914	ROBERT McCART	39	Crushed by cage while working in shaft
08.05.1915	JAMES BROWN	44	Roof fall (severe head injuries)
02.11.1915	ALEXANDER NELSON	37	Roof fall (crushing fractures of ribs and thorax)
24.08.1917	WILLIAM KILPATRICK	47	No details (fracture and dislocation of neck)
28.07.1919	JOHN CHALMERS	46	No details (fracture and dislocation of neck, multiple injuries)
09.04.1920	[EDWARD McGINTY]	23	Crushing accident (no details)
09.03.1923	[MICHAEL McGINTY]	53	Rock fall (1ton, fractured skull)

The above two miners are father and son)

Date	Name	Age	Cause
11.12.1925	JOHN C. BARRIE	36	No details (fractured spine)
03.10.1928	SARAH CUNNINGHAM	14	Crushed by conveyer belt
16.12.1930	THOMAS McCONAGHY	48	Fall of coal from face
17.06.1935	JAMES ROBERTSON	28	Runaway hutches (head injuries asphyxia)
28.11.1936	JOHN COUSINS	---	Roof fall
31.03.1938	ANTONY STRAIN	16	Entangled in machinery at screening tables
12.12.1938	ALEX. P. GILMOUR	18	Killed on surface (fractured skull)
07.06.1939	PETER MCLEOD	53	No details (fractures of spine and skull)
27.12.1940	GEORGE McFARLANE	---	No details
08.06.1942	RICHARD ANDERSON	39	Ch4 gas poisoning
14.01.1943	JAMES I. KERR	--	Explosion
26.07.1944	JOHN R. HUNTER	30	Dragged into a revolving shaft on the surface
19.02.1948	JAMES SKEWIES	64	Roof fall (2 tons, killed instantly.)

HAMILTON PALACE COLLIERY

Hamilton Palace Colliery was developed by the Bent Colliery Co, in 1884 on 800 acres leased from the Duke of Hamilton's trustees. The company was owned by James Dixon. In 1910 the colliery employed 1120 men, with 995 working underground and the other 250 at the surface.

The pit was sunk near Bothwellhaugh Farm steading and Dixon also built a pit village consisting of 458 houses for his workers. The village consisted of 79 single ends, 349 room and kitchens, 27 three roomed and 3 four roomed houses and it was given the name Bothwellhaugh after the steading but to the locals it was never called anything other than the Pailis. The Pailis was a very close knit mining community and former residents are extremely proud of having lived there.

The colliery closed in May 1959 and the village struggled on for some more years but was eventually demolished and the residents rehoused.

THE LAST PIT PONIES

Redundant pit pony waiting to learn its fate in a Quarter field, September 1966. Photograph courtesy of
The Hamilton Advertiser.

WEE PIT POWNIE

Wee pit pownie, harness and a'
A hutch at the bottom, ready for tae draw,
Ile flask, tea flask, piece boax and a'
And we'll no' be hame tae the mornin'.

Scotland's last pit ponies worked at Knowetop Mine Quarter near Hamilton until the mine closed at the
end of August 1966. They remained for sale for some time but appear to have been eventually sent
south to a Durham retirement home for pit ponies.

The following article written by Larkhall's "Lav'rockha' " was published in the Hamilton Advertiser on
the 14th October 1966.

PIT PONIES AND DRIVERS

So the last dozen of Scotland's pit ponies have worked their last shift….and are now on offer for sale by
the National Coal Board. They served the mining industry well, these little beasts of burden of the pits.

For many miners and ex-miners in the town and district, the end of the pit pony as an integral part of the mechanics of coal transport underground will bring back memories of their own early days in pit work.

For hundreds of pit-boys it was a natural step to leave "faither" or an elder brother to work at the coal-face and seek the status and freedom of being a driver.

Being able to handle a horse gave the young driver a feeling that he was growing up and as he progressed in his new job he soon found---provided that he had plenty of stamina and courage --- that he had joined the most "clannish group" in the pit. Pit drivers, when they got together, could often lay down the law on such things as pit "bens" (the allocation of empty hutches for single facemen, pairs, and often two men and a boy); "free cleek" (or priority at the pithead in the morning); and whether or not it should be an idle day if the drivers felt they had a complaint which the gaffer refused to remedy.

Most of them were kind to the pit ponies, some were not; but all were governed by the single word "cleek" (underground transport) and gaffers and cleek-hunters made it perfectly clear that if a driver wished to hold his job, he had better see to it that plenty of empty hutches were speedily sent on their way to the main lye for the link-up with mechanical transport.

Colliers and other workers had their "piece time" but drivers took their piece at "cornin'" round about mid-shift, when the ponies got their bag of corn.

HARDY AND TOUGH

The cocky wee Gordon had nothing on the pit driver; he felt he was a man among men when he stepped forward to enter the cage in the morning, with his big piece-box showing in his jacket pocket and a long whip tucked in his belt. He was hardy and tough, with strength and stamina developing rapidly as he emerged from boyhood to young manhood. He was a good man for the local football club; he was always first on the floor at the "jiggin'," and he was game for any ploy at the miners' row when the working day was over.

But as years go by quickly in early manhood, the driver, when he came to around twenty, had to think of "courting seriously" and to consider what marriage would mean on a driver's wage. For most of them it meant giving up the driving for a job at the coal-face and a bigger wage; few regretted the years of pit work as a pony driver.

THE LAST HUTCH OF COAL
KNOWETOP MINE, QUARTER,. SEPTEMBER 1966

Pit ponies were hard working little animals and without a doubt they deserve a place of honour in the history of coal mining. There was a bond between the drivers and their ponies and many a driver owed his life to his pony after it refused to enter an area just prior to a roof fall and in the pitch darkness of the mine when the light from a lamp had failed, the ponies would lead the miner back to the pit bottom.

On 9th November 1911 the Hamilton Advertiser published a letter from Robert T. Wallace, manager of Greenfield Colliery and former undermanager at Fairhill Colliery condemning music hall artiste Harry Lauder's allegation of the ill- treatment of pit ponies by their drivers. Wallace's angry letter gives us an insight into the lives of ponies and their drivers when he writes that "The *stabling accommodation in Fairhill Colliery, the last Lauder worked in before adopting his present profession, were the pride of all concerned in the colliery, being roomy, dry and comfortable in every respect and thoroughly well ventilated. They were looked after by Alex. Scott, Ostler, still in Hamilton, a man who knew well how to treat a horse and one who would not have them abused, while last but not least they were worked by a class of young lads who vied with each other as to who could keep their horse in the best condition".*

For more than one hundred years the whorles on the pit heads turned and as they turned, countless thousands of men and boys were lowered down into and up from the deep pits sunk into the rolling fields and glens of Lanarkshire. The whorls also brought to the surface the millions of tons of coal which these men and boys had sweated blood and tears to remove from the bowels of the earth and it was this coal which fired the engines that powered the industrial revolution.

Despite the vast fortunes made from coal, the only winners were the aristocracy, the landed gentry, the coal barons and the coal companies and their shareholders, who, in their greed for wealth and power, ruthlessly exploited the miners and looked down on them as if they were some kind of unintelligent, emotionless, human sub species. For working in conditions which at best were appalling and at worst indescribable, the miners were rewarded with starvation wages, chronic ill health and an early grave.

The descendents of the coal miners still retain an overwhelming sense of pride in their ancestors even although it is now more than 70 years since the last deep pit closed in Hamilton Parish. The old time miners are all gone, but their voices still echo down through the years each time one of their descendents repeats a tale first heard from their lips.......and so the story of their suffering and heroism is passed on from generation to generation.

Coal mining in Hamilton came to an end when the last miner's lamp was extinguished at Knowetop Mine, Quarter in August, 1966. The above pony was the last pit pony ever to draw a hutch of coal in Scotland. The name of the miner with the pony is unknown, but this book is dedicated to him and to my father and your father and to all of our coal mining forefathers, who, without a shadow of a doubt, were a uniquely brave....... brotherhood of men.

THE MINERS' LAST SHIFT

When the last pit is closed, and to the sun
  The miner turns his face, erect and free,
The last shift worked, and the last black ton won
  What do you deem the miner's speech will be?

How will the master-world greet him then?
  I tell you, for I know his mother well,
Stronger than metals she has reared her men,
  I've seen his father carve his bed in hell.

He had no soul to sell, I've heard you say,
  You with your centpercent had naught to buy,
Now he is here, fronting the light of day,
  What will you plead the answer to his why?

Far o'er the age-long pits he stood alone,
  A world where none but he might live and rule,
Midst the dead million year's his image shone
  One day you called him hero, next, the fool.

Hero or fool he stands before you now,
  That man with whom the sun you would not share,
The dews of stars fall on his rugged brow,
  The wandering winds weave music in his hair.

The last pit closed, his last mate starved for bread,
  He stands erect amid the race of men,
The bleached, the broken, and his myriad dead,
  The way he came, alone his kingdom then.

I tell you, for I knew his mother well,
  Stronger than metals him she nursed had soul;
By this sweet light, where God meant men to dwell,
  What will ye do now for your bloody coal?

EDWARD HUNTER c.1926

How many people driving past these ruins on the Carscallan Road, Quarter, are aware that they are the monumental remains of Quarter No.6 Pit, which piece by piece, are slowly decaying and vanishing,........ into the mists of time?
Photograph courtesy of Wullie Kerr, c. 2007

The Past

The past is here
The past is there.
Look around and see,
The past is everywhere.

Sometimes it's secret,
Hidden by nature or
In old books and maps.
Sometimes it's obvious and
Will stop you in your tracks.

Let your eyes be opened
So you can see
The traces of time
The changes of the years.
View the splendour and glory,
The moss and the stones.

Gone or is it?
Forgotten, not quite.
If you see it, you've lit the light,
Joined time and place.
The modern, the old.
The perpetual fight.   *Lesley Farnan c.2001*